THE "NONSENSE" PAPERS

THE "NONSENSE" PAPERS

2012 AND BEYOND: UFO ANTHOLOGY, VOLUME ONE

JAMES W. ASTRADA

iUniverse, Inc.
Bloomington

The "Nonsense" Papers
2012 and Beyond: UFO Anthology, Volume One

iUniverse books may be ordered through booksellers or by contacting:

iUniverse
1663 Liberty Drive
Bloomington, IN 47403
www.iuniverse.com
1-800-Authors (1-800-288-4677)

ISBN: 978-1-4759-4669-7 (sc)
ISBN: 978-1-4759-4671-0 (hc)
ISBN: 978-1-4759-4670-3 (ebk)

Library of Congress Control Number: 2012916330

Printed in the United States of America

iUniverse rev. date: 09/07/2012

Contents

For my mother *Alexandra*; may her journey on Earth lead to ascension in consciousness to surpass the human condition.

And for my boys *Rupert* and *O'Higgins*:

O'Higgins, you have been a crucial part of my life and partly responsible for the positive changes in me including this book. Even though you passed away too soon, your spirit is still with me. The other half is due to Rupert who is still here to help me ascend spiritually and mentally

IN LOVING MEMORY OF O'HIGGINS—NOVEMBER 2ND, 2002—May 5th, 2010.

Preface

The Message

Aliens and UFOs have always been a central point in human history and life in general. Whether the idea is completely ridiculed, scorned, or glorified, there seems to be a definite speculation on the existence of other worldly races and/or beings. What is the fascination we seem to cling to when discussing something that is only seen as pop culture and entertainment in this new age of digital technology? The *digital age* is truly among us and perhaps our preconceptions of where alien life will change based on new discoveries. Although the subject is mostly ridiculed and portrayed as fantasy, many hundreds of people over the course of this country's history and worldwide have claimed contact or abduction by UFO entities giving detailed description about the events. The results range from different entities such as *Reptilians, Greys, Arcturians, Pleiadians, Andromedans, Nordics, Sirians, Lyrians,* "little green men," and so forth.

Although the majority of the cases are debunked, some of them are usually very well documented displaying that there is something transpiring. The common population's trust in corporate run media outlets never really a full disclosure without a biased view. The government itself denies any strange phenomena and usually attribute the events to "natural" occurrences, weather balloons, RC helicopters, swamp gas from Venus, Chinese lanterns, military flares attached to individual parachutes, optical illusions, military exercises, or completely deny the events (even though many small towns have numerous witnesses).

The dilemma is the lack of information when paranormal events transpire without proper explanation. If anyone tries to disclose an event, they are slandered by the media and debunked by experts in various fields. When we consider something real or *nonsense*, the individual is left to decide which road to choose based on their current belief system and/or culture. Most humans seem to believe with absolute certainty, that we have no visitors or neighbors in this vast galactic universe filled with planets, stars, solar systems, and even identical galaxies. Most Americans believe in one deity responsible for such a complicated and unusual design of this universe. Scientists have already speculated more than three hundred sixty-five planets could harvest life similar to our own. With the final disclosure considering the Gliese 581 star system and Kepler 22b, there are planets that are exactly like Earth only bigger harboring water and possible "life." John P. Mills PhD recently stated that over 50 billion planets exist in the Milky Way Galaxy with 500 million living within habitable zones in their perspective star systems [1]. With this result, we seemed to be very disillusioned with the fact of universal loneliness and might have company right near our doorstep or even in our midst.

This idea of nonsense will explain why we must change our views based on culture, society, and religion due to the digital age. Many key speakers, authors, and ex-military personnel will explain to us their point of views displaying a human world vastly more complicated than potentially believed. It will question our current belief systems and force us to use the muscle that we may have been neglecting over many centuries of religious rule: our brains. These speakers also warn of dangerous events that are to transpire in the coming end of our current cycle in 2012. Whether we believe them or not, this idea must be investigated and researched. They will also perhaps force us to question our craziness and unwillingness to believe outside our fear driven culture, and introduce us to alien interest groups that they consider regressive or beneficial.

This step could also mean the search for intelligent life is far from over as we are just beginning to discover our place in this vast universe. Humans are so accustomed to simplistic and mundane explanations that it seems we do not have the ability anymore to rationalize. Everything has become a theory, and is described as "controversial" or completely discredited depending on what right-wing religious faction plans on attacking first. We must realize that we need skepticism or opposition in order to gain profit or a heated debate. Let us not forget that selling this idea of UFOs is a tough sell on Capitol Hill as well. Just imagine the result of full disclosure as the president of the United States decided to tell people that aliens were. Many would see this as a "godsend" and others would be mortified.

The impact on the religious community and the shroud of deception would be lifted, paving the way for a new consciousness. Frantic fear will drive the population rampant causing chaos and the systematic dismantling of what we call normal life. Corporate interests would have to alter their entire structure with the possibility of multi-dimensional expansion due to new alien factors. The Vatican is planning for something, as they have changed their idea overnight considering aliens [2].

Just until recently this belief was not supported by the church, however, it is now ok to believe in aliens and UFOs. A senior Vatican priest by the name of *Guy Consolmagno*, declared seriously in an interview on September 17, 2010 that if aliens landed here on Earth and requested baptism, he would be delighted to offer the service to them [3]. To further their delusion, Jesuit Father *Jose Funes* Director of the Vatican Observatory, considered aliens our "extraterrestrial brothers" and were excluded from "Christ's redemption" on Earth [4]. This of course was only possible if the alien life form was of a different composition than human. Why an intelligent life form would ever have the need to adapt to primitive cultural beliefs is confusing to say the least. This idea of partial disclosure may be to prepare for some upcoming event(s) that will transpire changing our human history forever. We must try to open our minds to understand why it is so important to see a new perspectives rather than relying on narrow-minded dangerous views that have prevented our ascension into a new world view.

We must try to act vigilant and use our inner power in order to decipher what is "right" and what is "wrong." We cannot allow globalization, culture, and religion to keep us in the shroud of ignorance that we have displayed over the last twenty-five hundred years. We are our own enemy, and how we raise our future generations, depends on our ability to rationalize, use common sense, logic, spiritual, and emotional realms. So far, it is quite clear that we have a lot to learn about ourselves, the environment/biosphere, and the proper use of energy resources without damaging the Earth. The idea of human rights in non-existent, the majority of animals are not loved and respected as they should be. They are seemingly viewed as food or lower species without "feelings."

Human nature has shown a sad reality by killing and displacing other organisms based on our greed and the lust for economic progress, fossil fuel energy, and lumber resources by destroying vital forests, and feeding the machine of industrialization. Although many movements have been created to "defend the planet," (I.e. ecofeminism, preservationists, conservationists, ecotheology, etc . . .) they are still based on the basis of human cultural beliefs that desperately need change. Our space of independence is non-existent as we are forced into submission by elite interests who are void of emotion, love, and spirit. How do we ever expect to be saved if we do not act? For this fact, we must accept that we are ruined and destroyed with no hope for survival. Perhaps this Native American prayer can help understand our dire need for change:

> *"O Great Spirit,*
> *Whose voice I hear in the winds,*
> *And whose breath gives life to all the world,*
> *Hear Me. I am small and weak, I need your strength and wisdom*
> *Let me walk in Beauty, and make my eyes ever behold the red and purple sunset*
> *Make My Hands respect the things you have made and my ears sharp to hear your voice*
> *Make Me Wise so that I may understand the things you have taught my People*
> *Let Me Learn the lessons you have hidden in every leaf and rock*
> *I Seek Strength, not to be greater than my brother, but to fight my greatest enemy—myself.*
> *Make Me Always ready to come to you with clean hands and straight eyes*
> *So, When Life Fades, as the fading sunset, my spirit may come to you without shame."*
> *Ahoe (Native prayer; the seven sacred prayers)*

We must fight ourselves from our own destructive nature in order to ascend into a new consciousness and possibly join our alien creators. These ideas are not to force you to accept these observations, but to question within and look around us at our everyday predicament. We need to challenge ourselves to new ideas. It seems that we want benign indifference, and separation of thought that would constitute unity is the major obstacles we have trouble overcoming. Humans tend to wrap ourselves in a busy, hard life so that we do not have the opportunity to discover our power. We need to give ourselves the chance to discover our inner power without having the thoughts of "sin" and "unworthy" in our vocabulary.

Ascension as an individual may take an entire lifetime or even many lifetimes to master; however it should not be an obstacle. Emotions, love, and compassion have to come universally, not fixated on one individual or many. Maybe then, we as humans can be viewed as more than a universal menace or lost child. We need to take care of our thoughts and those around us. We are on our own, and must be responsible for our own actions now. A very heartfelt suggestion from my mother was to focus on the present, and enjoy the moment for they are never to return. Living with no regrets and opening my mind to new ideas. This is a great task for our humanity; however could be achieved with the proper guidance from our alien forefathers who are no doubt intertwined within our society.

Many of these key speakers attended the *Awake and Aware Conference* held by Project Camelot back in 2009-2010. Having the privilege to view each lecture in detail initiated interest in the field of Ufology and paranormal activity. Adding travels to the Pampas in Argentina a few years back, the opportunity arose to view phenomena that were just simply unexplainable. Examples were anything from seeing orbiting lights circumventing windmills to red/yellow lights following individuals. With the Pampas being void of any light besides the stars, one was surrounded by complete darkness. The distance between neighbors were far too great to view any additional lights in what the townspeople called *Chacras.* Surprisingly, they were accustomed to these phenomena and even baptized with the name *luz malas.* Many of the people either refused or were too hesitant to explain the history or their own personal experiences due to fear.

Adding to personal research and furthering studies were due in part to these specific men, their presentations, and personal experiences in the paranormal. An ascension of sorts transpired after learning from those who have much to offer regarding UFOs and the history behind them. Growing and learning are essential to become a more informed and vigilant person that everyone has the opportunity to do. This opportunity has become one of the best experiences that will be shared with the rest of the human community.

End notes

[1] John P. Mills PhD. "How many habitable are in the Milky Way Galaxy?" *About.com Space/Astronomy* (2012).

[2] Nicholos Wethington "Vatican Holds Conference on Extraterrestrial Life." *Universe Today* (November 2009).

[3] Alok Jha. "Pope's astronomer would baptize alien if it asked him." *The Guardian U.K* (September 2010).

[4] John Thavis. "Vatican astronomer says that if aliens exist, they may not need redemption." *Catholic News Service* (May 2008)

If you are one step ahead of the world,
you're a genius. If you are two steps ahead,
you're a crack pot.

—Sterling Alan

I

Alex Collier and the Andromedan Holographic Model of the Universe

As we take a look at the marvels of the planet Earth such as the pyramids of Giza, the Inca Civilization (including Machu Picchu), the Olmec statues, and Tenochtitlan (whose entire layout happens to fashion the solar system), Stonehenge, the Cambodian pyramids etc. we happen to attribute them to human design. This accepted theory states that *humans* have shaped these wonderful, complex and mystical designs by our own hands. To be accurate, most of these creations believed to be created in our sequential time, are in fact much older. The Sphinx for instance, is much older as opposed to the common belief of thirty-five hundred years by Egyptologists. In the 1960s, mathematician and symbolist R.A. Schwaller de Lubicz postulated the following theory from his book *Sacred Science: The King of Pharaonic Theocracy* :

> *"A great civilization must have preceded the vast movements of water that passed over Egypt, which leads us to assume that already existed, sculptured in the rock of the west cliff at Giza that Sphinx whose laconic body, except for the head shows indisputable signs of aquatic erosion . . .*

Schwaller de Lubicz then suggested ways to prove that a civilization way beyond the capabilities of Egypt 4,500 years ago existed many thousands of years prior to that time:

> *"If the single fact of the water erosion of the Sphinx could be confirmed, it would in itself overthrow all accepted chronologies of the history of civilization; it would force a drastic re-evaluation of the assumptions of 'progress'—the assumption upon which the whole of modern education is based. It would be difficult to find a single, simple question with graver implications . . ."*

With this overwhelming evidence like the Sphinx, the arguments of the experts are seemingly crumbling and eroding. As humans need to feel important in the cosmos, we attribute the mysteries of the past to simple explanation when it fact it requires more. The universe as we will cover in detail is a vast place filled with stars, planets, galaxies too grand for the human mind to understand. In turn, we seem to create an illusionary world where humans are the center and the rest of the universe looks upon us for we are the only "intelligent life form" in the solar system.

This of course even not attributing to Jungian archetypes, gives the feeling of being insignificant and the desire to be the center of attention (transitioning into something great in our lifetime). Humans seem to need this attention due to the lack of a general purpose. One could defend this theory by focusing on the natural system. Mammals on this planet seem to instinctively develop equilibrium with their surrounding environment while humans move from one area to another. When we have exhausted all resources in the area, we have to multiple to sustain our species and move elsewhere to another area continuing our cycle of destruction. Overall, it seems our purpose is to destroy based on our natural instincts.

To add to this description of humans, we also have such a delusional idea of ourselves including which planetary bodies in the solar system are considered planets and others not, which species are more important than others, and which areas of the world should be spared and others used for resources etc . . . Looking at these observations and our situations, humans should strive for truths and a better understanding.

Through history, most iconic constructions given credit to ancient civilizations complete accuracy, articulation and quite frankly a work of art (as we see in these wonderful structures), could not be humanly possible. According to the ancient alien theory, our alien ancestors may have had a big part in the design, technology, and construction of these great wonders [1] [2]. Let us study the pyramids of Giza for instance; the three pyramids are so perfect, that a sheet of paper cannot fit between the blocks. All three of them are lined perfectly with the Orion-Osiris belt and seem to move with the stars trajectories. Graham Hancock theorized in conjunction with Robert Bauval that whoever built these great wonders, had knowledge on how the stars would look eight thousand years before they were actually built [3]. There seems to be an in depth connection between the stars of Orion and the three pyramids according to the *Orion Correlation Theory*. First presented by Robert Bauval in 1983, he believed through observations, which the three main pyramids and their layout coincided with the three stars on the belt of Orion:

> *"We have demonstrated with a substantial body of evidence that the pattern of stars that is "frozen" on the ground at Giza in the form of the three pyramids and the Sphinx represents the deposition of the*

> *constellations of Orion and Leo as they looked at the moment of sunrise on the spring equinox during the astronomical "Age of "Leo" (i.e., the epoch in which the Sun was "housed" by Leo on the spring equinox). Like all processional ages this was a 2,160-year period. It is generally calculated to have fallen between the Gregorian calendar dates of 10,970 and 8810 BC." (The Mars Mystery, pg. 189)*

In order to accomplish a feat such as this, one would need to have the technology to fly, have knowledge on how the stars would correlate with these wonders and view from a celestial point for a finished product. Some in the scientific community offered other evidence that the "perfect" match claimed by Hancock and Bauval was not so. Scientists by the name of Ed Krupp from the Griffith Observatory in Los Angeles and Anthony Fairall an astronomy teacher from the University of Cape Town South Africa argued that the angles were somewhat different from that of the stars [4] [5]. Either way, it could still be theorized that primitive men existing from that time period had little to do with the construction of the pyramids.

Others who strictly believe in their faith or religious doctrine attribute these colossal wonders to "slaves" or local inhabitants. The Sinai Peninsula has no archeological evidence of any bones, artifacts, or even Egyptian weapons lain out on the desert floor [6]. We have to t ake in consideration of how Egyptians also claimed that they were able to transport these humungous blocks that weighed tons, up sand dunes on simple pulleys and carts. After they were placed on top of each other with laser precision, (that even technology now cannot even produce) the magnificent structures were created. Why is it that only three of the pyramids have withstood the passage of time, yet others supposedly created by the same craftsmanship, crumbled to the ground? The only logical explanation is that the originals were not created by the Egyptians, and the Egyptians arrived to this location to find these objects (the Pyramids of Giza and the Sphinx) already here.

The Egyptian Antiquities Organization and Egyptian tourism cannot afford to admit this due to the obvious blow it would cost them in tourist dollars. Is this a money making scheme only, or do they have something else to hide? Recently, no one is allowed to enter the pyramids for unknown reasons [7]. Are they afraid that someone will discover something that is not supposed to be seen? Many "experts" that claim to have an understanding in prehistoric archeology and physical anthropology, refuse to believe that these magnificent structures were built by other beings. They also claim to have "tons of evidence" based on history.

History, as fragile as it is, changes almost every day as researchers are finding more and more discrepancies in their structured belief systems. Having a degree does allow one to discuss the topic in an arena or debate forum however, at the same time could be fundamentally flawed, especially if it is based on a system that can be changed every day by discoveries. Is it too difficult to believe that there exist beings more advanced and powerful than humans in the universe? All of the past civilizations from Sumer to the Native Americans share their encounters with gods from the stars. How much more evidence do we need; a spaceship landing, worldwide enslavement by an exterior source, or the annihilation of humans in general?

If we are to accept this controversial truth of alien life engaging with humans on a day-to-day basis, we have to ask certain questions. If they are here, why is there so much effort to block disclosure about a subject that most consider nonsense? This could be a direct result to what could be called power control. The hierarchy that we contain in this human world must be maintained with no intention of change. In order to claim two important roles (power and rites) bestowed upon the powerful elite, the mass must be made to see a certain view, otherwise chaos ensues. This is not uncommon as all organisms have their own caste system and the powerful have no intention of sharing what they have with anyone at any cost.

There will always be those who have everything and those who have nothing; the only problem is the powerful who gain their position seem afraid to fall. This is how the system has worked for over five thousand years; an unbalanced system masquerading as a balanced one, ready to crumble at any time on the brink of failure. All those who gain power are afraid to lose it. Those who do not have it have a hunger for it, which is why they are always on the losing end. This cycle of self-destruction must stop in order for "change" to occur, introducing a new system. The question is now what kind of system will be created to allow a real balance to occur where the "bottom rung" supports the elite without a time bomb attached. In the long run, humans must come in terms with the painful reality that we refuse to face: not all of us have a sense of worth that is equal determined by our own prejudices. Due to this belief system, not everyone can be spared.

Project Camelot's Message

Project Camelot, a private established organization claiming to *alert* humanity about the truth concerning UFOs, interviews certain individuals that will be covered during the course of this book. This group also considers themselves to be an active part of the exopolitical community (being considered UFO special interest group beforehand). The group leaders are two individuals called *Kerry Cassidy* and *Bill Ryan* who fund the entire organization on their own, with generous contributions from followers. Another individual David Wilcox is a third member, claiming to be a psychic medium with an understanding of the spirit world and its mechanics. The group supposedly focuses on creating awareness for the rest of humankind to "wake up" from their mental sleep and see the *truth* for what it really is. Their main belief system is centered on the belief that an advanced race of aliens known as the Draco (reptilian), are using human beings as a natural resource (food, energy, slave labor etc . . .). According to their Intel, these beings exist in the same galaxy and have been here for about eight hundred thousand years or so. There are few speculations that in fact a race of intelligently created bipedal reptiles did exist at the time of the dinosaurs called *dinosauroid* (taking in consideration that *if* the dinosaurs survived, they would evolve into this species). In the 1980s, a paleontologist by the name of Dale Russell introduced the idea that if the dinosaurs survived they would evolve into something similar to human beings with their own language [8] [9].

Although the idea was completely ridiculed after its publication, many still believe this may be a possibility. Human beings are not the only species to evolve in any environment. It may be a little hard to imagine that other organisms may have evolved elsewhere in the universe far beyond our imagination. Why is it such an unbelievable concept that humans refuse to admit? Do we feel threatened? Will this concept destroy our egos to display that we are not in control and important? Have these beings existed thought our history and worshipped in ancient cultures? Almost every ancient civilization (Incan, Aztec, Egyptian, Phoenician, Sumerian, Babylonian, Native American, Rama, etc . . .) has had a reptilian deity that they have worshipped and considered all powerful. *Sebek* (*Sobek*), *Nimrod*, *Quetzalcoatl*, *Apep* (Apophis), *Hong* (rainbow dragon) *Medusa*, *Nagas* (Hindu), and the *Chitari* (African), are just a few examples of the many gods that the ancients feared and worshipped over the millennia. They believed that they were descendants of these reptilian entities that bred with their humankind to create the kings of men and women.

Is Project Camelot trying to inform us, or is there something bigger at stake here? Cassidy's *passion* is to eliminate the Draconian influence on the human race so that we may be free to rule ourselves. She is bent on the belief that we humans are all going to be *saved* and ascend into greatness without doing any effort. In the author's opinion, practicing a dangerous technique of alerting the unprepared population is not such a good idea. A system that humans have been dependent on for the last five thousand years is to be replaced with Cassidy's dream it seems. Are we ready to rule ourselves and decide which humans are worth supporting and which are not? We all believe we are unique and our idea of the *sanctity of life* is based on cultural and personal beliefs. We do not seem to possess the mental skill or ability to decide for ourselves at this point in time. It is apparent that maybe we humans are too weak to decide for ourselves which is why we allow systems to control us, and our independence is something that is lacking in our beings (to take responsibility seems to difficult a task).

Alex Collier and the Fate of Humanity

One individual known as Alex Collier is a close friend of Project Camelot and offers his insight on a new system given to him by an extraterrestrial race known as the *Andromedans.* He considers himself an extraterrestrial contactee that is able to transmit the message that this alien race has for human beings. This race supposedly originates from the galaxy Andromeda and according to him; they are a benevolent race only here in the interest of our benefit. Since everyone seems to have an agenda, Collier may mean well to lift the human spirit; however a fresh analysis is required. Collier stated that these beings operated on a *holographic* level in terms of government and society. The term holographic implies that fourth and fifth density are dominant and can intervene with lower dimensions at will that human beings currently operate on (second and third densities) [10]. Acquiring this technology and utilizing it can be very useful for societies to grow and establish a balance of sorts. Human corporations and governments would not accept this technology or system for the fact that their firm control on humans could be eliminated. Unless there is profit for this system on a public level, the secret and special interest groups will continue to conceal this technology until they can establish a monopoly. Collier strongly believes that the governments cannot afford disclosure of this precious technology until preparations for the public population are established.

Sometime in 2012, Collier claims that major events and changes will occur on this planet. He doesn't imply that there will be an end of the world scenario; however, he states and *end* in human consciousness would occur. In any case, somehow humans will alter themselves or be altered artificially through frequency. He also stated his belief that China or India would be the first countries to expose the UFO conspiracy theory and the cover up behind it. This speculation could be accurate since as of February 2012, China's *Chang'e-2* released photos of an "alien base found on the moon. According to *messagetoeagle.com*, China is trying to undermine NASA by stating that there are in fact UFOs on the Moon, and that NASA is purposefully airbrushing photos and misleading the public media:

> *"I was sent some pictures by a source who claims China will be releasing Hi Res images taken by the Chang'e-2 moon orbiter which clearly show buildings and structures on the moon's surface. He also claims NASA has deliberately bombed important areas of the Moon in an effort to destroy ancient artifacts and facilities . . ." (messagetoeagle.com)*

During his 2009 conference for *Project Camelot*, he presented information concerning many aspects of the UFO agenda. He discussed the Cassini Project launched by NASA was supposedly only a probe to study the aspect of Saturn. He disclosed that the probe was really present to monitor an alien ship that was orbiting the planet for unknown reasons. He further stated that the project was black ops because no one in the government was willing to discuss it. Raising a few questions, we must wonder why this craft is stationed there and for what purpose? It is Collier's Andromedans? It is the Draco that Project Camelot seems to fear? Is the ship going to make its way here in 2012, or are they just an observing ship to monitor human behavior? Could this be the ship that *Skylab III* monitored in 1973?

Considered an excellent contribution to the discovery of UFOs, NASA claimed that this was a man made satellite reflecting red light off of Skylab, however, the data found displayed that this "explanation" was inconclusive proving that this structure was anomalous. The structure according to the three astronauts *Bean*, *Lousma*, and *Garriott*, followed them for ten minutes very close to the Skylab. If this was a satellite, it would be traveling too close to them (uncomfortably) not to detect, and NASA or NORAD would have been able to identify it. Since the astronauts were startled by it and maintained a trajectory similar to their own, this then proved that the object was either an alien craft of sorts or some unknown sentient intelligence [11].

Another craft of unknown origin according to Collier is orbiting the South Pole with a structure twenty miles long. Ships and other "objects" enter and leave at will which should be causing questions and concerns. Collier unfortunately, was unwilling to discuss this any further bringing the speculation that this was either fabrication or a more serious issue [12]. If these speculations are true, how are the government and NASA able to block out these objects from being seen by telescopes and binoculars? Even more bizarre was another claimed alien craft supposedly orbiting the planet Neptune at eighteen degrees right ascension, looked like a "death star" that one would see on Star Wars [13]. According to Collier, this structure is friendly although the United States government has been keeping an eye on it. If the government was interested in this structure as a threat, this could mean that they might not be human allies with our best interests.

Could these finds threaten the power hierarchy that we have covered? Who determines which are benevolent races and dangerous ones? Collier himself adheres to the *Draconian* agenda and offered his intake on what they planned to do with humans. His information again stems from his supposed contacts the Andromedans, who could be an opposing force to the reptiles. This doesn't mean the reptiles are necessarily *enemies* of the human race, it could mean that these two alien factions are at war and plan to use humans as an intermediary. The propaganda angle between two warring races or empires proved to be useful in times of war as seen during WWII. We as humans could be caught in the middle of a galactic war being used as pawns. Whoever wins this war doesn't signify that humans will benefit from either side.

According to Collier's Intel, the Orion Wars have ended about thirty-six thousand years ago in result of the Draconian (reptile) race controlling and continuing to control planet Earth and the neighboring planets around us. He did not go into detail on what the Draco were; he just considered them a dominant race that views humans as pathetic creatures only meant for manual labor and food. Collier strictly believed that the Draco along with the power elite here on this planet were already in league. This of course could resemble the Hollywood portrayal of John Carpenter's movie *They Live* (1988). The movie is based on a short story by Ray Nelson called Eight o'clock in the morning, which dealt with an alien race from Andromeda colonizing Earth using humans as a commodity and ruling us with an iron hand. They cloaked themselves to look like humans while they dominated the globe alongside the human elite. Grotesque in nature, the Andromedans were the supposed enemies, not the reptiles. The only way to discover them was to utilize special shades to "see" the true identity of these alien creatures. All humans that opposed the rulers were eventually killed expect for two heroes who made it to the end eventually scrambling the signal, and showing the true identity of the creatures to the whole world.

Hollywood usually portrays any movie with humans versus an unknown enemy as the victor despite the obstacles.

Although this may be what we all desire, this doesn't transpire that way. Since the conception of this movie in 1984, could it be that Ray Nelson and John Carpenter were trying to hint to the human race an ongoing reality all these years? Collier also stated his thoughts during his speech at the conference especially concerning politics and the space program. Collier hinted at the ongoing conspiracy that happens to center around the Moon. He stated that the Moon itself was a base only inhabited on the dark side (due to the reality that we can never see that side) by governments who are in league with an alien race. He didn't clarify what alien race was involved; however, assured the listeners that world governments (United States, Chinese, and European "interests") had their prospective bases set up in a place of atmosphere on the Moon. Is Collier speculating that the Moon has an atmosphere, gravity, and life? Why then would there then be a conspiracy that the United States never landed there in the first place? Is he nothing more than a motivational speaker embalmed in his own delusional fantasy?

The human condition was also a central focus as he described what he believed to be the purpose of human beings: that we are destined to colonize the stars and expand. Was it the Andromedans that gave him this message? We as humans know through our history that we are a destructive species. Whether or not we act alone or with the help of some outside influence, it seems we are not capable of ever establishing a fixed or peaceful environment. This result is due to the underlying need for power, greed, and competition. Some of these human qualities are unavoidable; however we act beyond the limit pushing ourselves overboard into madness.

The key is to push for balance; however, we are stopping ourselves in doing this and need guidance. Who is to guide us? It is Collier's hailed saviors the Andromedans? Are they able to understand that we are a primitive race yet to reach the consciousness of balance, love, understanding, and compassion? Are they willing to wait for us as we continue to destroy everything living in the environment around us? Whatever the outcome may be, humans as a whole will not be helped in making conscious decisions. We must do this on an individual basis with the selected few who surpass normalcy and substandard human behavior. Will the rest of humanity look to these champions for guidance? Should they give it to us? Can we handle this type of responsibility?

Collier believes in the power of the human spirit, and declares that because of this untapped power, the governments and pharmaceutical companies fear us and use vaccines like the swine flu (*H1N1*) and others to permanently damage our DNA that cannot be repaired or damage healthy cells [14]. Collier also reiterates his belief that two-thirds of the population would be eliminated sometime by 2012. What are some of the ways humans can prevent this, or do we allow the push for our demise faster than normal? His Andromedan source also indicated the fall of the dollar and the emergence of a new monetary system of global capacity with a one world government. This government will be run by the same thirteen families that controlled Rome for the last twenty-five hundred years. Along with this system, Collier stated that an involvement with gene therapy and programs to create super soldiers (that are created from a hybrid of human genes and *unknown* genes) to establish order [15].

The Martian moons *Phobos* and *Deimos* along with Earth's Moon would be prevalent in this matter as bases for the assumed soldiers that Collier believed in [16]. He even went as far to explain this model as a story similar to Star Wars (hinting at clone units bred for military intelligence).

Believing a story like this will be almost impossible without any reliable sources and the public population viewing this as mere fantasy or science fiction. This could be the reason why humans fail to ascend or improve their situation. Collier may be trying to send a message that we are thousands of years behind in technology, intelligence, awareness, and understanding causing our ultimate failure as a species (some signs may show otherwise).

According to the model of *galactic structure*, the super advanced civilizations exist within the center of the galaxy while the less advanced exist farther and farther away towards the outer rims. Within this large group of civilizations, Collier claimed that there were numerous groups of aliens with their own interests and agendas [17]. *Who* they were and *what* they wanted, were not on Collier's agenda for explanation during the conference. With this scenario, we humans must eliminate this illusionary concept of "good" and "bad" due to the blunt realization that we could be on our own. Collier stated that the more troubled and disillusioned human beings were the religious ones; along with their fantasy that has caused more damage than good [18]. The reason would be due to a false reality they have created based on a perception of fantastic beliefs; which in turn has reinforced this illusion with their reality. This ***does not*** exclude Collier and the belief that the Andromedans will assist us. Without the proper evidence and lack of credibility, Collier may be a victim of his own reinforced illusion [19].

Andromedan Mentorship

During the conference, one concept came into being that merited investigation: "focus goes and energy flows."

What exactly did he mean by this? How do we define the terminology *energy* in ways to make sense of this? Collier could be describing humans controlling their environment with proper techniques. We have been taught over the centuries that we are powerless, and that a god is the only entity that can create *miracles*. The matter of truth is that we could be gods in our own rite due to the result of being created from alien species [20]. Does this mean our capacity for power is infinite? Is this the reason that the elite fear the poor and public population? Untapped power they cannot control? Are they purposefully destroying our DNA to hinder certain powers that could essentially change our species for the better [21]?

Not all of the humans undergo these changes, meaning that a certain few are allowed access to explore their potential (on an individual scale). Unlike the three cults that have dominated the globe under a shroud of ignorance and shame, most humans unfortunately believe whatever they are told and surrender their power losing it. We are all supposedly assured that the responsibility is not in our hands and a god will assure us salvation deciding everything for us. We as humans have to stop leaving our responsibility in the hands of nonexistent entities, and take control paying for the mistakes we make. *We are not sinners or unworthy; humans are prone to mistakes and very big ones!* We have to learn not to repeat them over and over. The major flaw we humans contain is the lack of faith within ourselves. We always attribute our success to a higher power neglecting our own potential.

Does this make us arrogant to adhere to this train of thought as most religions would state? Not necessarily, because we finally take a step into a larger world of doing things on our own without fear, lies, and false promises. Collier seemed sympathetic to this concept and reiterated these other forces will not take an active interest in aiding us or more, unless we reach a certain level. Then and only then, they would conveniently "help" humans ascend into the next level. For this to work as a species, everyone (meaning every single human body) must ascend spiritually (not religiously), intellectually, compassionately, and lovingly as a whole. How can this be realistically attainable? If Collier is correct about the elite purposefully destroying us at all costs, when are we going to start? How long will this take years, centuries, or millennia? It doesn't seem along our current path, that this reality will ever leave its illusionary state.

We must remember that he mentioned that the Andromedans followed a *holographic model* as exemplary in superior races. What does this mean for humans? We all supposedly wish for a utopian society where everyone and everything is bliss, harmonious and error free; could this new unknown model help us? Collier described his utopian model as possible only when as a species, we alter our consciousness and "move up." This of course would mean that all human beings would receive all basic needs at no cost (health care, food, amenities, water etc . . .) without "strings attached." This could be a possibility if every human individual would look out for one another in the betterment of the entire race. Could this be the standard model for a one world government? Isn't this what the elite are pushing for the unity of the human race under one banner?

What makes Collier's Andromedans so different, the fact that they are not human? The Andromedans supposedly use this model which displayed their superiority over humans. Their system focuses on the young and teaches them all the known knowledge while presenting it to them regardless if they are ready to receive it. This in turn makes the younger generation wiser than the older. The older generations are not concerned with this, due to the younger generation carrying the same structure improving it in many ways (thus altering its basis for a more advanced existence). When this is achieved, the mind expands as well as the body and the spirit [22].

Humans on the other hand, employ the exact opposite: firstly, we do not teach our young anything at all; in fact we teach them *fear*. We limit their thought processes, claiming that they are not ready to hear certain information until they are older (or when we feel they can be told), and further this practice by controlling their education. The concept of wisdom goes to the older generation, thus keeping the young ignorant until the *time* is right. This concept doesn't happen globally as we would expect it to transpire; instead it is done in a caste system causing separation of classes (giving the privileges to the elite carrying information, meanwhile the poor unfortunates die with little knowledge whatsoever). The older person is valued as wise and is afraid that the younger generation will toss them aside hence the asinine commandment "honor your mother and father." *Next*, supposedly only a few individuals are aware of anything around them, making the elite just as vulnerable (less impacted) to this stipulation as well.

Their pyramid structure varies from the regular standard version where capital and living systems are replaced by *knowledge* and *power*. Collier lends an example stating that the president of the United States was not aware of the forty-seven levels of security above him in making decisions for all of humanity; as he believes disclosure is far from reality. Lastly, international bankers have created a system of control based on a debt system, making money necessary, owning water, resources, and basic human needs. This only means that one must pay to enjoy these gifts for a comfortable existence. Now the question remains as to why must one pay for water when it is part of this planet and so readily available to humans. The answer is simple: because if one monopolizes water, one will control the people since we cannot function without it.

It would seem obvious then that a monetary system must be eliminated if humans are to try to reach what Collier's utopian principle. What would the transition look like in the meantime? We have buried ourselves in this system and have allowed it to control us; bonding to our human culture transforming us into slaves. Unless there is a global uprising, it doesn't seem possible that humans will ever break the bonds. We must imagine though that if we humans ever break free and this system is destroyed, another system would gain control with their own interests and power (bringing humans deeper into another chaotic result) causing a never ending cycle. This could theorize that humans are like lost children; we have no direction and must be told what to do and when to do it. As far a benevolent races go, we really do not know what their agendas are or what their interests are. Collier stated that "the needs of the many outweigh the few." If this is the case, then the few are the ones in control and a balance must be reached.

Interestingly enough, Collier speculated many key points about human beings and what exactly the mystery may be surrounding our existence. According to his personal research and the Andromedans, humans are made of three elements: *color*, *light*, and *sound*. He also stated that the DNA can be repaired (contrary to his original statement concerning the vaccines) but he doesn't know how (or could be refraining to expose how). The Andromedans have their DNA perfect according to Collier, and due to this, they are able to remember their past lives and memories [23]. Humans on the other hand, are very ignorant of their past lives or memories as we lose them with age (or with chemical alteration due to foods, drugs, and other elements). It can be suggested that maybe the damage done to our DNA is for this reason, so we cannot remember who we were or are for that matter. It is quite possible we experience these phenomena from time to time using the phrase *déjà vu*.

This is very difficult to determine due to the fact we acquire some distant memory of the current situation we are dealing with. This could come at any random time and happens because supposedly, we have done this already. Could it also be possible that due to the complexity of the mind, that these recalled events transpired in this current life or are they the "streams crossing?" Collier also maintained a more realistic view concerning self-responsibility when faced with decisions. This concept fell under what he called the *domain of knowing*. This theory called for the human to question why we believe the things we do. It also called for humans to look at ourselves and realize that we are not just physicality, but two beings existing simultaneously [24]. Despite all of the religious jargon surrounding the issue, it is known through scientific research by Dr. Duncan McDougall that the human "soul" weighed approximately twenty-one grams and that we are connected to it even though it remains dormant [25]. All of the experiments, mistakes, trials are known to us buried deep within and surface when we are conscious about our actions.

We know this phenomenon as having a gut feeling, as we are creating our own adventures and now must take responsibility for them (i.e. decisions). We must shy away from praying to the heavens at an invisible father figure to rescue us every time we are faced with a challenge. This act could be the main reason for our failures and in turn we hinder our growth. We must help ourselves by detaching from the *addiction of physicality*. Once we do acquire a three hundred sixty degree perception of all things around us, the result will lead to self-empowerment and introspection (which according to Collier must be voluntary) [26].

Most of Collier's speculations as profound as they were, claimed to help humans achieve a better understanding of UFO and the vast universe we live in assuming his contacts are legit. In order to discover for ourselves whether we as humans can trust these *enlightened* races, we must find their origin. Where do these Andromedans originate from? He stated that he was told that the Andromedans arrived from an ancient universe separate from our own. The Andromedans created wormholes and pathways to distinct universes encountering ruins and civilizations. If we are to follow this model, the multiverse theory comes into play. Collier also mentioned that their traveling capabilities grossly exceeded ours due to them utilizing eight, ninth and tenth densities of the twelve known densities shown to humankind. If we accept the scenario that the Andromedans have mastered the space-time continuum, accurately travel to any known universe with proficiency, time is of no importance, and other parallel dimensions are easily accessible. The very idea (if true), astonishes our feeble human minds as we are accustomed to seeing this done by Captain Kirk, or Picard.

The very perplexing fact according to Collier is that all advanced and intelligent races have no idea where they came from. This causes a bit of confusion due to the fact that their supposed mastery of the DNA being undamaged, would give them access to their past lives. As Collier's story changes, the outlook on the issue is called into question. Could this mean that the Andromedans have an agenda that we humans are not paying close attention to? Collier means well, however, he does not relay details as to purposefully withhold vital pieces of information. Could this be a test? Must we discover the rest on our own? Are the Andromedans afraid of what we might do with this newly found knowledge?

Another idea given to him by his Andromedan masters was the idea of mentorship. He believed that humans were meant for more than just being servants and bonded slaves of extraterrestrial races [27]. This could hint at the speculation that we were created in a laboratory of sorts; moreover by trial and error like any science project. Collier expressed much hope on the idea of positive change and shifts of consciousness that will alter our thinking process. The result will allow humans to ascend into fourth and fifth densities or dimensions. Although this may not explain why humans have not dominated the third density yet, Collier failed to explain in detail with lack of information. He seemed driven as a motivational speaker of sorts, trying to ease the suffering by offering hopes and speculations of possible solutions concerning the "human burden" to the audience. This could fall along the line of religious dogma that the three major cults employ in our everyday lives. This idea coupled with refusal to believe humans as a natural resource also seemed to be among his passionate arguments.

An agreement with Collier's point on this system that we have created now doesn't benefit us and must change, however, nature works in cycles. If the current system is replaced by something new and improved, would this system become corrupted later in its evolution? We have seen history repeat itself many times over giving more and more damaging effects as technology advances at an alarming rate. Just because one dogmatic view is erased does not mean it is ok to instill another view that might damage humans even more. Every organism must recover from damage (mentally or physically) and given time to heal before implementing another program. If we are not given time to heal, the effect could be more destructive than anticipated. Love, peace, right, and wrong are only ideas as well and many different humans have their own distinctive definitions about them.

Eventually, if the system grows and changes, these ideas we thought so positive of, could change into something more detrimental. This stems the idea of a *vision quest* that Collier mentioned in his argument. We must go beyond what we have here in the physical state and break away into the unknown without fear, ignorance, or doubt. Humans must shed this "sugar coated" dream world of fantasy and enter a more realistic state. Will we be able to do this due to the fact that we have been so immersed into this fantasy? How can we tell the difference, and will we be able to become more useful to the Earth or cause more damage? This answer will not be easy to obtain and we can expect a lot of failure.

Light and darkness were two concepts that Collier also mentioned were important regarding humans. He attributed darkness to religious doctrine not understanding its true power; however, centered his point that learning about darkness was important not fighting it. This is true as most of the universe is composed of dark matter, one must imagine the power one can harness if humans learn to understand it without fearing it. Collier also stated that there was a dimensional/spiritual location or realm that was unknown, and to judge it as a human was impossible and unrealistic. His main point centered on intention and its necessity to create what humans want. How do we know what we want? Our desires usually do not include the species as a whole, rather an individual want usually attributing to one's own desires. The problem stems from the reality that humans do not think as a collective, we tend to think of our own survival from an individual stand point.

Although this is an ideal way, we do not care about those around us; our existence is the top priority. If most humans who are selfish and greedy intend to build a new system of belief, then the outcome would result in a similar model we have now. We are creatures of habit and it takes great suffering, pain and cataclysmic events to really change our points of view. Asking questions are the basis of change; as questioning the illogical around ourselves cause humans to enter a different mind state. The only problem with this belief is that most people are out of their comfort zone and are not ready for this type of self-responsibility.

The Unveiling of Free Alien Technology

According to Collier's belief, the Andromedans and four other races (that he mentioned towards the end) are here to help us empower ourselves to reach a new level [28]. Who are the other newly added races he mentions without names? Why is it in their best interests to help us if he stated we must act on our own first? If the claim is that the regressive Draconian race utilizes our bodies here on this physicality for slavery, are these benevolent races going to replace them? Would they go further as to do this on a spiritual level? Could absorbing our spiritual energy be their agenda to so eagerly help us? It is no doubt that Earth will undergo changes in 2012; however Collier didn't specify what date exactly. He either seemed unsure or just invented the story as he went along The solar system we live in is moving through a plasma belt and galactic plane very soon.

What does this mean for humans and our survival? Collier already hinted that our amazing technology was given to us by UFOs, could they help us survive these changes? Cold fusion, which was thought impossible, is being utilized by the DARPA program according to Collier. The DARPA program was and agency created for defense purposes by the United States for the improvement of technology for the military founded in Arlington Virginia. It is responsible for most major improvements in technology with funding over the last thirty years. The creation of the program in 1958 was due to the Soviet's launch of Sputnik in 1957. At the time the program called *ARPA* (Advanced Research Project Agency) was only established to keep the United States technology above the "enemy" in order to prevent any "technological surprises."

Now the game has changed and the defense was added in order to remain above the rest in terms of technology for a few surprises of our own in case other countries decide to attack us. ARPA has undergone many changes with the name from 1972, 1993, and finally 1996. It seemed that defense was necessary during the Vietnam war, the Gulf War, and finally after 1996, where the name remained DARPA. Since the program centers on our technological advances, we must discover where the ideas for this rapid technology emerged from. The idea of using *micro turbines* by DARPA could (with only two million dollars) provide fifty thousand people with energy to power a city of great size like Los Angeles, New York or Miami indefinitely [29].

Traveling to other planets would in turn be easier with this technology as well. Using a *Space X Kestrel engine* developed by SpaceX would allow for easier propulsion. Governments according to Collier have been given this technology to create propulsion systems that can allow for space travel. Since these rockets were used for the *Falcon* and *Draco (dragon)* spacecraft, it would be likely that this may be accurate information. Since these projects developed by *SpaceX* (operating out of Hawthorne California) are used for transporting crew and supplies to the space station, it is safe to assume that a more advanced model could send crews farther into space.

According to specs, these transport modules would be ideal for Lunar and Martian mission later on due to their heat shield's ability to withstand reentry velocities [30]. A magneto engine once installed into an automobile will make the car last indefinitely [31]. Why isn't the public allowed to utilize these examples of technology when we are paying for it with our tax dollars? The obvious fact that private companies and special interest groups cannot allow this to surface due to the fact that all profit would be marginalized. They have purchased this knowledge for their ownership and the delegation of it entirely. When will the public benefit for these modern marvels? Will it be too late to enjoy these few mentioned advancements due to the crumbling foundation we rest on? When will disclosure initiate, when UFOs descend from the skies?

How are humans ever going to connect into the "Galactic family" if we are not going to survive this initiation program? Collier believes that they are not here to babysit us, but to mentor us by showing us possibilities. They will supposedly show us what really happened, how we got here, and where we come from. Alas, this is the main goal is it not? Showing us these so called truths will either elevate us or damage us depending on how we take it. They also plan to remove the concept of time by showing us that it doesn't exist, thus removing it from our belief system. They will also show us that we are not inferior, and will discuss the topic of spirituality from four different points of view. This of course is much better than the ignorant one sided view we have existing now.

How this works according to Collier, is that the four major races will display their expression of how they see the soul and how it really is. This would obviously destroy the original belief of the theoretical "two sides of the story" scenario. The concept also known as the science of the soul could provide some answers for a greater understanding. What it claims to do is help the human being retain consciousness, recall cellular memory, and certitude. We then do not have to fear the mythical hell, purgatory, or even the guileless view of heaven; which expands our rationality, common sense and logic.

Karma is another question to tackle; does it exist or is it another ruse to lure us into ignorance a well? Collier stated that Andromedans are very reserved when it comes to our religion and politics. They believe that they are the same and limit their help to us when it comes to these two problems. Could the reason be to let us emerge from our own ignorance? Did they at one time suffer the same childish beliefs? Can we and will we let go of tradition and dogma to embrace the unknown? We as humans a naturally afraid and *fear* creates a wall to shield us from reality and possibly knowing more knowledge of our past. Are the eyes of the universe desperately watching us to ascend because they were once in our position? Have others tried and failed? Humans could be compared to stars: memories of the past trying to catch up with the present. Humans cannot proceed into the future until we settle our past. As stars, we are old photographs of what we used to be and we cannot access it due to our stubbornness and/or fear to explore outside of our beliefs.

Collier believes that the Andromedans are waiting for us to accept responsibility for our own actions. The trouble that comes from this dilemma is do we let the powers and governments of the world represent us when the destruction and chaos result in their decisions? Have we helped them accomplish this by surrendering ourselves to them? Do we want them to continue to represent the voice of all humans globally? It is true when the Native Americans state that humans have a hole in their heart that can never be filled, as we constantly need to fill the void within us. If this is the case, we all have sacrificed ourselves at the present time for nothing. It seems that we are building the wrong life on a weak foundation. How can we continue to allow this to transpire?

Alex Collier has shared a lot with us in terms of a brief look into his belief system of alien technology and the way of life of just one race of beings. He went even further as to say he has been aboard one of their ships and has experienced this phenomena firsthand. Whether we can believe this is entirely up to personal research and opinion. We must take in consideration that the Andromedans operated on fifth density and with this technology, they had a sort of holographic camera that he claimed they used on him to take "pictures." With these pictures, a "snap shot" contained the entire human life of the individual from conception to the present time on what he called holographic negatives. Basically, we can see our body as it went from birth to where we are now currently with every single disease we've had every change, and all of our memories. They were also able to view our bodies with precision and pinpoint when we were most healthy at all levels. They also had the ability to extract this part and re-insert it into our physical state to heal ourselves (using our own genetic imprint or "photo") [32].

Can it be done? Is it feasible? ABC's remake of the show *V* gives us an example of this kind of technology. In the first season in 2009, we saw Chad Decker (the reporter) looking at his entire medical history after being scanned by the reptilian visitors. They were able to see all of his sicknesses, operations, and future problems with their technology. The *Visitors* mentioned that the cell carried a history each time it changed, and left an imprint of its past form. So in fact this information is true regarding the cell; now we have to ask can the next step be possible. Collier stated that we do in fact have this technology, however only in its raw form not fully developed. Should we allow these Andromedans to scan us? Or will the agenda be as shown in *V*? Could the show represent propaganda against the Draco in order to sway us away from them? This unfortunately must be answered diligently and with care. Help is never free and everything comes with a price; it is a matter of just how much we are willing to pay.

In closing, a deep insight on the perceptions of the Andromedan race and their way of being was presented. The purpose of this conference was supposedly concentrated on *Nibiru* (the proposed *Death Star* that would come and end the Earth by 2012 per the Sumerians) and its impact on the UFO community. Collier did not believe that this would take place, because he felt all of our sacrifice and pain we have endured cannot end with this result. Hope as we call it is our greatest strength and weakness according to the fictional Architect from the Matrix. Are we prolonging our destiny of self-eradication believing that we were meant for something more than this? Or are we in fact creating our own life as Collier has mentioned on human feeling of hope and despair?

Collier is not willing to accept the fact that we may be nearing our extinction, and he further exemplifies this by mentioning that we are being studied by alien races. So are we an experiment or a human habitat? Are they the Jane Goodall's of the universe and we are their monkeys? Collier believed that due to this unique mixture (which isn't third dimensional) and the complex ecosystem that we contain, we must have a unique purpose. Passing through this galactic plane in 2012 will resulting dangerous global earthquakes killing many according to Collier. Many dangerous earthquakes did result during this year; however global catastrophes are yet to surface. Even more bizarre was his answer concerning disaster and the possible lack of intervention by his Andromedans masters.

Once this planet undergoes these effects, the *Schumann resonance* will change with the planet entering the plasma field causing time itself to stop [33]. All of the indigenous animals of this planet will have to change their harmonic frequency in order to "match" the newly transformed Earth. Some species will meet the change, however some will not. Nature will decide on what organisms will adapt to the change, not humans. Collier even concerned himself with the notion that most humans would not meet the requirements either! The third dimension would eventually merge with the fourth dimension with the end result of humans operating on this level. Humans realistically have trouble dealing with the two dimensional plane as it is, so it perplexes the mind on how we will surpass this obstacle.

After these changes have taken effect, our young will become the teachers according to Collier. He also added that he didn't know how the end would result leaving an array of doubt and speculation. As we look at the twenty-six thousand year cycle coming to a close, one can ponder what it is that humans need to alter their consciousness quickly in order to meet the requirements for survival. This question puts the individual at stake even if Collier is incorrect in his claims. Either side of the playing field takes a risk. Humans cannot anticipate the future nor see the past the choices they make. The choice is already and now we as responsible humans must understand it. Whomever we choose to guide us out of our current predicament, we must ask: are we replacing one master for another?

End notes

[1] Michael Lieb. *Children of Ezekiel: Aliens, UFOs, the Crisis of Race, and the Advent of End Time.* Duke University Press, p. 250 (1998).

[2] *Cithara.* (St. Bonaventure University 1961), 12.

[3] Graham Hancock. *Mars Mystery: A secret connection between Earth and the Red Planet.* Three Rivers Press (June 1999).

[4] Anthony Fairall. "Precession and the layout of Ancient Egyptian pyramids." *Journal of Royal Astronomical Society* (June 1999).

[5] Ed Krupp. "Pyramid marketing schemes." *Sky and Telescope* (February 1997).

[6] Michael Slackman. "In Sinai desert, no trace of Moses." *New York Times* (April 2007).

[7] Jimmy Dunn. "Tours to the pyramids of Egypt." *Touregypt.net* (August 2011).

[8] Russell, D.A.; Seguin, R. "Reconstruction of the small cretaceous theropod stenonychosaurus inequalis and a hypothetical dinosauroid." *Syllogenus* 37; 1-43 (1982).

[9] Naish, D. "Dinosauroids revisited." *Tetrapod Zoology* (April 2011).

[10] Project Camelot. "Alex Collier at the Awake and Aware Conference." *Projectcamelot*.org. Los Angeles California (September 2009).

[11] factfictionandconjecture.ca/files/skylab_3.hmtl (2006).

[12] Alex Collier. *Defending Sacred Ground: Letters from Andromeda and Diversified Enterprises.* Val Verian Press (1998).

[13] Laura Tyco. "Massive Derelict Spaceship found beyond Neptune." *Before it's news [indyinfo.com]* (November 2011).

[14] F. William Engdahl. "Nano Particles used in untested H1N1 Swine flu vaccines." *Infowars.com* (September 2009).

[15] projectcamleot.org/Duncan_o_finioan.html (January 2007).
[16] alienshift.com/id213.hmtl.
[17] bid 12.
[18] Ibid 10.
[19] Horm, M. "The Alex Collier Hoax is now over!" *www.truthcontrol.com/articles/alex-collier-hoax-nowover.* (2009).
[20] Gregory Brewer. "Could the human race have been created by aliens?" *examiner.com* (March 2010).
[21] Terrance Aym. "DNA-Destroying chip being embedded into mobile phone." *Pakalertpress.com* (April 2012).
[22] Alex Collier. "Andromedans and Mentorship." *Earth Transformation Conference.* (Hawaii 2010).
[23] Ibid 22.
[24] Ibid 22.
[25] Dr. Duncan McDougall M.D. "Hypothesis concerning soul substance together with experimental evidence of the existence of such substance." *Journal of the American Society of Psychical Research* (May 1907).
[26] Ibid 22.
[27] Ibid 22
[28] Ibid 22.
[29] Ibid 22.
[30] spacexlaunchreport.com/falcon9.html June 2012.
[31] Ibid 22.
[32] Ibid 22.
[33] Ben Tremblay. "Zero Point and Schumann Resonance." *Dailycommonsense.com* (April 2008).

Of course it is possible that UFO's really do
contain aliens as many people believe,
and the Government is hushing it up.
-Stephen Hawking

II

The Human Spark of Divinity and Robert Dean

Henry Higgins once said "*I have the milk of human kindness by the quart in every vein.*" This message gives us a chance to further study ourselves to see if we fit this model. Robert O. Dean is a retired Command Sergeant Major of the United States Army and one of the top advocates for exopolitics and the quest for UFO understanding. He has worked for the government for many years and has actually taken part in some of the most notable incidents with human/alien contact during his time in the military. Dean even furthers the claim that he actually *met* aliens face to face. Whether this man is speaking from the heart or just becoming another disinformation obstacle, many interesting topics were discussed in his forty-five years of personal research and experience.

Dean attended the Awake and Aware Conference of 2009 in Burbank California as a major speaker for Project Camelot. He stated that he was a recluse for quite some time, however surfaced to bring a sort of message to the human race who decided not to take anymore disinformation and dishonesty from the governments of the world concerning UFOs. For the last twenty of the forty-five years, he has presented the community willing to learn information that he claimed breached his "national security oath." This of course could be defended since he served in the U.S. military. As sincere as he seems and chalked full of bizarre out-of-this-world information, we must ask ourselves: what is Dean's agenda and can it really benefit humankind to ascend into the so called Galactic Family principle?

It is currently known that Dean has served during the Cold Front lines, during the time when the U.S. government engaged in secret black ops experiments like *Project Blue Book* (dealing with mind control), and the *Brookings Report* dealing with UFO impact on the mass population. It is also known that Dean worked for FEMA for fourteen years, and through research we find that this organization is not really out to help the human race for positive results (although they claim). Examples include FEMA hiring *Kenyon International* during the hurricane Katrina incident for "body dumping;" by setting up a mobile morgue for handling the numerous bodies the aftermath contained [1].

It was documented that Kenyon International was scandal ridden enough being a subsidiary of *SCI* (Service Corporation International) based out of Texas. It is run by a friend of the Bush family with cases already dealing with desecrating and illegally discarding corpses [2]. The *Menorah Gardens* chain of cemeteries owned by *SCI*, were broken into desecrated and bodies were removed from two cemeteries in Florida. They then dumped the remains in the back woods frequently inhabited by wild animals that investigations found in 2001 [3]. SCI had to settle a lawsuit for the amount of $200 million filed by the family members of the deceased. Even more interesting was that Peter Hartmann, manager of Menorah Gardens at the time, was found dead due to carbon monoxide poisoning outside his parent's apartment in a case resulting in suicide [4].

Can we be certain that Dean is a man we need representing us for the betterment of humankind? FEMA claiming to help the

Rwandan people during their genocide in 1994 didn't add to their credibility either. An investigation by the Virginia attorney general's office discovered in 1999 that planes provided by Christian Coalition founder Pat Robertson supposedly were used to fly supplies to Zaire under *Operation Blessing,* were really used for transporting mining equipment for a diamond operation run by a company called *African Development Corp.* The most bizarre fact that presented itself was that the prominent stockholder of this corporation was *Pat Robertson* himself along with Zaire Dictator *Mobutu Sese Seko* (who assisted in the setup of the operation) [5]. These few examples are just how atrocious and uncaring FEMA really is. Since Dean worked with them for fourteen years, can we assume that he helped partake in some of these "relief efforts?"

Human/Alien Interaction

Dean admits that he doesn't like to speak publicly, travel, or even bother anymore in dealing with the lies of the government. He stated that he only spoke now, due to the fact of the many people that came to the conference. He was also heartened that the audience was willing to hear what he had to say concerning "change" for the betterment of humanity. Dean started off with the statement: "the UFO story is the greatest story in human history" and he may be right. It is speculated by ancient astronaut theorists that UFOs have interacted with humanity for the last ten thousand years developing an interrelationship. He even goes as far as to stipulate that two or more of these groups are responsible in creating and manipulating the human gene pool to make us the delightful creatures we are today. Dean added that this process began well over one hundred thousand years ago.

During this conference, Dean clarified that he had a sort of sympathy with the U.S. government when it came to disclosure concerning aliens. This was due to the fact that he believed that the people on top do not know how to "remove the lid" of *Pandora's Box*. The story is too large and the government is incapable of preparation to the masses. The Brookings Repot that we have mentioned before, is an actual study completed by the government. NASA gave a contract to the Brookings Institute in 1950 to discover what to do in the future in case of extraterrestrial contact with humans. The study lasted three years, was published, and delivered to Congress in 1961.

The study concluded that if humans were to encounter this situation of alien intelligence, it would be wise *not* to tell the masses [6]. At that time, Margaret Mead was on this committee and suggested the same advice. Mead had a lot of personal experience during her time in the South Pacific dealing with primitive tribes. Her conclusion was that *if* and *when* the tribes encountered society at the time with the technology and power (the United States), they became useless and ineffectual. The result would be the natives dying in the process due to fear and the incapacity to assimilate [7]. Ever since 1961, Congress read the report, and this became national policy still employed to this day.

This would obviously transpire in our current situation due to lack of information we contain dealing with the unknown. When powerful race encounters an inferior race, an assimilation or complete eradication as we have seen in our own history (Columbus, the Spanish Conquistadors, the Vikings conquest, the English colonies with the Native Americans, the Roman Empire and the idea of *Pax Romana* etc . . .) transpires. Is this to be our fate? It could be suggested that Dean may be correct in the fact that alien disclosure would result in the systematic destruction of the social world, the theological world, and the scientific community. Although the eradication of the theological, scientific and social worlds would not be a negative result, one would have to wonder what would replace them.

Dean elucidated the fact that the question about alien presence is not just limited to the visitation phenomena, but actual integration into the human primitive world. He also stated that they have portals where *inter-dimensional* beings are able to travel to multiple realties simultaneously, making them the most advanced societies of alien civilizations [8]. These beings are the ones Dean believed were worshipped in ancient times. This could be true considering the fact that we have mentioned the amazing and enormous ancient ruins clearly not built by humans. As we have covered, it would take technology far beyond our imagination to conceive how they were built. Dean described this as "godlike technology" that the United States government now has access to [9]. He was sympathetic to their nondisclosure; however, his "patience" runs out in the quest for full disclosure.

Obama according to him will not disclose any information of aliens or UFO phenomena during his presidential term [10]. He attributed the reason for this apprehension due to the president not being properly briefed. Dean mentioned President Jimmy Carter who at the time promised if elected, would reveal all UFO information that was deemed top secret to the American public [11]. Unfortunately, this was not possible due to the fact at his national security briefing; the director of the CIA at the time was *George Herbert Walker Bush*. Bush explained to Carter that he did not have a high enough clearance and that information was on a "need to know basis." The result ended with false promises unfulfilled and questions unanswered. Could there be a direct connection between the U.S. presidency and UFO phenomena?

Bush became president himself later on and if this was the case, he was well informed on the information that Carter was supposedly trying to disclose. Why did Bush not disclose the information that he knew during his time as a CIA director? It seems that the presidency knows absolutely nothing on this subject matter and conveniently so. But then again, *Kennedy* wanted to sincerely follow the guidelines of the constitution on informing the American people concerning UFOs. Maybe it wasn't in his best interests to play the *human hero.* As the result show, it doesn't seem to get one anywhere in life . . . . only death [12].

Dean shed some light on a parable that he considered very important when talking about aliens and understanding them. His philosophy centered on what he called "*The Three Steve's of the Apocalypse.*" When we hear this word, usually religious fanatics and the latter attribute the Christian mythical "end of times" scenario. Also the nefarious four horsemen are mentioned as an extra melodramatic touch to partake in this scheme as well, heralding the end of the world. Is this what *apocalypse* really means? Apocalypse or *apokalupsis*, is of Greek origin signifying three things: the revealing, uncovering and disclosing of the truth. This terminology of truth also seems to be a problem when it comes to religion in general. Could it signify the uncovering of lies by religious dogma or uncover the facts concerning our origins?

Dean himself stated that we were in the middle of the apocalypse of revealing, uncovering, and disclosing of the vague concept of truth, and that another twenty or thirty years would pass before we were introduced to this. Two of his colleagues Steven Bassett (executive of the *Paradigm Research Group*) and Dr. Steven Greer (an American physician, Ufologist, author, lecturer, and the founder of the *Orion Research and Disclosure Project*) have tried tirelessly for the government and Washington to disclose information concerning UFOs and their presence on Earth [13]. They have both set up congressional meetings year after year to push for this idea, however, the results ended up not in their favor. As of 2012, they have failed in getting the Obama administration or U.S. government to admit any programs or admit anything concerning UFOs.

The last Steve that Dean referred to is working in Hollywood as part of the entertainment world. Steven Spielberg somehow fits into the subject of UFO phenomena simply because through his works, he has shown a sort of disclosure as he releases aliens in our presence through movies and television shows. Spielberg went as far as stating that his purpose was never to entertain the people, rather to discuss current pressing issues in our time [14]. Three examples of the most profound evidence would start with his movie *E.T.* created in 1982. This was obviously intended for children to view aliens as sort of non-threatening, wonderful entities that everyone could befriend and relate to. The main character E.T., who looked rather harmless, needed to find his way back home, as he was stranded here on Earth. The movie overall message portrayed aliens as softhearted and passive. Is he employing the method of softening the truth of taking something dangerous and replacing it with a non-threatening version?

Coincidentally, Spielberg's second interpretation was the film *Close Encounters of the Third Kind.* Although this movie was made first in 1977, this film was intended for the adult audience. Richard Dreyfuss starred in this film as it took us into a world of benign aliens, quests and the concept of family. The movie focused on the theory that music could be used to contact aliens. The government actually does this successfully and comes into contact with alien intelligence. They then engage in a sort of alien exchange program as we the viewer's actually have the privilege to see an actual "mother ship" as Dreyfuss' character board towards the end of the movie.

Could these events based on actual events that took place (i.e. abductions, first contact) or do we stick to the normal reaction of fantasy and science fiction? The movie also displays almost non-threatening entities to adults as well, portraying us adolescent naïve humans. Could the Brookings Report be accurate that we would suffer greatly if we uncovered the truth about an alien presence? We as Americans are so dependent on TV programming, that we cannot live without it [15]. This tool happens to be a powerful instrument when taking control of thoughts or ideas; especially when the subjects concerning UFOs and paranormal phenomena are presented.

The last project Spielberg did before his new show in 2011 Falling Skies was *Taken,* which Dean considered to be the best example yet. This series in 2002 won many awards for being one of the best miniseries on TV at the time. The main plot dealt with the Roswell crash and the actual subject of alien experimentation on human beings that actually led to the creation of a human hybrid; which could determine the future for human kind. Portrayed as a more believable scenario that some might consider true, the Roswell crashes did take place despite government cover ups and disinformation [16]. Dean mentioned that *Taken* was displaying some classified information during their episodes as entertainment. When we watch these movies and shows, how can we distinguish from actual information that might be true, to the information that is only there to keep us numb to what is happening around us?

Another producer who has shown great promise for releasing classified information in the guise of entertainment was *Chris Carter.* The creator of X-Files, Carter had discussed information about UFOs at the *Mensa Regional Conference* in

2009. The show was of course a success and Dean mentioned three episodes that actually displayed true classified material. Dean also hinted at many shows like *Stargate*, *Star Trek* and the latter from time to time, injected little pieces of facts into material that go unnoticed by the viewers. Why don't we see these little facts or pieces of information? Why are we blind to the little bits of information that might answer many of our questions? Dean attributed this to something called "*subliminal educational programming* [17]." What does this mean for us? Are we being brainwashed at a level unconsciously and continue to be so now? How can we snap out of this programming to finally pay attention to the details?

UFO technology

Lockheed Martin founded in 1995, is one of the U.S. foremost advanced corporations dealing with military, technology, defense, security, and even aerospace. Located in Bethesda Maryland in the Washington metropolitan area, a merger between *Lockheed Corporation* and *Martin Marrieta* took place in 1995. They are considered to be the top company having greatly advanced technological capabilities that we would only describe as fantasy. An individual by the name of *Ben Rich*, whom Dean mentioned as a key important figure, was a major scientist at Lockheed. Before his retirement, he was able to comment that we humans were "one hundred years ahead of established science." If his claim was true, that would mean that as of now (like religion), we are being fed lies about how scientifically advanced we really are. Could it be that all of this scientific research has an equally existent shadow program that deals with the real technology we have acquired? According to Dean, Rich had clearance and was well imbedded in special programs. He actually used the phrase "we can take E.T. home" meaning that they either had *zero point energy* or reverse engineering based on alien craft technology. Rich was the second director of Skunk Works from the years 1975-1991, and also nicknamed the "father of stealth" for being responsible for the development of the *F-17 aircraft* [18].

Skunk Works, is a top secret program dealing with advanced stealth technology which included the U-2 spy plane. This meant that with this sort of developed technology, there would be a safe assumption that the origin was not Earth based. Since the 1950s, technology has grown at a geometric rate leaving the old world behind. Before WWII, the idea that we as a nation would surpass the rest of the world was unheard of. The sort of technology we are dealing with today just didn't pop out of nowhere, it was either given to us or we have recovered it from some elusive force. Where did it come from? How did the U.S. amass such a wealth of technological advances within the last sixty to seventy years? One can suggest other worldly influences are in this solution looking for answers.

Whenever people have seen a black triangle UFO, the mass media usually attributed it to secret government craft such as the *F-117 Nighthawk* or the *B-2 Spirit* [19]. If this is the case, where did the idea for this model and development design emerge from? Was it due to creative inspiration of top scientists, or were they possibly based on an earlier alien prototype? Is it possible that Rich could be responsible for the development of these craft on his own? Unfortunately, he died due to cancer in 1995 which leaves us with many unanswered questions. When the mention of technology comes into argument, when is the public going to receive full disclosure on how technologically advanced we really are? If the technology can indeed take "E.T. home," this possible colonization of space in our current timeline may be a reality.

Other information that Dean mentioned were advanced systems development programs dealing with the likes of *modified propulsion*, *matter/antimatter conversion*, *exotic field tension*, *wormholes*, and *transluminal* (or hyper-luminal) flight meaning "faster than light [20]." All of these wonderful and near impossibilities may be experimented on and finally mastered by these top scientists at laboratories around the country. In order to have these capabilities, we would need an alien craft with reverse engineering to even begin to cross this threshold of science. It would seem now the term *science fact* could be used in this instance. Rich stated at his retirement in 1991, that the term UFO stood for "unfunded opportunities" as well as aliens. Most of the scientific community thought he lost his mind, but there could be a hidden message within his statement [21]. Could Rich be hinting silently for the investigation of forces unknown deep within our government?

Dean like most of us has a "hate list" (as the late comedian George Carlin once had). The list included politicians, and NASA. As far as politicians went, he believed what most people thought in terms of their honesty. He described them as "clowns, liars and thieves" that the people elect to represent them [22]. He recommended that before the "voters" rush to the polls, we must examine who we are allowing to represent us for the greater good. We are told constantly by government and mass media what is "good for us." We have been stripped of our freedom to think and make rational decisions, and these politicians are the best money can buy. It seems they are actors paid to entertain us while they work for someone's interests other than our own.

They act like mercenaries working for the highest bidder, and it seems obvious that they aren't here for the people's needs, rather for the needs of the corporate interest masquerading as government policy. The people as we have seen are at the bottom of the list in terms of any type of policy [23].

NASA or what Dean calls "never a straight answer," is far more interesting. Dean disclosed some information concerning how he speculated they operated and still do operate. NASA is one of many government agencies who lack explanation or seem to purposefully destroy any evidence they have concerning alien artifacts or UFO sightings [24]. Dean doesn't trust NASA and suggested that the people do the same. He agreed with the fact that yes they went to the moon (due to contrary beliefs); however, they haven't really disclosed what they found there. There was even speculation that the U.S. never landed on the moon based on evidence by Japan's *Kaguya Lunar Orbiter* that photographed the supposed areas of the Apollo 15 and 17 in 1972. There was no equipment found nor and evidence that any astronaut walked or operated rovers in the area. The photos that the Japanese rover took claimed to support this speculation contrary to evidence given by NASA [25].

NASA a few years back had admitted that they had inadvertently or "mistakenly" erased forty rolls from the Apollo program which contained thousands of photographs [26][27]. Was this purposefully done and were forced to eliminate evidence that could compromise the lies of the entire space program? This mistake was of course done to the Apollo 13 mission; the craft that supposedly never made it back to Earth for "technical purposes." What did Apollo 13 capture or discover from their rolls of film to be systematically destroyed? Dean shed some light on the subject giving us what he considered good news in terms of locating the "missing" film.

According to Dean, NASA forgot that they had a contract with the *JPA* (Japanese Space Agency) back in the 1960s who also recorded the Apollo missions. Every single negative of the entire Apollo missions were purchased and then recorded on computers located in Tokyo. Dean described that his "hatred" was not entirely for all of NASA, just the policy makers and administrators that he labeled as "bad guys." If the Japanese did record everything as he had claimed, there would be no mistake that they had the forty rolls of film that NASA conveniently erased or "forgot" to keep. During the conference, Dean surprisingly had two negatives given to him by top research scientist *Junichi Yaoi* in Japan at the time he attended on national television in Japan [28]. If NASA or the government interests really wanted to eliminate any evidence, it would be a safe assumption that they would have remembered important contacts made dealing with top secret or sensitive material. It would seem that even the best sometimes slip and produce errors.

Dean presented two negatives labeled *Apollo 13 negative 9* and *Apollo 13 negative 10.* Although the negatives were only in his possession, trying to authenticate them would be impossible (or to examine them). The cover story that the public receives about the mission according to NASA was the following: one faulty oxygen tank exploded causing the mission to be unsuccessful, even promoting a movie back in 1995 with a bevy of star actors including Tom Hanks. Contrary to NASA, these negatives show otherwise. *Negative 9* displayed many odd objects labeled *A*, *B*, and *C*. The first two objects are disc shaped entities signifying alien craft not man made (*B* and *C*). The last object *A* was to Dean the most interesting object of them all. This object was approximately five miles long and shaped like a cigar with intricate details [29].

The size alone for this sort of thing was enormous and obviously prompted NASA to avoid any engagement due to fear. Could it have been an alien fleet watching humans to make sure we acted accordingly, or worse yet an invasion preparation to inhabit the planet Earth? The other negative showed the objects moving and displayed another object of similar shape about two miles long. Dean attributed these objects to be similar to aircraft carriers here on Earth. According to his Intel, the smaller ships were leaving the bigger objects and returning to them as if they were portable bases. This could be possible due to the fact that objects that size obviously carry more than a "few green men."

A brilliant scientist by the name of *Norman R. Bergrun*, and also a close friend of Robert Dean, may have evidence to prove that NASA is being covert about their findings. Bergrun was an alumni for *Ames Research Laboratory*, *NACA* (National Committee for Aeronautics), and *NASA* where he worked for twelve years. During his time at Ames, he led the way to the design criteria for "airplane thermal ice prevention" and the development of "roll stability" laws for airplanes, rockets, and missiles [30]. This man was obviously a credit to genius and creative inspiration as he was also a photographic expert and engineer. Bergrun was also responsible for putting together the *Voyager* programs. During the 1970s, astronomers and NASA were discovering anomalous happenings with the rings of Saturn. They labeled these as "unexplainable occurrences" and they could not figure out what to make of them. With this result, Voyager was sent during the 1980s to discover what to make of these anomalies.

There were many photographs taken and Bergrun being honest (according to Dean), wanted to disclose those original photographs not altered by NASA. He was unable to publish his book anywhere in the United States concerning the photos of Voyager 1. Fortunately, he received publication of his book in Aberdeen Scotland. On the cover of his book, he displayed the *B-ring* of Saturn and next to it a self-luminous artificial object larger than our Moon. It appeared to be the color orange and could not be considered part of the planet's rings due to the fact in the photos; it changed location periodically as if driven by an artificial force [31]. The *A-ring* photo containing another strange object portraying a sort of "electromagnetic vehicle" that was an enormous two thousand miles long and four hundred fifty miles in diameter. An object of this size was definitely not part of the planet's origin and was deemed artificial.

Bergrun suggested that they may have constructed the rings, themselves hence the title of his book. Dean on the other hand, suggested that they may have been mining the rings in order to extract minerals from them. Either suggestion could be accurate. What if in fact they were mining the rings in order to extract a sort of mineral that was vital to them? We as humans do it here on Earth, it be possible with the right technology being utilized to do this in space. Unfortunately of late, Bergrun cannot be found hinting a number of things: he passed away, went into seclusion or was made to disappear. Either way, a genius will be missed in attempting to find a way for all humans to know the wonder and mysteries that established science has hidden surrounding just our own solar system.

The *Phobos* missions during the Soviet space program also offered us another example of strange phenomena that happened during the Mars missions. A cosmonaut by the name of Maureen Popovich took part in one of the Soviet Union's greatest finds in UFO history next to the Apollo missions. Phobos is one of Mars' moons that NASA and the

Soviet Union have been looking at during this time of the march for the discovery of space. While only twelve miles in diameter, this moon holds of lot of mysteries. The *Phobos 2* was sent out to view the moon and take pictures of both Mars and the moon itself. Among the amazing discoveries this probe discovered, one photo displayed a city-like structure the size of Chicago generating heat under the surface of Mars [35]. This photo was supposedly taken in infrared detecting strange heat signals.

Many experts have argued, and have tried to debunk this stating that the photo was a close up of a roach's belly, but of course it is known that these allegations were done purposefully to stir away the attention from the possibility of truth. Dean claimed that he has personally known that Mars was blooming with life along with Martian inhabitants. If this is the case, NASA is wrongfully playing with our time, taxes, and livelihoods. Why would they deliberately show photos of no importance or altered photos of Mars if not to give us a hint of deception and treachery? These photos were published along with others in Germany due to its classified nature at the time [36].

Another photo that the probe took before it was compromised was a strange object leaving the surface of *Phobos* slamming into the probe and decommissioning it permanently. This object was an elongated cigar shaped craft alerting the Soviet's to its presence as to warn the cosmonauts operating this machine to back off [37][38]. Could H.G. Wells be correct about his assumption of an alien race concerning a "war of the worlds?" *Michael Hesemann* was the German publisher responsible for these photos. It seemed strange that the United States would aide in their findings of alien intelligence when they already had the proof; however dismissed it. Why did they publish in Newsweek 2009 that

NASA is actively searching for extraterrestrial life [39]? Are they mocking us? Wouldn't this a shameful act on their integrity?

Engineering Humanity

Dean suggested that there are laboratories countrywide that are actually military, for example *Sandia National Labs* in California, *Los Alamos National Labs* also located in California, and *Brookhaven National Laboratory* located in Long Island [32]. According to Dean, these labs deal with alien races besides their claimed activities and purposes. Dean mentioned four distinct races that have worked with the government since his retirement with these beings classified as humanoid (but with distinctions that any normal human would notice if they came into contact with them). One of the four races looks very similar to us, and would not be noticed in our midst. Although he mentioned President Eisenhower coming into contact with this race nicknamed the "Nordics" due to their appearance of Aryan likeness, it is now verified that this transpired on *Edwards Air Force Base* [33].

Nevertheless, Dean believed that this race is here to help humans make a transition from "adolescence" into "adulthood." Why should they help us? What agenda do they have and what can they gain from our ascension into a larger world? Could we be allies against a common enemy, or do they have plans for us genetically? Dean suggested that they were part of the *human genome program* for that last ten thousand to a hundred thousand years ago [34]. *Christian O'Brien* also suggested the same idea in his book *The Genius of the Few*, that the human race was part of an alien creation of races that engineered us. There could be a more complex explanation to what the bigger picture really is. The question now would be to evaluate the accuracy of the *Brookings Report* and Margaret Mead's analysis on contact.

Dean's dislike for the theologians brought mixed messages. Organized religion itself is dangerous to the human being due to the creation of faith that could be used to justify illusions of the human mind. Dean stated a factually that "religion tends to divide people" and for a good reason. Although Dean promotes the concept of spiritual life, he mentioned a few bizarre things about his past life regressions. He considered the human being as a "masterpiece" along with being divine in some way. His personal opinion seems to omit our past behavior and the grotesqueries of our current actions to contest this exaggerated belief. He also went on to state that Jesus was one of his closest friends from one of his past lives, and still is a good friend. Religious studies and research have shown that *Jesus* is a symbol rather than a person based on older myths predating the story [40]. Adding the doctrines, birth, death, and teachings of *Gautama Buddha* (who existed six hundred years before him) supported that the foundation of the Christian myth was founded on Buddhism [41]. With this evidence, Dean doesn't support religion; however he doesn't seem to go against it as well being silent on the subject.

The Problem with the American Public

Dean's last group on the list was the American public that he stated was a "big problem." He focused on the attention span of the common person and their fascination with mindless entertainment such as "worthless sports" or Dancing with the Stars. This could attribute to Dean's idea of *subliminal educational programming,* and could better explain why the people have short attention spans [42]. He presented many examples of why the mass is just letting government do what they will with their essence. In 1959, a scientist by the name of *Wernher Von Braun,* (who was a former Nazi employed by the United States government) was quoted about the happenings that occurred in 1954 concerning Eisenhower, and the near death experience he almost fell victim to due to a heart attack. Why would the president have this sort of experience if it was not due to something that impacted him greatly? Von Braun was exceptionally bright and practically developed the Saturn V program and stated the following:

> *"We find ourselves faced with powers that are far stronger than we hitherto assumed, and whose base is at present time unknown to us. I cannot say more at present, we are now engaged in entering into closer contact with those powers." (News Europa, 1959)*

Why didn't the American public demand to know what he meant by powers? No one it seemed pursued this and investigated on what he meant to say with this. It resulted that the public allowed this to pass by missing an opportunity for disclosure. In the 1970s, German professor *Hermann Oberth* stated another interesting message:

> *"We cannot take credit for our record advancement in certain scientific fields alone. We have been helped by the peoples of other worlds. Flying saucers are real and spaceships are from another solar system." (American Weekly 1954; 1974)*

If the great professor is not clear enough, he is telling us that we are not alone and that other forces exist out there. These statements came from two men who worked at NASA and were prominent geniuses dealing with rockets and space exploration. What more do we need to ask for about disclosure? No one of course was curious enough to question the good professor on what he meant, and this quickly disappeared from the minds of the American mass. Amazingly, a sort of disclosure went as far as congressional and still no one decided to question these men on their statements or even bothered to investigate further to disprove these accusations. In 1987, Hawaii state senator Daniel K. Inouye addressed congress and stated on file in the congressional record this following statement:

> *"There exists a shadowy government with its own Air Force, Navy, and its own fundraising mechanism, and the ability to pursue its own ideas of the natural interest, free from all checks and balances and free from the law itself." (Iran-Contra special committee 1987-89)*

This senator actually representing our country and protecting the people was hinting at something very important and very dangerous. Why didn't the American people bother to investigate or support his claims? If they did not want to believe him, the least the public could do was to research to prove him otherwise. Here is an obvious lapse in the human brain of the American public as they seem to allow the events to pass throughout history unnoticed. Dean also stated his concern for the direction that the human race was going in terms of future promises. An example of this concern was an event labeled the *Hudson Valley Sightings* from 1982-1995. It was an event so bizarre, that it would be impossible not to notice what transpired during that amount of time. The *FAA* (Federal Aviation Administration) during these events conjured the idea that "little planes" were in formation at night to disprove the boomerang shaped discs and triangular craft flying low over the valley (this of course being a direct violation of FAA policy) [43]. At one point, a triangular craft flew over *Indian Point Nuclear Power Plant* located in New York for about an hour. Why didn't the public demand answers about these strange happenings?

Why didn't the American public question the FAA and its policy to understand that planes are not allowed to fly in that formation (and in that fashion) unless ready for war? With the number of years these events transpired, there wasn't a cry for disclosure from the people for answers. This proves a sad reality that the public is susceptible to any belief system without question as long as it doesn't threaten their simplistic beliefs or affect their comfort zone. Could it be the grip of fear that hinders us to push forward? This goes contrary to Dean's belief that the human being is a "divine spark" due to the fact that we are not ascending because of our fear and our ability to see events in a different light. We must realize that sometimes things cannot be explained rationally. Dean believes almost foolishly that human beings are some sort of masterpiece, when in fact evidence shows we are not. With the evidence present along with understanding these events, it seems that this "*masterpiece*" has a long way to go before it can fit into Dean's idealistic description of a wonderful creature.

The Mckinnon/NASA Fiasco

A British amateur hacker known as *Gary Mckinnon* created a fiasco for both the U.S government and NASA in terms of defense systems and national security. In 2001, Mckinnon hacked into NASA and Defense Department computers with little effort. Apparently, information that he was not privy to nor had clearance for was uncovered. Almost immediately he was arrested, and was planned for extradition to the United States for his "crimes" along with seventy years in prison [44]. Only two countries do not require evidence to prosecute their own citizens being *Ireland* and *England*. In this case, since he wasn't a U.S. citizen, he had to be tried publicly in front of judge and jury. What exactly did he download from those computers who obviously had sensitive information? Why with his little knowledge about computer systems, was allowed access so easily?

Before he was captured, he was able to gather all evidence, compiled the information, and then gave it to top U.K researcher *Timothy Good* before he disappeared in 2006 [45]. Project Camelot had a chance to interview him in 2006 before he went "missing" without a trace. Concerning NASA, he found many photographs that eluded to the United States containing "non-terrestrial ships" orbiting the planet Earth and the transfer of military personnel to and from those ships. He also mentioned that he used a dial up modem which he why he claimed he was unable to download the photos in time.

During his short interview, he described the event with terminologies such as "non-terrestrial officers" and "off world cargo" with operations elsewhere in space [46]. The idea of "non-terrestrial" signifies somewhere other than Earth. Ben Rich already mentioned that we were one hundred years ahead, meaning there could be a correlation here. Dean went further in the investigation concerning the vessels used for these transports. According to Dean, the ships names were the *U.S.S. Curtis Lemay;* who was known as the planner and executor of the bombing of Japanese cities during the war. He then established the *SAC* (Strategic Air Command) into a "nuclear instrument" for war. The other vessel was the *U.S.S. Roscoe Hillenkoetter*; who was known for being a four star Admiral and the first director of the CIA in 1947 by President Harry Truman. According to the Navy manifest in the United States, there are no vessels with these names on Earth, implying that these vessels are either fictional or covert projects outside the planet Earth [47].

Either way, the information was not privy to Mckinnon or anyone else for that matter to read or discover. Dean believed strongly that these vessels are above the Earth as well and stated that the taxpayer's money was responsible for this. Why was this information so easily accessible for Mckinnon? According to him, no passwords were required to gain access, he considered himself an unprofessional hacker, self-taught, and somehow was able to discover UFO files and what he described as "hidden technology [48]." Something doesn't add up here if this were to be considered fact. Mckinnon wasn't at liberty to disclose too much during the interview due to his "situation;" however he did mention that there was *free energy* that he believed humans were destined to have.

He also mentioned *Bulldog 8* from NASA, which was a special building they utilized to airbrush photos for the mass public erasing any evidence of UFO or unexplainable objects [49]. Viewing the photos that inaccessible to the public, he was able to see many crafts that were not man made orbiting the Earth's atmosphere. Even without the photos or proof that he may be fabricating this information, the government agencies acted quickly to stop him. According to Mckinnon, his "journey" ended in 2002 as NASA finally cut his internet connection to their network. He did receive press in England with the *Financial Times*, *BBC* interviews, and the *National Press Conference*, however naturally did not receive proper coverage in the United States. It seems this trend happens all too frequently when people have tried to uncover suspicious activities by the United States government concerning UFOs.

Mckinnon wasn't able to disclose the names of a list he acquired of military personnel aboard these vessels, however, he did mention that the list of names had about twenty to thirty individuals with ranks but no destination (only terminologies such as "fleet to fleet" and "ship to ship" transfers). Mckinnon believed also that these were not Earthbound but "Space Marines" considering origins from NASA or the United States Navy but did not elaborate. Dean however elaborated further as to name the shadow space program that the U.S. government has calling them *UAC* (United States Aerospace Command) [50]. Dean using his military background as justification, described this agency as being "joint" which included all branches of the government including *Navy, Army, Air Force, Marine Corps, and British interests.*

Could this be the reason that the British government was so eager to rid themselves of Mckinnon and aid the United States in prosecuting him quickly before he disclosed information to uncover their program? Dean disclosed three major activities that the UAC engaged in and still do. Firstly, they are responsible for launching satellites at numerous locations around the globe using the "Cape Canaveral" theme as a cover up. Secondly, they maintain an entire fleet of vessels in orbit above the Earth and possibly elsewhere. Lastly, utilize a technology of *zero point energy* and *antigravity* which he believes will not be available to the public until 2020 [51].

Dean mentioned a quaint theory that during the years 1998-2000, funds in the amount of $1.7 trillion per year that "disappeared off the books" was used to fund this program.

He also stated that the day before the events of September 11, 2001, the department of defense secretary noticed that $3 trillion was also "missing" over a period of three years [52]. Adding this figure to the already gross amount of funds, this resulted in an enormous amount of money from the American public "lost" for unknown reasons. Could it be that the staged events of September 2001 were used to excuse the loss of money, precious metals while forcing the public to focus their attention elsewhere [53]? This would be the only ideal way for the money to "disappear" safely and conveniently be forgotten. Whatever the case may be, Mckinnon has been fighting extradition as of late and given a diagnosis of Asperger's syndrome to probably discredit his findings [54].

Dean closed his presentation at the conference stating that 2012 is not the end, but the beginning of a new age. Although he doesn't disclose what comes from this new age, he stated this would be a transitional period on two levels: as a *species* and as a *planet*. We also must investigate his claim of the idea of the "spark of divinity" that he strongly believes we humans have within us. He claims that we are not a mistake, not an accident, and has great hope for humans accentuating that we are a "beautiful race" with a bright future. This however could be speculation after all the information we have uncovered. How can we be a "beautiful race" if we are constantly destroying everything around us such as the environment with GHG emissions, mistreatment of ecosystems/biomes, and mistreatment of each other for the sake of our needs and human growth [55]? We as a species keep on procreating at a rate that we cannot sustain in the future. The abundance of resources are being depleted, we are genetically altering our foods, and the vegetation around us unconcerned about the effects on nature and the reaction she might have. Humans are trying to control nature and this will not go unpunished.

How can we be divine when we treat each other without love, care, or compassion? Where is the desire for universal understanding? This evidence clearly displays a greedy, self-righteous, and hopeless organism that has ever been created in the history of sequential time. We are an unguided mistake only bred for destruction and consumption of all around us. While we are searching for our supposed purpose in life, we eradicate everything in our paths in the name of ignorance and Dean's idea of "adolescence." Dean could in fact be describing another humanoid race he may have come in contact with. Even he could not ignore what we have done as a species historically and still attribute us to "godhood" or of divine nature. If it is true that certain beings have genetically created us, they should be ashamed at our almost handicap-like growth in the realms of spirituality and mental wellbeing. The "spark" we supposedly have is nonexistent and in order for it to sustain itself, humans have to take a different direction than we are now presently on, otherwise the light within will drive us into madness and the eradication of our species. Will our alien masters allow this and start over with a new creation? Will we be only a *footprint in the sand*, or will we leave a mark that we can be proud to show our creators? Currently, we are far from it . . . .

End Notes

[1] Miriam Raftery. "FEMA, La. Outsource Katrina body count to firm implemented in body dumping scandals." *Therawstory.com* (September 2005).

[2] Ibid 1.

[3] Mike Levy. "Careless undertaking." *Jewishjournal.com* (January 2002).
[4] Staff Writer. "Central figure in cemetery probe found dead." *CNN News* (December 2001).
[5] Bill Weinberg. "FEMA promotes Pat Robertson's charity—despite Congo diamond scandal." *Ww4report*.com (September 2005).
[6] nicap.org/papers/brookings.pdf.
[7] Margaret Mead. *Sex and Temperament in Three Primitive Societies*. Harper Perennial (May 2001).
[8] Project Camelot. "Robert O. Dean at the Awake and Aware Conference." Burbank, California (September 2009).
[9] Ibid 8.
[10] Ibid 8.
[11] Timothy Good. *Above Top Secret: The Worldwide UFO Cover-up*. Quill (September 1989).
[12] Richard M. Dolan and Bryce Zabel. *A.D. After Disclosure: When The Government Finally Tells The Truth About Alien Contact.* New Page Books (May 2012).
[13] Disclosureproject.org.
[14] Project Camelot. "Jordan Maxwell: The Takeover of Planet Earth." Los Angeles, California (September 2008).
[15] Don Reisinger. "Study: Americans, Japanese watch the most TV." *Cnet*.com (November 2010).
[16] Rob Waugh. "It was a craft that did not come from this planet: CIA agent speaks out on 65th anniversary of Roswell 'UFO' landings. *Daily Mail U.K.* (July 2012).
[17] Ibid 8.
[18] Ben Rich and Lee Jones. *Skunkworks: A Personal Memoir of My Years at Lockheed*. Boston: Little Brown and Co. 1996; pp. 316-341.
[19] Phil Patton. "6 top-secret aircraft that are mistaken for UFOs." *Popular Mechanics* (February 2009).

[20] Robert Dean. "Whistleblower: 60 years if UFO denial." *Awake and Aware Conference*, projectcamelot.org (2009).

[21] Ibid 18.

[22] Ibid 18.

[23] Dylan Ratigan. "Get money: we the people, not the politicians." *Huffington Post* (September 2011).

[24] Jeff Peckman. "Whistleblowers evidence of NASA UFO fraud might kill UK hacker case." *Examiner.com* (January 2009)

[25] Pravda. "Japanese Orbiter finds no evidence Apollo missions landed on Moon." *Prisonplanet.com* (May 2009).

[26] Maggie Fox. "Moon landing tapes got erased, NASA admits." *Reuters.com* (July 2009).

[27] Daniel Nasaw and Richard Luscombe. "Houston we have a problem: original moon footage erased." *The Guardian U.K.* (July 2009).

[28] Ibid 8, 20.

[29] Ibid 8, 20.

[30] Ringmakersofsaturn.com

[31] Norman R. Bergrun. *Ringmakers of Saturn*. Edinburgh: Pentland Press 1986.

[32] Ibid 8, 20.

[33] William L. Moore. "President Eisenhower meets aliens." *The Gazette* Hollywood, California (March 1989).

[34] Ibid 8, 20.

[35] marsnews.com/news/20020920-phobos2images.html.

[36] Philip Mantle. "Russian Pilot—Cosmonaut Aleksei Leonov and UFOs." *Americanchronicle*.com (January 2010).

[37] Zecharia Sitchin. *Apokalypse: Armageddon die Endzeit und die Prophezeiungen von der Wiederkunft*. Kopp Rottenburg (April 2007).

[38] Ibid 35.

[39] Andrew Romano. "Aliens Exist." *Newsweek* (August 2009).

[40] Mark Amaru Pinkham. "*The Truth behind the Christ Myth: The Redemption of the Peacock Angel*. Adventures Unlimited Press (August 2002).

[41] Jerry H. Bently. *Old World Encounters: Cross-Cultural Contacts and Exchange in Pre-Modern Times*. Oxford University Press (January 1993; p. 240).

[42] Ibid 8, 20.

[43] Philip J. Imbrogno, Allen Hynek, and Bob Pratt. *Night Siege: The Hudson Valley UFO Sightings*. Llewellyn Press (May 1998).

[44] "Project Camelot Interviews Gary Mckinnon." *Projectcamleot.org* (2006).

[45] Ibid 8, 20.

[46] Ibid 44.

[47] Ibid 8, 20.

[48] Ibid 44.

[49] Ibid 24, 44.

[50] Ibid 8, 20.

[51] Ibid 8, 20.

[52] Ibid 8, 20.

[53] 911research.com/WTC/evidence/gold.html.

[54] Associated Press. "Hacker loses extradition appeal." *BBC News* (July 2009).

[55] Susanne Posel. "US Government Study: Humans are National Security Threat to Oceans and our Planet." *Blacklistednews.com* (June 2012).

The UFO phenomena being reported is something real and not visionary or fictitious.

-General Nathan Twining (Chairman; Joint Chiefs of Staff 1955-58)

III

George Green and the New Pleiadian Paradigm

The quest for UFO understanding happens on many levels of consciousness. George Green maintains that we focus only on our physical level; however, in order to really get a clearer picture one must do this on a spiritual level as well. Green is retired United States Air Force and claims to have contact with another benevolent race of alien beings known as the *Pleiadians*; whom are in contact with a chosen few in order to wake up our consciousness and bring humans above third density beings. We have yet another group who seems to be in our favor to allow us closer to the path of ascension into a larger unknown world. We must investigate these claims as to find out who is really here for the benefit of humankind, and who is here to gain something from our destruction. Green invites us to see that our individuality is more important in the grand scheme of things and in order to *save* ourselves and others. In order to do this, we must first focus on the internal soul. To better understand this idea, we must question whatever we may think and understand about life based on religious dogma or personal beliefs.

Another interviewee of Project Camelot, Green offered another view on UFOs and their purpose in our existence. He offered many interesting theories and personal experiences in the interview while covering many bases. *Kerry Cassidy's* preconceived ideas took a different pathway of understanding than Green's initial message. By applying this new train of thought process, humans now venture into a different mindset leaving our culture, religious views, egos, and fears behind to start clean.

Nuclear Tensions

Green was fairly wealthy all of his life working for the United States government and also engaging in certain projects that included the construction of buildings and facilities. He also mentioned that he was in corporate banking, so he had a wide range of knowledge of how the system worked as was able to utilize that in order to stay on top. After a while, he began to see that the system he once believed in was not there to help humanity. He believed it was meant to enslave it not only in the physical realm, but the spiritual realm as well [1].

Green stated many key figures such as special bunkers that one would need a *ticket* for in case of nuclear fallout or worse. Most of these underground facilities are based within mountains and Earth's natural topography. As of late, tensions have been heating up with countries such as North Korea, China, India, and Iran [2] [3]. Iran also boasted they could destroy their enemies within matter of minutes after attacks [4]. Nuclear programs have been launched and testing has created tensions with the United States and South Korea [5]. The self-declared state of Israel who has been aided by the United States is also causing tensions between Iran since the Olympics started as sources state an impending attack by the final quarter of 2012 [6].

The recently released movie *The Divide* (2012) portrayed survivors of a nuclear attack in New York with the devastating aftermath of dealing with their humanity. As time wound down, each individual became trapped in the reality of being alone with no hope in sight. Eventually everyone met their fate of death by radioactive poisoning or madness. The main character Eva was able to escape to the surface only to find everything is a state of disarray. There was also the look of disbelief and shock as she was hopeful of a different outcome. Green strongly believes that with impending attacks planned for enemy countries in the near future that might take place, government officials and VIP would the need to escape leaving the rest of humanity to our fate due to their actions.

An Altered View of Consciousness

During the beginning of his interview, we found Green discussing how he interacted with the elite and government officials during the time of Kennedy and how during this moment, he changed his path in terms of who he really worked for. He mentioned a meeting with *Ted Kennedy* himself, along with other members of a committee that would name him the "President of Companies [7]." Unaware of just exactly the job was all about; he decided to inquire on what he would actually do. According to Green, he was told he had to liquidate the expendable containers, raid assets, and then split them. At the time Green had no idea what the "expendable containers" were however, at the meeting he had been told that this meant human beings.

He met with these officials in Aspen Colorado where on top of this new title, he was to become the next financial Chairman for the next president who at the time was to be Jimmy Carter. Green like most voters believed there was a distinction between the two parties Democratic and

Republican. After he was told that the government controlled both parties, there really wasn't a choice on who ran since both parties were controlled by the same source [8]. Beyond this explanation, Green was most curious on why he was considered for this job that he knew nothing about. He credited himself to be a builder of cities helping *Steven Levitt* the American economist with cities named after him in New York and Pennsylvania. What was told to Green in response of his curiosity on why he was selected for such a task was that he was diligent with money and they "owned him favors."

All curiosity aside, Green's major duties involved attending all state democratic functions, raising money for these democratic functions, and meeting women. According to Green's beliefs, this was identifiable as Ted Kennedy and his whole persona [9]. At one instance Green told very disturbing occurrences when he brought his own daughter to these meetings. Kennedy according to Green was very interested in his daughter who happened to be fourteen at the time. It went as far as Kennedy wanting to be sexually involved with her regardless of her being underage. After this incident, Green expressed that this was the turning point in his life where he decided that he did not want to partake in any more "government" or elitist practices. Green witnessed drug use and paraphernalia at these so called "social" events and expressed his disgust for them as well.

If Green was to join, he was to take part in the program introduced by Carter at the time called the *Global 2000 Agenda*. This agenda planned to eliminate three hundred billion humans by the year 2000 in order to sustain natural resources and the planet itself, because realistically it could only house five hundred billon inhabitants. This course of action has not been implemented yet due to the fact that there are more people now than ever; and the growth rate continues to climb.

Officially there are approximately seven billion people worldwide, and environmental scientists predict near ten billion by the year 2050 [10]. Green himself expressed that due to this staggering number of human beings, forty percent of people globally are living on only two dollars a day. Realistically, every organism has strong bodies and weak bodies. Only "favored" groups in a natural selection depending on their capabilities may survive with mutual support instead of competing according to Kropotkin [11]. This could be attainable assuming that most humans work together; however, this is not the case as most of us are bred with the goal of attaining personal success over the rest of our human companions.

Many of the normal population of the world do have the capacity for good and can definitely be considered different from the rest. In the case of selecting who becomes a candidate for survival in the wake of a nuclear/chemical attack is a dilemma to say the least. To even begin to decide what qualifications are needed to meet the prerequisites or which agency decides could bring arguments from all sides. Who gives the government the initial decision making on which life is more valuable than another? Is it the "god" excuse? Is it based on financial or education? It seems though sadly that whatever moral decisions be made, this plan will eventually come to fruition:

> *"We are going to get Global 2000 implemented, one way or another by famine, starvation, or by choice... We need real economic shock, a depression to get our message across." (Statement made by*

Zero Population Growth spokesman, 9/18/81—The Spiral Report Vol. 111, March 31, 1982)

This may be a cruel statement, but the decision makers are forgetting the error of their ways. The ignorance that inhabits the world, destroys it, pollutes it, and disregards it is learned from leaders and governments. The governments are responsible to teach the masses how to conduct themselves in the proper manner. Whether it is Green Imperialism, Neo-Malthusianism Theory, World Systems Theory, or Neoliberalism; if they are planning to abandon these lost children (which are reflected in their statement), this means that they are not taking responsibility for their own actions [12]. The parent must take responsibility for their actions in regards to their children whether or not they succeed or fail; for it is the parent that brought the child into existence. The governments are acting irresponsibly and now wish to erase their mistake by terminating three hundred billion lives in order to justify their actions. This is not a favorable method of action because life works in circular repetitive cycles; and this crossroad will eventually arise again. Do we continue to apply this method every time our species grows to an alarming number? Is this the magic of being human? There is no doubt a perversion of Darwinian law at stake here, disrupting nature's flow based on our own failures.

Green discussed how the United States government have already taken measures to ensure the survival of selected groups of human beings in structures called domes or m*onoliths*. These structures are being considered for shelter to house humans in case of natural or unnatural disasters. These shelters are composed of concrete and "foam" that Green described was used for insulation. Constructed up to standards, these domes can withstand up to three hundred forty mile per hour winds [13]. According to Green, he stated "they will be coming for us;" but did not mention if it was winds of those speeds or something else in the near future.

Another interesting fact is that these domes can be heated by ten 100 watt light bulbs (although he didn't mention if they were mercury or LED). The only problem that Green saw with these structures was the concept of proper air circulation that he stated the government hadn't figured out yet. If the air remained stagnant, humans would only breathe in the refuse from their own bodies that we exhale result in death if more than one human occupied the space. He stated as of 2009, the structures were only prevalent to the Midwest and California [14]. This could mean a number of possibilities: either the disasters are only made to strike in the areas of the Midwest, they must test them first to see how many survive, or this is just a contrivance to give people the illusion that the government is desperately trying to salvage as many people as they can.

The company *Monolithic* (who operates out of Italy, Texas) that constructs these domes assured the public they were built to last and were affordable. They have two options of floor plans with one being the "*president's choice*" that have ten different designs, and the "*resident's choice;*" that allow one to choose dome size, diameter, floors, bedrooms, and all amenities that a regular house would contain [15]. The resident choice floor plans start from about $1,350—$2,250 for just the set of drawings; with price increasing as floors and rooms are added. The main fact is that every single detail is considered when one places that *special* order. The president's choice models were surprisingly cheaper, considering the drawings range from about $750—$1,500 to start [16].

The price also depends on the design and finding the contract company to create the structure for the buyer.

Realistically evaluating the situation, one must have the necessary funds to create this bunker to save them from disaster. As an added bonus, there are separate links on the company's web page where safety equipment can be bought, concrete additives, and other tools necessary to maintain the dome to its full capacity. The message here is clearly that *certain* people are allowed to take action in terms of ensuring their survival, while the others less economically unfortunate, will have to seek other methods in order to survive. The concept "money can buy anything" still stands strong and will continue to do so for those who plan to stay after the disasters occur.

When citizens perish, what will be done about the workforce/manual labor and the working class that these elitists so desperately need and have been using as the backbone of their collected wealth? Will the issue of stagnant air be addressed here with Monolithic? As far as planning to purchase one of these domes, maybe playing the lotto or a bank loan might be an incentive, but alas, the "economy" is suffering and the dreams of survival will have to pass as other dreams have passed in our lives. It seems that nothing can be done and one must embrace for the event(s) to come without *fear* or *regret*.

Religious and Spiritual Implications

Green mentioned his only contacts were the Pleiadians, however, now he stated the situation went beyond contact. Adding to this notion of contact, Green offered interesting outlooks on the Judeo-Christian bible as well. His belief centered on the book of John in the New Testament myth. His belief was that the book was wrong in its claim that the word was the beginning. According to his source of higher knowledge and power, the beginning was conceived by thought [17]. The thinking process should work before any words are spoken to relay it outside the brain's mechanism clearly. Green exemplified that thought was the beginning along with meditation and the "creation's thinking." This process occurred through different dimensions and manifested into an illusion that we call our reality now: the third dimension or density.

In greater detail, we find that our physical body and our human reality are merely illusions or holograms that have been manifested in order to house the more important part the *soul*; which is composed of vibrations and light [18]. When these two elements are connected, they form a pattern of sorts that created the image that we have in front of us today. In turn, the soul or whatever energy is composed within the human body, acts as a carrying case that holds our physical bodies together. This of course is a speculation based on the fact that the spirit itself would have to be composed of hydrogen since the universe contains over 75%. Being creations of the universe, it is only logical that the material from space resides in humans [19].

Hydrogen or *H* is very necessary within the universe for many things and processes containing seventy five percent of its initial mass. Life itself consists of hydrogen as it exists in organic compounds and water. It can also be used as a fuel and has considered part of the metallurgic process as it can weaken metals and cause them to fracture [20]. Established science believes that the abundance of hydrogen is very rare here on Earth, however, with this new theory of how every human soul is composed of hydrogen, this could mean that we ourselves are the greatest source on the planet. Could this be the reason we are considered a commodity?

What if some humans don't contain a soul? Through some of our experiences, usually sometimes we see humans acting inhumane towards themselves and other life forms displaying the elimination of emotional feelings within them. These humans are sometimes known as people without souls. Is this the example that Green was trying to tell us? How would the physical or holographic model of our third density be possible for those without energy? How do they maintain their existence in this density? Green speculated that there are two methods for affecting the body without a soul: one being fluorescent lights, and the other being thought [21]. While light remains a mystery to science but somehow affects the human body, thought is more powerful even though its concept is fairly unknown to most humans.

Green during the interview used Cassidy as an example for the thought process. He used *kinesis* as the basis for its ground on manipulating her body just using hand motions. Maintaining a base of energy with the proper technique, one can manipulate and "cut off" energy from the extremities of any human. It acted as a sort of parasitic bond that sucked the energy from the host, as Green displayed with little or no effort his domination over Cassidy's arms and bodily functions. Although she tried to maintain her stance, her arms moved and bent at his will as he made certain hand gestures around her body. This method could be used for purposes of personal power and gain over weaker humans if it actually works.

Green mentioned that priests use this practice as mind control in order to possess the willing participant and extract their energy from them making them dependent on the church [22]. The religious agenda along with the manipulation and extraction of the human soul or its energy for control leaves humans trapped. Priests themselves display control using the sign of the cross and cutting the energy off in four places, affecting the chakras [23]. It is no wonder that the religious devotee is always drained or "thrown back" experiencing illusions that god is within them. The result is not a spiritual force entering your body, it is the priest or pastor extracting and manipulating one's body using this parasitic technique with the permission of the individual.

Green stated that the body and mind itself were controlled by three different processes: *light*, *color* and *action* [24]. In this case we are allowing them to take our spiritual energy that we already contain within us! Through action, the individual opens their chakras of color and light and allow the energy to dissipate. With the proper technique, the extractor could absorb this energy for himself/herself to manipulate the body. The only way Green speculated to hinder this action by the master of the technique is to keep balance of the body by vibrations.

He maintained the idea of keeping everything in balance, meaning condensed light backed to frequency. With this idea manifested, one could travel to distant stars without the use of spaceship or craft in mere hours (his example of five hundred light years could be achieved in mere hours). Through this theory, our spirit is a teleportation device that could travel to the source or anywhere we allow it to go. Space itself maintains the constant temperature of about—270 degrees Celsius, which Green proposed was the ideal environment for the human soul [25]. He clarified the process included the manifesting, condensing and recreating of light into different shapes, allowed us to experience astral travel.

The process looks very promising; however the techniques themselves are not easily done. Humans have grown dependent on their holographic illusion and have eliminated the need for their spiritual reality. Adhering to an organized religion is not the answer due to the surrendering of one's own power and replacing it with an illusionary concept given by another human. In turn, one allows the other human(s) to absorb the energy and leave the surrendered victim powerless and confused (with a sense of false euphoria). The more we embrace what the Pleiadians consider to be victim consciousness, (not taking responsibility for one's own actions and the complete surrender of internal power) humans in turn leave their actions to a "higher authority" and expect redemption in the end with no effort taken during their entire sequential lifetime [26].

The Fate of Synthetics

What of the fate of those without a soul? Are they classified as humans or something else? Green explained that these beings were lab created through a technology given to them by the Greys [27]. Scientists have been developing them for some time now and have labeled them synthetics. These entities are defined as not real, signifying that they themselves are not holograms run by a spiritual engine, rather an empty artificial engine mimicking the soul. For more information, Green recommended the movie *Boys from Brazil* (1978) as a reference to the subject. In the movie, the subjects of cloning and replacing world leaders (ninety-four targets) with copies to follow orders of the Fourth Reich was the main plot.

The United States government along with eight other nations was "making people." Green described the creations as having a plastic feel to them; however scientists are using a newer technology to make them feel more human-like. The Soviets as well have their own special technique for creating synthetics. He explained that only two cells were required to make a carbon copy of an individual subject. With a small electrical charge, the fetus begins to grow and all that is needed is a food source [28]. At one time, Green explained that the government was hypnotizing women to use their eggs and invented alien abduction stories for inducing memory loss. After fourteen weeks when the fetus disappeared, it developed on its own growing its own blood supply. At this point, the scientists injected a pituitary hormone (melatonin, serotonin, 5-hydroxtrytophan, or an alien source) to accelerate the being's growth.

Green mentioned the major benefits from having these clones; one being the additional "spare parts" one could have in case of accidents. Since the clone is essentially a duplicate from the original human, there would be no rejection of the parts, since they originated from the same cells. The other benefit would be replacing key figures whose interests conflict with the ruling elite. Although this does sound like a movie, Green assured that the doppelgangers were being stationed where the leaders once were. He even went as far as to use George Bush Sr. as an example for one of these clones [29].

The United States government also cloned Hitler (as described from the movie) as he supposedly flew to Barcelona Spain along with Eva, and charted a plane to Antarctica. He then died a few years back in Brazil, Argentina or Chile according to many theorists such as *David Icke*; who went as far as to link him to the lineage of Rothschild and the being Jewish himself [30]. Green stated that there were documents to prove this; however he did not provide them himself. He did however provide the example of how Stalin himself performed the autopsy on the body of the supposed body of Hitler and noticed that the ears were different and testicles were a "bizarre form [31]."

The year 1938 was the starting point according to Green that clones have been used in special scientific programs by the eight nations [32]. If adhering to the one world government agenda, these cloned leaders would be adequate to run the program smoothly. The *soul memory* was different from the body or *hologram memory,* which might be able to identify who was classified human and who was synthetic. This also meant that we have two separate recorders of memory both existing simultaneously with separate drives like a computer system. Is there a reason that the soul keeps a separate sort of database that doesn't interact with the body hologram? According to Green, when an individual went into a hospital to get an encephalogram, our conscious memory would be downloaded onto a "disc" that is then given to our synthetic copy to manifest speech, memory or basic motor functions making the clone an exact duplicate of the original host [33].

Another film to accentuate this idea was the *Sixth Day* (2000) with Arnold Schwarzenegger whose main focus covered the subject of cloning. Upon creation, each unit remembered the previous memories of the deceased clone before it including the pain or experience prior to death. Although it resembled the original host, it lacked the "soul," making it a separate entity. If the clone is able to mimic every detail of the original host, how would one be able to identify it? Clones in the Sixth Day all carried markers underneath their lips to display how many times a copy was made.

Green believed that the operation was not completely perfected and that all units required maintenance. The process was not "foolproof" with the units taken to Camp David Bethesda Hospital where nurses there according to Green, called them "the others" or *no soul humans* [34]. If this speculation was to be true, then the playing field was at another level that could end up severely problematic if left unchecked. Alien interests were also occupying these "empty suits" for their own agendas. This could explain some of the phenomena that religious community mentions as possessions that require exorcisms. This assumption could be valid due to the fact that aliens can manipulate a clone or synthetic controlling its mental and physical aspects. One could also theorize alien manipulation in our own relationships (i.e. soul mates) for agendas beyond our comprehension [35]. The main point Green was trying to portray was that all of the world leaders were bought and recreated to think a certain way and conduct themselves accordingly. What then does this hold for the future fate of human beings?

Blade Runner (1982) was considered another portrayal of reality for human beings in the near future. Will all humans be replaced by exact duplicates not capable of making conscious decisions from our spiritual memory? Will we be converted into obedient inanimate beings made for following certain guidelines? It could be argued that organized religion is following this plan already along with schools and education programs. Perhaps the Global 2000 Agenda is completed, as human emotions are almost non evident and "synthetic" behavior is more a reality as people turn the cold shoulder. After the cataclysmic events to follow soon, the synthetic population has a chance to thrive and replace the loss of human life. The elite could maintain control indefinitely with the absence of the spiritual engine; which could be the only last hope of human defense we have left.

UFO Contact and Green

In 1958, Green was stationed at Edwards Air Force Base and witnessed strange events he decided to share with Camelot. One anomaly was an ion powered engine that was utilized by disc-shaped craft that according to his commander was created by Sikorsky for use in outer space. Green described the base itself as a "crossover base" that contained eight hundred men and twenty-five civilians. Since the discs were deemed "civilian projects," it didn't receive the attention it would if labeled something else. Green also mentioned two dead aliens that could reference the Roswell incident of 1947. When he questioned his commander about this anomaly, his investigation led him to a dead end as his commander told him he didn't have enough clearance for answers. Shortly after, he was transferred off base due to his curiosity [36].

Green worked with a partner for a while concerning investigation of UFOs and being a contactee of sorts. A man named Bill Meier who in 1975 according to Green started his ascension and interaction with UFOs. It was Green's understanding that the aliens needed our own individual permission to contact us, although he didn't specify how. He stated that the Pleiadians themselves *chose* Green to be their representation so to speak here on planet Earth to help them accomplish their agenda of waking up people on Earth [37]. The planet is described as a prison of sorts where all races from different species are housed together. Could this be a sentence for crimes committed by aliens in the cosmos? Could this be punishment for something they may have done to occupy a third density hologram and live their lives as humans with no memory of their past life? This could fit within the realms of *cosmic punishment* and the need to "serve time" until one is ready to learn about their spiritual body. If reincarnation is real, one could imagine the number of times one need to live in order to learn their lesson(s).

Is there a sort of review board that determines the prisoner's availability for a sort of *cosmic parole* when the physical body dies? Green mentioned the book the *Teachings of Jmmanuel* where Meier supposedly went back in time to contact this man called *Jmmanuel* who in fact resembled Jesus in his belief [38]. This contradicted Green's research as he did not agree with this. After four days with this supposed character, Meier was sent back to the present and wrote this book of his encounters. Many critics disclaimed most of what Meier proposed, however, there are others out there that believed his word and braced themselves for a failed prediction of a proposed WWIII in November 2011. This book was later investigated by a man called Jim Deardorff; who in essence was able to find many faults with Meier's structured belief.

The concepts that humans hold onto dearly ("good" and "evil,") are not legitimate and needed to be investigated under a different light. Green stated that we are given free will to explore and learn [39]. *Serotonin* wakens our body in the 3D world or light, and *melatonin* works in darkness can causes the body to sleep. According to Green, between the hours of twelve and four in the morning, some "downloading or uploading occurs." If one is successful, one can be in touch with a higher power or creation and create a sort of communion to set goals and "be it [40]." The main point Green stated was that the planet is important, and the illusion of *good* and *evil* are really utilized to see what works and what doesn't. Nature itself is a self-correcting system, and if lower organisms tamper with it, it will react in a more violent manner. Balance is important in maintaining a perfect being in proper order humans are in the learning process to achieve that goal.

Future Preparations

The Laws of Attraction are very important in maintaining this perfect being in proper order with the following steps: *attraction*, *intent*, *allowance*, and finally *balance*. Time sequence is inadequate and hinders progress for human beings. Green believes this concept as well stating that if humans remain on the illusion of time, we will be setting ourselves into a reality that doesn't allow for expansion and we allow this limit ourselves by putting restraints. This means that the past, present and future are now and we must live the now and focus. This doesn't mean that the future potentials aren't there; it just means that they can be changed very easily in a matter of minutes based on decision making. The moment we expand on an idea or thought, the message is then creating another life line that is then put into play. The moment we abandon this idea, the life line ceases and creates another pathway to a completely different world.

In regards to Meier's mind, he traveled to the past to meet this character Jmmanuel, but he also mentioned that he traveled into the future. He implicated that the future destruction of places such as San Francisco where many people are dead and the damage along with destruction are clear. Green expanded and mentioned that Meier himself took photos of these places and many landmarks, however refused to show up in an U.S. court of law to show this evidence [41].

It is known at this moment that he lives his life in seclusion due to many possibilities. Was it the failed prediction of his WWIII? If in fact he did have evidence of a nuclear post-apocalyptic future, could San Francisco fall along with other great cities like Atlanta and New York in the near future? If this happens, the U.S. in general will lose all of their defense networks, computers, financial institutions, and will likely not rebound. Meier mentioned the dissension in the Middle East to spread to the United States. According to Green however, San Francisco is destroyed before the initial war and not a result of nuclear fallout [42]. This is obviously happening now as of 2010 where Egypt, Libya, Bahrain, Iran, Iraq, and Afghanistan are still in unrest due to U.S. presence and dictators believed to placed there by U.S. interests [43]. Green mentioned that as a species, we are right on the precipice of this event and that when California is affected as the San Andreas Fault will move about one thousand feet. The fact that only eighteen feet would destroy southern California only makes this staggering figure beyond comprehension. The safest suggestion Green stated was to move out of California immediately.

Continuing on the Global 2000 agenda would include for the United States the reduction of the American population for the progressive agenda [44]. As the population in the U.S. is constantly growing, one ponders how this would possibly be done. Nuclear fallout in crowded cities could be an effective method; however, all of the chosen few would have to leave the area before this "attack" would happen. Where would they go? Wouldn't they have to be safely transported to underground cities such as the one located under Denver International Airport (DIA)? The city itself spans one hundred miles and runs into the Cheyenne mountain chain that would house enough people to survive a planned attack.

A strange coincidence such as from the 1977 movie *Encounters of the Third Kind*, has possibly made a connection between DIA and alien activity. In an important scene, scientists received a message from the alien ship with a coded number sequence 104443040361O. Coincidentally, this number sequence happens to also be the location of DIA. Although the movie was in 1977, sixteen years later the airport was built on thirty-four thousand acres of undeveloped land [45]. Could it have been that the Spielberg was pointing out coordinates for a future bunker for the elite, or are we looking too deep into coincidence?

The base itself is no ordinary base, as it contains very peculiar artwork and designs that when paying attention to the details, is closely tied to Masonic symbols and doomsday predictions. Several paintings murals that display children over looking burned cities and destruction are placed there for certain reasons. Not to mention a strange stone structure with Masonic symbols, also looks like a control or some sort of futuristic device. With examples like these, this may be a location fit for establishing a new life for those meant to live beyond the destruction? Just on the construction alone, describes how this airport is not a typical airport for those flying out of the country or even coming in:

> *"The airport has a fiber optic communications core made of 5,300 miles of cable. That's longer than the Nile River. That's from New York to Buenos Aires, Argentina. The airport also has 11,365 miles of copper communications network. The fueling system can pump 1,000 gallons of jet fuel per minute through a 28-mile network of pipes. There are six fuel hold tanks that each holds 2.73 million gallons of jet fuel . . . the huge, main terminal is Jeppesen Terminal, named after Elfry Jeppesen who was the first person to create maps specifically for aviation (the company is still in business today). This area is known as the "Great Hall . . . ." It's said it is 900 feet by 210 feet big. This is over 1.5 million square feet of space. All told, there is over 6 million square feet of public space at DIA. The airport brags they have room to build another terminal and two more*

> *concourses and could serve 100 million passengers a year. The airport flew 36 million in 2001 . . . . (anomlaies-unlimited.com [Denver airport], 2001)*

Green didn't elaborate on anything concerning underground bases or locations that would be compromised. He only stated that the Pleiadians would not disclose to him who he really was on the "other side" because he would have not selected the "job" he was given now. For this reason, he explained he was not allowed to pursue past life regressions. Does this mean these missions or jobs are against our will? This poses a problem for those who want to be informed before taking a job; because it might put the "volunteers" in danger. It seems that the aliens are playing with humans in the sense that we are selected to fulfill their agendas only, without any clear understanding of the tasks at hand. If this is the case, then most of the conscious human beings would not help aliens in "waking up" the rest due to the probable danger and high improbability of success.

Green stated the mere fact: "people who wake up do not want to accept their job, and want to go back to sleep." This can be compared to the Matrix when *Cypher* attempted to make a deal with Agent Smith to be reinserted back into the Matrix; where he would live in ignorance that he called "bliss" without dealing with the reality of his current life. Are humans all like this, or do some like the sense of adventure? Can we trust each other to work together to wake people up and offer them a "red pill" to escape the current enslavement we are all in? Or will there be some humans bent on completing their own agendas outside the "greater human good?" Whatever the case may be, we as a species have to do this on an individual level due to the low probability of success with humans working together without the result of competition or disagreement. All the progress made together could be destroyed by only *one* human. All hopes, dreams, goals and foundations made by the many would be crushed.

Our situation, our way of life, and everything we think as humans is simply a tiny fraction of a bigger understanding. Green himself was especially impacted about twelve years ago when he was contacted by the government to help them construct prisoner war camps in Las Vegas. Green was hesitant at first, but then contacted a friend at the time *Ted Gunderson* (who also happened to be head of the FBI), who told him the exact same idea and went even further to disclose that these "camps" were being built all over the country [46]. Who does the U.S. plan on making concentration camp prisoners? This has happened before with the Japanese during WWII, so it comes to no surprise that the U.S. would make this possibly happen on a countrywide scale. Could the enemy be the American public or some elusive enemy not yet discovered? Green didn't specify on who exactly the enemy was or any idea except for the fact about a war.

Supposedly according to Green, the year 2000 was the time that the Middle East would fall and initiate the Global 2000 Agenda; however it was not successful enough. This failure would initiate phase two for this year 2012 and also herald the end of the twenty-six thousand year cycle. Green was worried at the time due to the limited amount of people "waking up" to make a significant difference for the global occurrences that will transpire. His exact words were: "we are running out of time." Time is a human construct and this of course is not valid if we follow what the Pleiadians labeled as *sequential time*.

Hidden Messages

Green added many points on our usage of language that cause us to look closer on what we say and what it means. For example, he used the question "how are you today?" This phrase is widely used all over the world in many languages or forms that initiate conversation. This seems to be automatic whether we are just using it to attract a mate or for introduction into other subjects for attention. What kind of message are we relaying when we construct these phrases? According to Green the right question would be "why are you today?" The answer of course being that there might not be a tomorrow. This is a great way to look and analyze the situation realistically, and wonder what one individual can do to continue this cycle. What kinds of incentives drive us to continue this cycle?

Answers may vary from individual to the next; however would they be equally important to the Pleidian master plan? The plan put forth by the Pleiadians' "creator" may not have human individual feelings in mind when it created the plan. Strangely, Green remained optimistic despite the little time for this change. The answer could be that one must be thankful for the single day we all have, because tomorrow might never come. We must not be thankful based on fear that there is not following day, we must feel this from the heart, mind and soul, sending out a signal to the universe as a message for a chance to prove ourselves.

It is true that entropy is necessary for the creation of things, so maybe this is our lot in life; to destroy things for a new beginning. Green ensured that this chaos would ensue very soon with everything collapsing around us; including the monetary system, government, social structure, and human decency [47]. Green also stated that gold and silver would be the new monetary system and that they are a must along with the passport. All of the U.S. currency with the statement: "Federal Reserve Note" would be useless. The new one dollar gold coin (although not gold) would have value because it does not have the Federal Reserve label on it. His explanation for such action was that the individuals "on top" would just destroy themselves. Green's perception on how gold, oil and drugs make up the world currency could be the case. The stock exchange itself has nothing to do with business; the CIA, FBI, MI6 are all professional liars in Green's eyes [48]. Topping if off, Richard Hoagland stated "the lie is different on every level." As those who plan the demise of their enemy groups eliminate the obstacles, new ones emerge from within the group. The group mentality is then destroyed and only one or a few are left with the power and control.

In times of desperation most would turn to faith and religious comfort in order to comfort the harsh realities. The major message among these religious cults is the concept of redemption in the eyes of their demigod. Many logical arguments could be made in terms of what exactly do we have to save ourselves from, who do we have to save ourselves from, where did we come up with the idea on the human being and the need to be saved in the first place, and when did we allow ourselves to surrender this internal power to an outside illusion. The answer lies with personal responsibility and the alien interests will not let us leave this "prison planet" to destroy others [49].

What happened to Robert Dean's *United States Aerospace Command*? Didn't he specifically state that we were already orbiting earth and traveling to other planets? The complexity of the matter resides on many alien groups existing simultaneously giving their own distinct "messages" that could come into conflict. It could be agreed that in order for humans to leave we must be balanced; and we have to do this on our own. This information given to Green he assured did not originate from him or his books [50]. He stated that this flow of information was channeled through him by aliens. The main point is to focus on the message and not who it comes from. Based on the Pleiadian belief system, all humans should reach a state of constant communion with the spirit.

Preparations for Attack

Bio-weapons which include manmade diseases and genetic warfare would be used. Enough diseases without the proper "cure" would leave a hole in the human population if done correctly. The only problem there is would be to control otherwise results will occur such as the *brucellosis* outbreak. Green urged those who wished to make prominent changes personally, to read the book *The Secret History of the American Empire* by John Perkins. In this book, Perkins stated exactly what the United States has done, in terms of laying the groundwork to plan their own changes to make the world how they want it. The objective now individually would be to "change one's own world" not the whole world. When one reads the book, the message we should receive is that it is too late to change, the game has been played and it cannot be stopped. The only real plan anyone can fathom is to prepare as best as possible for a transition. If this is all an intricate plan that has been done meticulously, then what chance does one individual really have? Does this plan have human error, or has it been conceived by a larger force like what the Pleiadians consider "the creator's plan?"

Green described that the change would initially happen quickly and decisively; he called it the "three day weekend."

This essentially would fall on a Friday and escalate on Monday. During the weekend, all banks are closed and money is inaccessible unless one goes through an ATM. If all the machines fail, all funds will stop and all of our "money" will become unreachable; when this happens, the chaos really begins. It only takes three days for people to run out of food, one week when people will actually start killing for food, and then after twelve days the crowd becomes uncontrollable for the governments or police to restore order.

If this plan is to transpire and the government is expecting chaos, then they have made the necessary plans to protect themselves when the plan reaches the beginning stages. There is good news to this forced/planned change, not all countries will be affected. This doesn't mean that these countries are going to be easy to find or get to, this just means that if one prepares, they can somewhat avoid all of this unwanted or sudden changes. When neutron bombs are used, (and according to Green they will be used), the radiation will cease in three days then allowing clean air and the locations free of "unwanted people [51]." These "clean bombs" would pacify the area and then make it available for future prospects or uses. When these bombs are released, all major cities in the surrounding area would resort to mere dust and rubble.

If this was to take place on American soil the best bet would be to leave the country and travel south as far as possible to avoid the blast zones. Argentina has been considered a very safe place when these events take place. Green also recommended to keep small bills ($1-$20) as Americans will need them to buy their way out of here if they have the chance. According to the EPA, *Plutonium-239* with MOX is said to have a life span of at least twenty-four thousand years [52]. Won't the radioactive dust still cause health problems for any survivors? Even if survivors were able to avoid major side effects, they would be unable to use the land for twenty-four thousands years. Where food would be grown, how this would affect drinking water, and where living arrangements would be made are just a few important issues that would have to be addressed.

There is evidence according to Green, that three Russian nuclear submarines are stationed on both the east and western coasts of the United States. These are prototypes that can travel eighty miles an hour undetected by radar which are targeting specific U.S. cities [53]. Are they supposed to strike at a designated time like a countdown, or in the event of a disagreement between Russia and the U.S.? Has the countdown already begun? The cities were Washington D.C., New York, and Atlanta. This could be a strategically good reason if one was planning to dismantle the United States. Since the capitol is located on the east coast, along with the financial center and the Center for Disease Control (CDC), it would be painlessly easy to destroy government and social structure all in one fell swoop by nuclear and germ warfare.

Once the financial means are eliminated (Wall Street) and the capitol is destroyed, the country would be unable to recover or fight back. Between the radiation and diseases, the population would reduce in a matter of a few weeks and then quickly spread all over the rest of the country. Within months, the U.S. would not exist; only shattered states or small communities that survived the first strike. Green has stated that China has the ability to shut down U.S. computer systems within two days. Could this be the horrifying truth, or a hoax led to scare the public? It is safe to assume that the U.S. government is privy to this sort of reality and have already made the necessary provisions to avoid a total disaster for them, not us.

Will China be the one to shut us down? About a couple of years ago, China stated the following: "it has been five thousand years; it is our turn to run the world." Who was running the world for the past five thousand years? It is known that Rome itself was in power for about two thousand years (including Christian Rome), what about the other half? Green considered China to be a "wild card." Looking at the facts concerning China this may not be the case. They now have one hundred million single men that are young, able, and useful to the government. The U.S. only has three hundred million people which are not men, and not all of them young. This also means that forty percent are over fifty years old. China is also involved in every major city all over the world in the public and private sectors; buying up oil fields and producing all major exports globally [54].

If they are still loyal to the communist train of thought, this would mean that every single Chinese citizen is still an acting member of the government and must follow orders if the government requires a task from them. Hypothetically speaking, could all Chinese citizens all over the world could be sleeper agents ready to strike when the time is right? The Chinese themselves speak the languages of other countries especially English; while this is mandatory, the average U.S. citizen is not required to learn another language unless they attend a university or high paying job that requires them to. This of course could all be speculation. Doing a demographic concerning all Chinese citizens all over the globe will show their wide distribution into all areas of life. Looking at all these points, it may be time for China to take over.

The New Paradigm and the Environment

Green tries to stimulate us to think more and more as we venture into his research concerning the *new paradigm of the human soul.* This mysterious entity has caused speculation on our whole existence and the very means of what we are composed of. Could the mere sensations that we feel physically affect the soul as well? We are mostly all aware of the pleasure of physical touch, sensations, actions, and pain. However, could there be an extension to affect the soul in the same fashion? We are told that the sun is hot for instance, is this due to some chemical reaction to the skin or could it fact affect us at a deeper level? Green suggested that the sun is in fact cold, and that it sends a frequency of light to the atoms of organisms which in effect creates heat [55]. This would mean the process does not take place within the star as established science insists, rather within our bodies. Where do we learn to awaken our souls and feed them the same reactions we receive physically in order to ascend?

This process can be done, as the Buddhist monks or Tibetan monks have shown. It seems that we must quiet our minds and live in the present in order to gain a deeper understanding about the chakras and the soul. The mind runs as a never ending operating machine that processes and calculates everyday occurrences at every second. We must learn how to give this machine the rest it deserves to ground ourselves and alter our consciousness. Even though we sleep, our mind is still working to process the information of the entire day and store it in the memory archives of the brain. This could be achieved by using the *law of intent*, but the concept is easier said than done.

Green described the secret U.S military installation *Pine Gap* located near Alice Springs Australia. He stated that about thirty-five thousand elite would be stationed there in time for this plan on worldwide environmental change. There are many flaws that must be addressed: if the machines break, where are the survivors going to acquire spare parts? Every working machine like our brain needs spare parts just in case of breakdown or malfunction. Maintenance is required for any operational program to successfully transmit according to plan, power, or information. How are the governments going to address these matters? There has been a suggestion of using greenhouse gases to correct the winds once these events have transpired [56].

Environmental scientists have been pressing the issue of climate change and the excessive amount of GHG emissions over the last 20 years. The over production of GHG emissions could be due to certain agencies preparing for an oncoming nuclear attack. As the ongoing debate is argued on both sides as some politicians consider climate change as "junk science," this may be part of a bigger picture not yet discovered. When one uses the law of intent (whether for adverse or favorable reactions), the agenda of the group mind affects how the events will transpire and what consequences will result in the aftermath. The idea for greenhouse gases will be due to correct what nuclear or neutron explosions have created after their use. If the elite plan to resurface, then they must be allowed to live in conditions that will not affect them physically.

Green stated that the key to gain all knowledge is to follow the laws. The two ideas are of course human inventions to formulate an attempt of understanding the complicated world around us. As long as we follow these laws, we should be in fact successful in all we do. In all fairness, Green stated that ultimately the "train is coming" and everyone has their own agenda. The idea of the "master plan" is not in effect real, due to the fact of human free will [57]. Plans will always change once a human changes their behavior or ideas. With each individual applying the law of intent, one can imagine the results every outcome could and would potentially have. With freewill, comes the ability to make things appropriate for all humans and organisms on this planet. This power could also have the opposite effect destroying everyone as well. Where do synthetics fit into this category? Clones are programmed to have the ability to think, so the game could change with the movie *The Island* (2004) as the perfect example. If they are allowed to use this law as well, we would now have an even more complex result in all events. Where will the alien presence fit into all of this?

As we look into the sky and see the stars, Green pointed out that all heavenly objects that seem to glow colors (red, green and blue) are in fact alien craft taking "photos" of humans [58]. Green believes that we are the focal point of their interest. Going even further, the Pleiadians are also doing this monitoring at a spiritual level as well as physical. Will humans surpass these obstacles? We should take his advice and be "happy for the day;" for as we know it, tomorrow may never come.

Versions and Opinions

Preparation is only allowed by those with means to initiate it. He explained how the president of the United States is given oath under a *Jefferson bible* rather than the King James/ Gideon version. The founding fathers of this nation were all masons and with Jefferson himself being one, was considered the most influential man of his time concerning religious issues. He himself wanted to remove the supernatural qualities of Jesus that he believed were added by four Evangelists. This would make more sense since there is no concrete evidence that a Jesus ever existed [58]. Why do we have so many different versions of this falsely created fantasy, and what do we mean by version? Version means opinion, and every single group has their opinion based on their preconceived ideas of the "divine" and its meaning. This could play a part in free will, however, it could be suggested in causing more harm for the mere fact of trying to understand the spiritual in a way that is not truthful.

For example, a man known as Enoch was not mentioned in the Hebrew myth at all because of several reasons: firstly, he was a black man, and in the Hebrew myths, the black man was subjugated due to the fact that the founding father Ham supposedly committed a heinous sexual abuse act towards his father Noah [59]. Secondly, the story of Enoch described a man in Ethiopia meeting a group of nonhumans and then boarding a spacecraft in which he never returned to Earth [60]. Another interesting fabrication would be the invention of Exodus. Through extensive research, it has been concluded that the whole story itself is a lie. The Los Angeles Times had presented an article of interest concerning this false story that does attack Hebrew interest and questioned it validity:

> "The whole story never happened. Some guy just made it all up, and then Muhammad and the Israelites stole the story. The whole history of the so called Abrahamic people is a fabrication. Muslims like to claim that the Jewish prophets were in fact Muslim instead. The Jews fabricated it and then the Muslims stole the fabrication. What does it tell you when you realize the *bourgeois* faction of the Jews have been fabricating stories about the persecution of since the Old Testament and continue to do so today . . ." (freemediaproductions.info, 04/14/2010).

Teresa Watanabe also composed an article that discussed the Exodus story fabrication in greater detail. She went on to quote Rabbi Wolpe who stated the following:

> "The truth every modern archeologist who has investigated the story of Exodus, with very few exceptions, agrees that the way the bible describes the Exodus is not the way it happened if it happened at all, Wople told his congregants." (*Teresa Watanbe Los Angeles Times, April 13, 2001*)

What does this tell us about the dangerous lie that ruined all of Egypt over the centuries accusing them of something that has no evidence or making audacious claims about slavery?

> "Ever increasingly a plague of scholars bears down upon the historicity of the Exodus. Jewish & non-Jewish alike, they are comrades in intellectual arms marching shoulder to shoulder to the refrain "The Exodus never happened." They might admit that they were perhaps modest waves of Hebrew nomadic wanderers seeking a better life in the land of milk and honey. But nothing like a biblical report of miraculous signs and wonders, upheaval and disaster, plagues and death— and liberation. One of the latest authorities numbering himself among those challenging the biblical testimony of the Exodus and rejecting the "scriptural myths" is Rabbi Burton L. Visotsky. His Passover article of doubt in the Washington Jewish Week of April 14, 2005 entitled "Pondering the Riddle of the Sphinx," assumes the scriptural account to be a fabulous

> fabrication; he gratuitously takes for granted and as self-evident that it is a myth." (Dr. Reeve Robert Brenner, *National Institute of Health*, Bethesda MD)

Because of these "versions," many victims have suffered and many events have transpired in the name of ignorant disastrous claims. History is changed by those who have their agendas. According to Green one cannot lie telepathically, and if this is the case, we are vulnerable in higher densities. Imagine an end to our physical life, we now would have to tell the truth to an alien being about our accomplishments or missions (communication would be telepathically due to the idea of speech being obsolete). How then would we be able to lie? The people here and now just do their jobs with no compunction. Even if we do plan to take Green's suggestions on preparing, initiating and desiring a recovered life after these events, what are some of the ways to succeed in doing so? Suggestions are always easy to speak about; it is the practical application that hinders most people. If this event is supposed to end our current life due to technology, how will it be restored for human life to continue?

Exodus from the U.S.

Green also stated that everything is controlled to extract more from us rather than supply it to us. The tax system is meant to take more out of the poor. So his best suggestions are to rent instead of buying. This may seem like a shot in the dark, but let us analyze this: if one *rents* during this time of chaos, then all one has sacrificed in the temporary location would cease and then would have to move elsewhere if one survived. Communication would cease, commerce would continue, however when the currency is null, concentration camps would arise. If one managed to avoid this prison camp and escape to another country, the idea of starting over would be the plan and being alive would be the reality.

If one purchased a location (townhouse, house, apartment, condo etc . . .) during the time of chaos, then all one has sacrificed in their own permanent location with everything bought and paid for, is destroyed and must be left behind. Most people will not leave their own investments behind and will stay if they can. During this time, communication will also cease, but commerce will continue. When the currency goes null, concentration camps will arise. If one chose to stay behind, they would be transferred to these concentration camps by force, leaving everything they have owned to the government. Which of these situations would be the most devastating? Some might argue this point and insist that renting is working and supplying someone else with the means to live.

The currency we use is just a legal tender meant to pay all debts public and private. This doesn't mean that we own this money due to the top of each billing having the statement: "Federal Reserve Note." Everything we purchase with the money we work for is not ours to keep, rather it is only used do the monetary system stays effective while people consume and purchase products. The worst case scenario, the government owns what one buys even though it has one's name on it; the bigger the purchase, the more devastated one will be when it comes time to abandon it. This is the case of highway robbery at its highest. If one has gold, Green assured that the individual would be better off than anyone else. What about families at a time like this? Are we all going to work together to survive this horror? Green's concept of family is that it is a unit; furthermore each individual has their own mission to complete. This is due to the belief that each family member is a different entity.

He stated that he doesn't worry about his family in the sense that if someone died, they have just completed their mission and have gone "home." Most of the common people might not agree with what he believes; attachment is a dangerous way of losing one's power and initially fall victim to it. The idea of enjoying the day comes into fruition, and we must enjoy the present no matter how short it is. Once we miss it, it never repeats itself. Most of us do not enjoy the present, therefore when it passes, we become miserable wishing they could have it back; acting upon psychoactive nostalgia. Green mentioned that "it was ok to look back, but don't stare;" we should not get caught up into the past and focus on the now because the situation is now. The soul energy is something beyond our understanding and becomes "mission impossible" to discover it.

In conclusion, what do we really need to prepare for this event? It seems that self-realization and the understanding of the human soul would be the best place to start. His definition of history is "his-story" which could only mean the events are accounts based solely on one's own interpretation. The Majestic Twelve program, which describes the people of Earth uniting against a hologram of an alien threat or some "creation," is another speculation of Green that could be possible called *Project Blue Beam* [61]. Although the FBI claimed that it was hoax according to their investigation in 1988, there is still plenty of documentation considering the opposite. Even more bizarre, were the ideas of Jesus and the stages of metamorphosis Green constructed about the myth. Green now stated that Jesus was not in fact human, but a hologram created by the Pleiadians to fulfill a purpose of doing things to wake people up. All of these "angels" and saints that the Christians deify are in fact alien groups [62].

Humans as a whole must change but only one individual at a time. Only then will we be able to join the rest of the Galactic family. The dream or illusion that Project Camelot has and most pro-human groups contain is noble on some levels, but very unrealistic at most. We must all accept the fact that eventually all organisms cease to exist and then are destroyed; either by sequential time or in our case, by our own actions. They fail to see the bigger picture than just the "good vs. evil" scenario or "saving" us from extinction. Evolution has its own life force and will continue to work as the machine it is to balance and maintain the system as it sees fit. Our only hope is to somehow adapt or understand how the system works and contribute to become useful members of our race. Doing this, we as humans become more powerful and then create a better understanding so that maybe our creators (whether they are the Draco, Andromedans, Pleiadians, Blues, Greys, Lyrians, Sirians, etc . . .) take pride in their creation as a proud parent and allow us to discover the universe deeper. At this time, the creation of a new paradigm for human beings is established pushing us ahead in the grand scheme of things.

End Notes

[1] Project Camelot. "Message from the ground crew: an interview with George Green." *Projectcamelot.org* Spokane, WA (2008).

[2] Xinhua. "India developing anti-radiation missile." *China Daily Europe* (April 2012).

[3] Jean H. Lee. "North Korea threats: Pyongyang warns south of special actions." *Huffington Post* (April 2012).

[4] Marcus George. "Iran says can destroy US bases minutes after attack" *Reuters.com* (July 2012).

[5] Ibid 3.

[6] Paul Joseph Watson. "Obama tells allies US will attack Iran by fall of 2012." *Infowars.com* (November 2011).

[7] Ibid1.

[8] Ibid 1.

[9] Ibid 1.

[10] Eric McLamb. "The day of seven billion." *Ecology.com* (September 2011).

[11] Peter Kropotkin. *Mutual Aid: A Factor of Evolution*. London: Free Press (2009).

[12] Charles L. Harper. *Environment and Society: Human Perspectives on Environmental Issues*. Prentice Hall 5th Ed. (July 2011).

[13] Ibid 1.

[14] Ibid 1.

[15] monolithic.com/topics/floorplans.

[16] Ibid 15.

[17] Ibid 1.

[18] Judith Kusel. "Your name: your soul, and what you are anchoring in . . . soul lessons . . ." *Wordpress.com* (March 2012).

[19] Gerald Grove. "We are literally made from stars." *Longleaf.net* (1997).

[20] H.C. Rogers. "Hydrogen Embrittlement of Metals." *Science 159* (1999).

[21] Benevolent Beings and George Green. *Handbook for the New Paradigm*. Bridger House Publications INC; Vol. I Ed (May 1999)

[22] Ibid 1.

[23] Ibid 1.

[24] Ibid 21.

[25] Ibid 1.

[26] Benevolent Beings and George Green. *Becoming (Handbook for the New Paradigm Vol. 3).* Bridger House Publications INC (January 2000).

[27] Ibid 1.

[28] Ibid 1.

[29] Ibid 1.

[30] David Icke. "Was Hitler a Rothschild?" *Theforbiddenknowledge.com* (2002)

[31] Benjamin Fischer. "Hitler, Stalin, and Operation Myth." CIA article, aboutfacts.net (2003).

[32] Ibid 1.

[33] Ibid 1.

[34] Ibid 1.

[35] Eve Lorgen. *The Love Bite: Alien Interference in Human Love Relationships.* ELogos & HHC Press (February 2000).

[36] Ibid 1.

[37] Ibid 1.

[38] Dietmar Rothe PhD. "The key spiritual teachings of Jmmanuel" *UFO Congress Seminar* (September 2001).

[39] Benevolent Beings and George Green. *Embracing the Rainbow.* Gazelle Distribution Trade; Vol. II Ed (June 1999).

[40] Ibid 1.

[41] Ibid 1.

[42] Ibid 1.

[43] Arnold Evans. "Dictatorships in Egypt, Saudi Arabia, Jordan, Kuwait, and UAE: how responsible is the United States?" *Middle East Reality* (January 2010).

[44] Robert Stein. "US population reduction is the root of progressive agenda." *Ourfuture.org* (July 2008).

[45] Lucus. "The mind-bending Close Encounters of the Third Kind/DIA connection." *Rabithole2.com* (February 2011).

[46] Ibid 1.

[47] Ibid 1.

[48] Ibid 1.

[49] Ian Sample. "Aliens may destroy humans to protect other civilizations." *The Guardian U.K.* (August 2011).

[50] Ibid 1.

[51] Ibid 1.

[52] epa.gov/radiation/radionuclides/plutonium.html.

[53] Ibid 1.

[54] Steven Hargreaves. "China: The new big oil." *CNN Money* (August 2009).

[55] Ibid 1.

[56] Ibid 1.

[57] Ibid 26.

[58] Steve Benson. "Did Jesus actually exist?" *i4m.com*

[59] Genesis 9: 24-27.

[60] Ashley Rye. "The Book of Enoch and UFOs." *Bibliotecapleyades.net*

[61] Serge Monast. "Project Blue Beam." *Educate-youeself.org* (1994).

[62] Ibid 1.

I don't laugh at people anymore when they say they have seen UFOs. I've seen one myself.

–President Jimmy Carter, January 1969.

IV

Richard Dolan and Exopolitical Human Responsibility vs. Dr. Steven Greer and Project Starlight

When the subject of *Exopolitics* and UFO research are brought to the table for argument or debate, there is one man who happens to fit the bill in terms of having completeness and coherence concerning this issue. According to Richard Dolan, there are certain events that have been transpiring within the governments of the world concerning aliens with an agenda. Richard Dolan is an investigative mind who is pushing for the truth for UFO disclosure and free energy technology that the U.S. government and other powerful enterprises seem to contain without the idea of sharing [1]. Dolan is a historian and as some people describe him as a "TV personality" with an expertise in Ufology. Since attending Oxford University and later becoming a finalist for the *Rhodes scholarship*, it is safe to assume that he has the proper education according to academia standards [2]. He might even offer a different outlook about this subject that most people take as more fiction than fact.

With his investigations and publishing three novels labeled *UFOs and the National Security State*, Dolan separates the dates of chronology in the fashion of certain times in history that we as humans have encountered these phenomenal events. The first dates were 1941-1973, the second volume covered the dates 1973-1991, and the final dates are covering 1991 to the present with possibilities of beyond. Dolan has presented the material to us in an orderly fashion with dates and undisputable evidence containing U.S. government documents, personal interviews, and just a wide variety of knowledge that places this more in the realm of reality. Moreover, he believes these books represent his thoughts and the push for disclosure. This may open humans to explore their past which is necessary in order to be responsible for our own futures.

The Push for Disclosure

Dolan attended the *Project Camelot Awake and Aware Conference* in 2009 in the attempt to discuss his findings and educate the small populace on the push for an immediate disclosure and the dangers of remaining in the current state we are in. He described the subject as *Exopolitics* and wanted people to create a new "roadmap" as he called it, so the subject itself would not be ridiculed by academia or the professional world. Since people in the current state only view UFOs and alien technology as merely fantasy or entertainment, there is quite of amount of work that needs to be done in order to change this point of view.

How does one attempt to try to convince the ignorant world in believing something this radical? He utilized examples of people's inability to see higher intelligent life forms interacting with less superior ones. For example let us presume that a couple of well-informed individuals from 2012 travel in time to the year 1400 and attempt to convince the known world that the Earth is indeed not flat, that the sun is the center of the solar system, and that religion is skewed and misinformed. What kind of reaction does one suppose these strange visitors from another time would receive?

Of course when this hypothetical is made, we are presuming that the individuals encounter an intelligent person from the time period like an astronomer, teacher, etc . . . We must realize that this is not far from the current realistic point of view. We as uninformed society now are definitely blind to other truths that lie beyond the simple concept of cell phones, computers, and American Idol. How do we react now when someone tries to alert the common population in understanding a more complex world? The same reaction would be relevant throughout history. The past in this case would be harsh using religious dogma to persecute and even openly kill the individual(s) who attempted to inform the world [3]. Dolan made an important point concerning history: in order for a society to be responsible, noteworthy, educated, and progressive, one has to remember the past.

Remembering the past allows for two important events: one is the ability to learn from mistakes in order to prevent a repeat, and the second being the ability to grow as a collective through education, experience, and energy flow (changing an adapting a new way of life to fit a more conscientious program for all life on this planet). This seems to fit the illusionary idea that Project Camelot is trying to accomplish: to awaken and aware the people of the world. The answer can only be completed once human responsibility is taken and the flow of information is allowed. Only then will those individuals who want to make a contribution for ascension should be successful.

Dolan used his books to explain his position and his belief about the need for remembering human history. Throughout his books, he explained the verified evidence that proves beyond a shadow of a doubt, that UFOs are and have been constantly viewing humans and their actions. His website *keyholepublishing.com*, offers all of his current books along with other writers who have information, or even share the same passion as he does [4]. His database according to him has over one thousand journals given to him by key witnesses and people of importance, contributing all the personal evidence they could. Dolan mentioned however, that many of the sources wished to remain anonymous; which could in turn cause a severe drop in authenticity. The reason for this move was due to the fact that the subject itself is already taking heat by skeptics everywhere. Most skeptics are quick to label any UFO occurrence as either a natural phenomenon or a military exercise. While some of this may be true, we do not know the extent of the type of technology that the U.S. military has, even though they display us repeated tests of obsolete equipment [5].

Nevertheless, one must view Dolan's work and by personal insight (not *prejudice* or preconceived ideas); then decide and research what they believe is worth investigating. Dolan's main mission is to try to provide a reliable guide to our human past; especially recent. With knowledge of the past, the author agrees that we can function as a normal or even decent society. Through his research, Dolan displayed to us that the United States' "past" is merely an archive of documents and memos. With this said, the majority of these memos and documents are and remain inaccessible to the public population. Despite FOIA (*Freedom of Information Act*) signed by President Johnson in 1966 which states a "federal law that allows for the full or partial disclosure of previously unreleased information and documents controlled by the United States Government," certain documents still cannot be disclosed. Why would the U.S. government defy a law that they implemented purposefully? Is there something so dangerous that it could shake the pillars of humanity if discovered? It seems a large part of our human history is still classified and "off limits" to the public.

Dolan's mission was to salvage as much information as he could from this conspiracy. He stressed that most of his findings originated from verifiable government documents. This meant these government documents do not and cannot require an argument. In order to prove these kinds of claims, these are the exact proofs one needs to finally destroy any skepticism. All of his journals (whether they be UFO organizations, on the spot investigations, or personal interviews), with little or few exceptions have been verified [6]. Most of these accounts remained anonymous which puts the reader in an unequal position. Dolan is an advocate for "good science" and the idea that "everyone should know." As we stressed the more anonymous information is, the less believable it will be. At this point, the investigation then becomes the individual's responsibility and must be thoroughly checked if one is ready to fathom the complexity of the situation. Dolan also stressed the importance of whom we are speaking to when we discuss subjects such as these. Like most civilizations of the past, the poor and underdeveloped mass that created the foundation of the social workforce, did not and could understand full concepts [7][8]. They are not informed enough to make conscientious decisions, nor ready to accept the truth/disclosure process unless they are informed from the "beginning." For this reason, religious dogma and social control programs are implemented to give the public a more "simple life" understanding; rather than explain things that could break the established structure. This is specifically why Dolan stated the following "be careful whom you talk to" recommendation. In his books, he covered not only the historical viewpoint as a whole, rather in parts with three major categories: encounters, politics, and global transformation.

UFO Encounters

Encounters are basically when UFO events take place where entities or unidentified craft have touched base with human contacts military or civilian. Examples included the "Hudson Bay sightings" of the 1980s and 1990s, or the *Travis Walton* abduction of 1973 [9]. The success according to Dolan, was that all of the encounters he covered had a quality of well documented verifiable sources making them indisputable. He separated them into five subcategories: *military cases, events in the Earth's orbit, abductions*, and *crop circles.*

With military cases and events in the Earth's orbit ranging in the hundreds; subjects like "fast walkers" (fast moving alien ships) or the *DSP* (Defense Support Program) satellite (a device used to spot UFO craft at high velocities even when the military describes it as an "early warning space defense probe") are abundant enough to make a case for UFO disclosure [10]. Concerning the DSP, why is a warning implemented? Is there an imminent threat in space that we can expect? According to Dolan's research, the U.S. government has located and spotted two hundred eight-three different occurrences during the 1973-1991 timeline [11]. One major occurrence transpired on September 18th, 1976 when Iranian fighter jets encountered a fast moving object in their airspace in Tehran. The witness being a pilot named Pirouzi had this statement:

> *"It was rectangular in shape at a height of about 6,000 ft. The right end was blue, the left was blue,*

> *and in the middle was a red light making a circular motion; the object was probably cylindrical." (Don Berliner UFO briefing document; Case ID 200. UFOevidence.org)*

With an example such as this, there is a case for UFO existence in our midst. The challenge now is to piece together all of the relationships between these five subcategories and try to identify if they are really visitors from an unknown part of the solar system and beyond or are they government schemes of undisclosed technology that they recovered from alien technology.

With abduction cases many are documented; however only one so far has ever been considered the best known evidence we have to claim these allegations: *The Travis Walton "Fire in the Sky" experience*. According to the evidence, this event took place in eastern Arizona on November 5th, 1975 when a bluish light from a flattened-disc shaped craft impacted Walton like a laser hitting a target and scaring off his six other companions leaving him there on his own. As they returned to check on his health situation, they were surprised to find no trace of either Walton or the craft itself. After numerous searches for this man (with helicopters, and police K-9 units) they were unsuccessful in finding anything [12]. Walton seemed to have vanished without a trace until the night of November 10th, when he mysteriously called his sister from a gas station incoherently as if he was drugged and distraught. There were polygraph tests performed by Cy Gilson on two of the crewmen Mike Rogers and Allen Dalis to prove that the events that took place were in fact genuine [13].

Many debunkers especially *Phillip Klass*, wrote two books which seemed to discredit most information; even studying the polygraph to find mistakes. Although he did bring up some interesting theories, they were not enough to simply dismiss the case as a complete hoax [14]. It was documented that another polygraph was used (state-of-the-art equipment) in 1993 as Gilson utilized the *CQT* methodology (Control Question Technique, a computer scored test) and the three men passed again. There was a debate between Klass and the whole Walton experience even though polygraph tests initially showed five of the six men passed with one test being inconclusive [15]. Walton however, stated the following in explaining his experience as the ship departed after dropping him off after his interaction with alien beings:

> *"I regained consciousness lying on my stomach, my head on my right forearm. Cold air brought me instantly awake. I looked up in time to see a light turn off on the bottom of a curved, gleaming hull . . . Then I saw the mirrored outline of a silvery disc hovering four feet above the paved surface of the road. It must have been about forty feet in diameter because it extended several feet off the left side of the road, a dozen yards away. I could see the night sky, the surrounding trees, and the highway centre line reflected in the curving mirror of its hull. I noticed a faint warmth radiating on my face. Then abruptly, it shot vertically into the sky, creating a strong breeze that stirred the nearby pine boughs and rustled the dry oak leaves that lay in the dry grass beside the road. It gave off no light, and it was almost instantly lost from sight. The most striking thing about its departure was its quietness . . ." (Fire In the Sky; Chapter 9—Human?)*

In his description of this supposed alien craft of human origin or is it in fact a group of extraterrestrials from an unknown world? His description of the alien themselves proved to be of humanoid quality even describing the males as "handsomely masculine" and females as the "epitome of their gender." Whatever the case may be the overwhelming evidence despite Klass' two books, points out more than just an elaborate hoax.

UFO Connection with Crop Circles and Mutilations

Mutilations are other phenomena that Dolan himself was interested in. He brought up the question of this fascinating practice although it is complete disgusting. Despite cases from all around the world (U.K, U.S., Puerto Rico ["Chupacabra"] Australia, Argentina, Brazil, etc . . .) governments are still unable to exactly decipher why these events are happening, or what/who exactly is behind these horrible acts. Is this UFO related or not? The exact definition for mutilation is "an act or physical injury that degrades the appearance or function of any living body, usually without causing death." Usually cases are reported involving cattle and have been since the 1960s; with reports usually stemming from the U.K [16].

The methodology of these phenomena had many speculating that it could be UFO due to the fact that the animal's blood was drained, the internal organs were removed, and there seemed to be no point of entry. Even more bizarre, were the removal of reproductive organs and anal coring which seem to be the most common and precise method (with no traces of being humanly and surgically done). When the bodies were found, most cases displayed the animal or (sometimes) human being was discovered without tracks around the body even in soft ground or mud. What then could be the reason for these allegations not being UFO related? If this was in fact not UFO like many claim, who would have the artisan's skill to perform such procedures without being caught over the last fifty years?

The most famous of human cases was reported in 1988 in Brazil. A mutilated man discovered near the *Guarapiranga Reservoir* by a police technician by the name of *Sergio Rubens* who took photos of what he thought was not naturally done; he then passed them to a cousin of his *Dr. Goes Rubens* to further investigate their odd nature. Dr. Rubens then contacted one of his close friends who was familiar with UFO/animal mutilations and then recognized the patterns done the man. As they investigated further, the man in charge Dr. Cuenca, gave his files and noted these striking facts:

> *"Although the victim had been dead for forty-eight to seventy-two hours there was no sign of being eaten by animals or starting to rot, as would be expected. There was no smell. Bleeding from the wounds had been minimal. The lips and flesh from the face had been cut away. The eyes, ears, and tongue had been removed. Neat round holes, one to one and a half inches in diameter, had been made on the shoulders, arms, head, stomach and anus and tissue and muscle had been extracted. The holes had not been made through which extensive digestive organs had been extracted. The scrotum, but not the penis had been removed, and all pubic hair had disappeared. The rectum had been cored out. Despite the devastating mutilations, there was no sign that the victim had been bound or had*

> *struggled in any way." (Inexplicata 2000, Las Luces de la Muerte)*

The simple fact that all of these graphic photos show a gruesome reality obviously not done by humans displayed a bigger conspiracy in terms of what the purpose would be to do this. Why specific body parts and not others? Were they using these parts for scientific study or is there something else that these body parts provided? Shockingly, the correlation between human and animal mutilations has a frequent number with the same results [17].

Crop circles happen to be the last phenomena that Dolan described as part of his UFO encounter theory, that we as humans have dealt with over the past sixty years. Crop circles are excellent phenomena clearly detailed, complicated, and above all done with precise fashion requiring skill beyond human measure. Although many debunkers try to credit the ancient ones (Nazca lines) to simple native tribes, there is evidence that this is definitely not the case. For instance, if one was to try to view these "drawings" in great detail, it would require an airplane for the lines to be seen in proper form.

If it was indeed the case of these phenomena done by simple natives, this would mean that they had in their possession a way to "draw" these lines using a flying device in order to construct its complexity. *Erich von Daniken*, a famous researcher, believes and has found through his investigations these "simple lines" that established science attributes to Indian tribes as simple religious practices, are not the case. He has discovered that the lines create a certain pathway that could be identified as a sort of landing location for either craft or airplane. Since the archeological community refuses to believe that the Incas had the technology to fly, the only other suggestion would be that beings of other planetary origin created and occupied this location for their base of operations [18].

The objects themselves were fashioned with a sort of mathematical symmetry that baffles even the most of experts also containing a sort of computer based astronomy. If modern science does not and cannot attribute these great mysteries to alien influence, they then should not attribute them to simple tribes. There is a greater unknown here that we must accept as rational and logical human beings. Something constructed these wonders long before the Inca civilization ever arrived; meaning the natives migrated to this location and came upon these wonders [19]. Whatever the reason may be, the author suggests it would be best to remain in speculation than attribute a common belief to something that doesn't add up. Interestingly enough, why would these alien visitors have the need to fashion animal drawings? Why would they need thirty-seven miles of runway to land? If this was the case, this must have been a central location with plenty of commerce or metropolitan area. Again, many archeologists would probably state that the Incas did not need alien or UFO artistic inspiration to create such a thing; they argue very well using the geological location of the desert and state the following:

> *"Stones (not sand) comprise the desert surface. Rusted by humidity, their darkened color increase heat absorption. The resulting cushion of warm surface air acts as a buffer against the wind; while minerals in the soil help to solidify the stones. On the "desert pavement" thus created this dry, rainless environment, erosion is practically nil— making for remarkable preservation of the markings." (Robert*

T. Carroll, the Nazca Lines. The Skeptic's Dictionary 2004.)

Although they try to argue this scientifically (and it would be accurate), they fail to explain why. Why would these native tribes take the time that costs thousands of people, long hours, an artisan's skill (that they cannot reproduce), and that specific location? If they stood the passage of time like all other ancient wonders, why then can these great mysteries done by a "simpler civilization" not be reproduced by our current technology? Archeologists fail to explain this by simply adhering to the religious importance of ancient times; however, the answer is still not there. With these explanations, there lacks the logical and rational viewpoints that are time and time again ignored. Nevertheless, archeology will soon have to accept that their financial future and reputation will be in jeopardy due to new discoveries that make them obsolete. Dolan addressed these interesting facts using UFO historical reference journals with documents that may prove useful.

Politics and the UFO Agenda

The subject of politics also enters the realm of UFO phenomenon in a profound way during the time of investigating the truth. Dolan expressed that this idea was worldwide, not only in the United States. He also included that the U.S. president and David Rockefeller were part of this equation [20]. Where does Rockefeller fit into the whole idea? Dolan has substantial evidence that he plays a big part on who is representing the United States of America. In his major analysis of politics in general, he mentioned many important parts of our government including presidential administrators, policies affecting research (like FOIA), infiltration of UFO research by intelligence groups, and larger geopolitical realties that many still believe do not exist or are a hoax. Control groups such as the *Bilderberg Group,* which is an unofficial annual "invitation only" conference, whose limit does not exceed one hundred forty people. Most of these people are in fields such as media, politics, banking, business, and military. Their press is undisclosed to the public and media, giving us a sort of mystery on why they do not allow the public to understand just exactly what they are discussing [21]. Another group is the *CFR* or Council on Foreign Relations, which insists that the creation of this "research center" is to better understand the world by comprehending global trends and contributing "ideas" to U.S. foreign policy. According to Dolan however, this is a "promotional ruling arm" of the New World Order of ruling elite. Their mission is to incorporate a "one group mind" in order to systematically destroy the ideas of freedom and free speech [22].

A Supreme Court judge by the name of Felix *Frankfurter* (1932-1969) stated "the real rulers in Washington are invisible and exercise power from behind the scenes." We may be looking at a shadowy government that has been mentioned by Inouye ruling the public into one mindset for easier control. By eliminating the Constitution, American sovereignty, and controlling the nation's money, one then has the power to rule the entire system under the guise of the original illusionary governmental structure. The council itself was incorporated within the American branch of government on July 29th, 1921 in New York, set up by *Colonel House* (Edward Mandel House; an American diplomat, presidential advisor and politician) amongst others that Gary Allen described as

> *"Such potentates of international banking such as J.P Morgan, John D. Rockefeller, Paul Warburg, Otto khan and Jacob Schiff . . . the same clique which had engineered the establishment of the Federal Reserve System." (American Opinion, 1972)*

Professor Carroll Quigley also added an in depth description of what the group actually represented according to his belief. They were basically a "front group for J.P Morgan and Company in association with very small American Round Table Group." If indeed Dolan has documentation of their involvement with UFO activities worldwide, this could mean that we indeed are being "cut off" from our need to know important information regarding our future and this world in general.

Another group that Dolan holds responsible for the continuation of the suppression of important information to the American public would be the *Trilateral Commission.* According to mainstream media, the commission itself was formed in 1973 as a private organization to create an initial bond of cooperation between Europe, the United States, and Japan. Their main objective was to establish within the private sector a "communications increase" between countries that were believed to be lacking. The group itself was founded by Rockefeller who besides the Ford Foundation is still its major fundraiser. It is no surprise that when the commission was founded by Rockefeller in 1973, he was also chairman of the CFR at the time. Do these two groups share the same mindset in destroying the American republic and the trust if the people?

In 1972 during his speech at the *Chase Manhattan International Financial Forums* in London, he stated an unusual idea requesting a commission be created for peace and prosperity. With this new creation, the commission would "be of help to governments by providing measured judgment." What exactly did he mean by measured judgment? Would this be another monopoly on the already unaware population around the world? Why are there only three organizations involved? Does South America no fit the requirements to join? Noam Chomsky offered us a different light than just "peaceful organization" for a better understanding:

> *"Perhaps the most striking feature of the new Administration is the role played in it by the Trilateral Commission. The mass media had little to say about this matter during the Presidential campaign— in fact, the connection of the Carter group to the Commission was recently selected as "the best censored news story of 1976"— and it has not received the attention that it might have since the Administration took office. All of the top positions in the government— the office of the President, Vice-President, Secretary of State, Defense and Treasury— are held by members of the Trilateral Commission, and the National Security Advisor was its director. Many lesser officials also came from this group. It is rare for such an easily identified private group to play such a prominent role in an American Administration." (Radical Priorities, 1981)*

If this is just a control group already placing their own interests within the government, there is little chance for change in terms of "voting" for an ideal candidate as the voice of the people. Although the very idea of a presidential candidate for the interest of the common people is absurd, the public seems to still believe in some way, that the illusion is still better than reality. Dolan himself also agreed with the fact that all of these groups have an interest in "technological considerations" and to "privatize the secret" of just how advanced we are in this day and age [23]. He also displayed the ideas of just how liberal President Carter really was at one point in his life. The political aspect also dealt with air space violations that Dolan suggested Carter was trying to disclose at one point. The very idea of UFO "fast walkers" spilling into the public eye could definitely threaten and undermine trust in the government. He also discussed how the breakup of the USSR could in fact be more than just an arms race between two countries that have a "difference of socially run governments [24]."

Why do we as people still believe the old republic exists here in America? Why are we stuck in conventional mindsets? We believe the president is still in charge, but the truth is no one knows who is in charge anymore [25]. As we have discussed, Rockefeller oversees mostly all of the U.S. in general. How powerful is Rockefeller really? To what extent does his iron hand reach? It seems that he decides just who exactly the president of the United States will be. Whomever we see get "elected by the people" is really done at the discretion of Rockefeller and his interests [26]. We still believe in the pseudo-democratic process Dolan still discussed as the public's main problem. An example of just how powerful Rockefeller is, one has to look at Gerald Ford who is the first unelected president of the United States in history (whom did not require a vote) [27].

Ford did not just "drop in the white house" as Dolan so eloquently put it, he was selected due to his track record of being not only close to Rockefeller, but he was a five time Bilderberg attendee [28]. Carter, who seemed liberal at first, was also selected due to his ties to the Trilateral Commission.

Ronald Regan at one time in the 80s, campaigned against the "elite," The Council on Foreign Relations, and George Bush Sr. quoting the following: "that man will never be part of my administration . . ." The campaign manager at the time was William Casey, (the head of the CIA from 1981-1987) head of CFR and a close friend of Rockefeller himself.

It seems that all of the "elected members" of the United States have one thing in common: they all work for the same team. Regan of course seemed to "change his mind" about his initial campaign and started in another direction; even changing his mind about Bush Sr. Painfully obvious, it is clear that Rockefeller has a big influence on how a president's views can be seen and changed. Dolan described to us just what a president is: nothing but a "sales rep" whose job is to sell us a lie. This lie could be many things including globalization, or "new wars" that really stem from international financial groups. One example Dolan used was the Gulf War which he branded a UFO event. Many soldiers have seen UFO activity during this time and have reported such observations:

> *"I watched this supposed satellite traverse across the sky when, suddenly it stopped in 'mid-orbit.' I thought I had been staring at the stars so long that my vision had potentially become blurred I shook off the confusion and got my visual of the object back. It was traversing the sky again. I thought to myself, "my eyes were just disoriented . . . ." (Jim Miller; 1991 Gulf War UFO mass sightings by American Troops. Rense.com)*

Dolan's "Breakaway Civilization"

The main point that Dolan tries to force us to do is question that was really is in charge and just exactly what the power structure is. Basically, we as uninformed citizens need to know who our governments are, and who is running the show. Dolan suggested we need to stop adhering to the "fifth grade civic version" of our government as he is correct. When we do describe UFOs and technology beyond our imagination, we must now ask a more important question: die "we" make it or did "they" make it? Dolan discussed that answering this question was very difficult; and we must not forget a clear answer on just the sightings taking place could be otherworld occurrences or man-made replicas. He attributed this conclusion on the fact that our "official" technological achievements have not been disclosed. This falls under the guise of "black budget" and classified federal spending.

When the term classified is used, Dolan discussed in greater detail the description of what this terms really meant: illegal money, "special access programs" (either acknowledged or unacknowledged), programs labeled "little to know basis" (congress and agencies), NARCO trafficking (including stock market/securities fraud), and money flow [29]. We remember discussing the privatization of the "secret" which meant that government agencies have unfortunately become dominated by private money with the UFO secret falling under the same predicament. Dolan stated the UFO idea as a "runaway nature" with private interest groups and contractors. They decide about what matters and what doesn't. Surprisingly, this would be the job of the *DoD* (Department of Defense) however, Dolan described them as merely "gatekeepers" to keep the money flowing [30].

This process is easier to administer than simply disclosing the truth and losing profit, which would negate growth and destroy the corporate interest. The process itself is simpler when the project doesn't become classified; instead becomes proprietary, like a trademark instilling ownership of the technology or idea. This way it would be easier to keep from the public and the corporations become more profitable with this new "exotic technology" not made by human hands. This process doesn't sound bad when one analyzes it; just imagine how many trademarks corporate interest have worldwide and imagine the amount if incredible "projects" they have access to while the public conveniently pays for it without ever seeing it.

The third part of Dolan's quest for the understanding of human history concerned the research of human development and human consciousness. According to the documents that Dolan disclosed, the U.S (1970-1980), has been trying to understand who our "visitors" were [31]. With these new visitors, there arose a problem that has been difficult to alleviate: firstly, abduction cases were rampant that needed to be investigated authentic or not (also the meaning of "abduction" had a new definition in the 1980s). Secondly, research on families who have encountered or reported these events had to be investigated as well (many were repeaters, and this phenomena had to be researched) like the McPherson family abduction of 1998.

Although it could be viewed as an actual abduction case, many skeptics mocked the video claiming it to be a work of fiction [32]. Dolan himself stressed about mutilations and the fascination/disturbing effect on humanity. And finally, crop circles and their fascinations as well. Dolan really attributed success to the internet itself; as what he described the UFO phenomena as being "the true pioneers of the internet."

With all of these events and data that have been received, Dolan concluded that cover up and researched data was undeniable. The question now remained on how this exactly affected human history.

When something is covered up or denied, the public falls into a lapse of information that shuts them of from a source that is need to know for people to gain knowledge and ascend. When the government or corporate interest take this information privy only to them, a "breakaway civilization" is formed (this meaning a separate coexisting civilization side by side). Dolan had researched this and had found that since the Cold War, this has been evident. Examples like separate scientific infrastructures with a shadow government with unlimited "money" as mentioned by Inouye. When this transpires, any scientific breakthrough that occurs would separate the public and the actual discovery more and more, bearing a separate entity with different set principles. For instance, Dolan mentioned time travel and how he or someone intelligent would tell people of the past what we know as our current reality. Do we think that someone from four hundred years ago would be able to handle whatever we tell them about now? Would there be the same kind of mindset that people would believe whatever their leaders told them?

Dolan also mentioned about the debate he had with Dr. Greer's "fiasco" concerning Roswell, the *GAO* (Government Accounting Office) and his disclosure project [33]. This branch is supposedly the "watchdog" of Congress that is an investigative branch. They supposedly have done investigations on the Roswell crash of 1947. Although they considered the object in question a "tracking balloon" or weather balloon, only two records were even found with regards to this event. This suggested that the other reports were either "missing or misplaced." In 1995, a detailed report was written to Congressman Steven Schiff giving the results made by the GAO supposedly explaining the situation by Richard Davis (the head of National Security Analysis) in a twenty page report. The report was supposedly investigated by major American agencies including the army stationed at Roswell base that seemed to change their story on exactly what they saw [34].

Within the report, Davis stated that most records were missing and only two were retrieved, however could not explain why the other reports were not recorded and who exactly misplaced or destroyed them. There seems to be an awful lot of clean up for something as trivial as a "weather balloon." The government is not directly stating that a craft of extraterrestrial origin was present, but the balloon story doesn't hold either. Something elusive was obviously at play here, and since the American public is under a different set of principles from "them," to discover any information from either now or sixty years ago is still not accessible.

Perhaps Dolan's idea of new age and higher consciousness could allow us to erase this invisible boundary holding the mass from discovering the truth. His idea of "death of the nation state" is a good reality and we need to investigate why. He discussed issues like the New World Order, and the basic question of what is a nation and does it exist [35]. He made an observation on just because we speak the same language in the same location does this constitute for being a nation? Who is sovereign and do we really understand the true nature of the power structure? The answer to all of these questions is no it seems, because everything we believe to now be hidden in obscurity. Since we do operate under the guise of breakaway civilization, the truth is we may never catch up to here we as informed citizens need to be. When and if we reach this level, then we may view life in a more cohesive, understanding, and unbiased way to really ascend into a new consciousness.

Dolan disagreed that all of the UFO visitors are benevolent as Dr. Greer and Robert Dean mentioned. We have to investigate to at least fathom any idea concerning esoteric principles. Exopolitics; which is what Dolan describes as UFO phenomena in general, must be taken into two variables: "us" and "them." We must be able to discuss them in great detail in order to understand them. Dolan presented a few questions that we should consider answering: how do we know what we know? Who exactly are we talking to? Are we making a clear distinction between our factual knowledge and our speculations? Another reality that could be considered would be the question of enough people to make a difference.

Who will force the government agencies to come forward about anything that has transpired in the last sixty years? Since the subject is generally ridiculed, he made the point that we must be disciplined due to Ufology and Exopolitics are not subjects in which one can be careless [36]. We must know the difference between "what we know and what we believe." The public usually relies on the propaganda of the corporate media and religious dogma. If we fashion ourselves to whatever they tell us, how can we be conscious enough to make a distinction on what we believe? How do we come out of the dark and illuminate our stagnant minds to understand the reality that we must learn?

"Us versus Them"

The group that is least informed and suffering the most would be the "us" category. The obvious is that the public is never informed about strange and unusual occurrences of dealings within the government structure. Why is it those special interests groups have to fear the public population? Why does the government need to act quickly when the retrieval of "exotic technology" arises? The need for a secret agenda is most questionable, because if the nation state is dead as Dolan predicts, then "enemy countries" are nonexistent due to a team effort. With everything on a secret budget or appropriation, the privatization of what Dolan calls "runaway technology achievements" leaves the public dead last on the list of need to know. Dolan stressed the time that the United States and USSR were in the arms race would be enough for a secretive agenda about everything. However, if we follow the belief system of a New World Order mentality, there really aren't any countries, only special interests groups that are playing the global "risk game" with real human beings as pieces.

The idea of this technological feudal system will always be evident in order to fulfill a powerful position. Dolan described how we as an uninformed, unintelligent mass view our current reality through a diagram he calls the "idealized view of our mental world." In this case, we are the supposed focus of society where the media provides us the information we want to know, the academia is represented as the value of truth and information with an intellectual exchange with us, and finally our ideal political system where politicians work honestly for the people and are the voice of the people [37]. Of course this is not true realistically and unfortunately we have to agree unanimously that these "ideals" as Dolan puts them, are only fantasy.

A more realistic view Dolan presents has a more complicated group of systems designed to put us at the bottom of the barrel in terms of achievements, news, technology, or any reforms whatsoever. In the realistic view, the tables are turned and we revolve around society. The corporation is in control and the only important factors are shareholder value and profit; not personal transformation or expanded consciousness. Behavioral engineering is implemented, not the illusionary academic or philosophical ascension, and the idea of a response or exchange of ideas back and forth is nonexistent [38]. The result is the "one guy with everything and the others has the rest . . . nothing" idea in play.

Dolan's harsh words are reality; it is up to us if we want to continue our social delusion. We must reject this idea and finally take a step into facing the hard, cold, and realistic social monstrosity that we have allowed to form due to our ignorance. Dolan offered a few tips on making this long trek into an unknown world easier with a positive attitude: firstly, we must disabuse ourselves of the notion that we have a truly open process politically, academically, or in our mainstream media. This of course is not happening now, albeit reforms and plans for changes. The lie as we have called it, is too deep and formed with a life of its own to destroy now. Secondly, Dolan believes this idea matters when discussing UFO/ET disclosure. This is truthful and he seems an honest man; however, does he really believe that the common layperson will rationalize, use common sense, and have a thinking process based on the current policy?

He also discussed the importance of this disclosure emanating from either a democratic government or fascist government. Sadly people still believe that we operate in a pseudo-democratic society; when the fact is we operate in a fascist form of society destroying the ability to think, philosophize on expanding the mind, or even discover our spiritual nature. Dolan stressed that the distinction between the two idealistic governments determined the disclosure factor in detail; he even furthered the idea that a democracy is a group of "uninformed citizens" that he believes isn't bad but dangerous. Ignorance of the populace brings fear and false hope that a supposed savoir will eliminate the threat and rescue the people in times of peril. The ideas that Dolan presented in determining how we as lost as we are overwhelming. The idea stems beyond deciding the benefits of democracy over fascism, the idea of either slave owners, or the public continuing to be slaves.

His idea of the escape of the masses into virtual worlds is the key. When things begin to deteriorate around us and our supposed savior doesn't not emerge to rescue us; the people will use fear, anger, and hatred to become a mob of violence. The people will be uncontrollable and there will be no turning back. Technology will become very useful and virtual reality will be needed to help the mass forget their reality completely (as religion may not prove useful any longer). In the digital age we now reside in, a mere delusion or fabrication cannot surpass technology on any level. Will these new virtual worlds become the new religion? We seem to be trading one master for another; and in this case a dangerous one. Dolan discussed the creation of a super race, or manipulation of DNA (or eugenics), quantum computing as well (NANO-technology) and the elimination of "redundant people [39]."

In order to complete this Global 2000 agenda, all of the redundant human beings must be eliminated; then the original Nazi standard of a selective breeding process will emerge to create a more stabilized group of mental and physical beings. Dolan stated this example as a sort of "postmodern dystopia" where the depletion of sources, ecosystem failure, and falling infrastructure will transpire resulting in the perfectly orchestrated "end game" scenario (or what religious fanatics call revelation). So far, it is realistic to determine that the "us" factor is on the losing end of this dangerous game.

The "them" factor of human destiny would be the UFO/ ET reality. This is where human beings are out of their league due to the lack of information on the subject. To become more informed about this subject, what can we rely on as concrete evidence? Dolan mentioned UFO literature (or sightings) as something to use as a reference. When we do this however, we must be careful on who to trust, since this can be used as a profit making endeavor. His next suggestion was using abduction literature; however at the same time he ushered a warning on what one must do in order to choose the proper cases due to the threat of manipulation. Lastly, Dolan mentioned collected data from experiences and information by remote viewers (but his exact words on this subject would be to use "extreme caution"). When we are dealing with the elusive idea of UFO and alien presence, we must ask very important questions. The main logical question would be who are they?

Dolan shared his research to tell us basic knowledge he had been able to acquire through data. He suggested they operate by stealth, that there is likely more than one species involved, and that they all contain diverse agendas [40]. This information based on research could be accurate due to our ability to rationalize and use common sense (that is assuming we can use these tools). He also stated that they were highly telepathic (meaning they had the ability to manipulate human thinking and human emotions). This dangerous ideal puts humans on the losing end due to the fact we are a less developed species. No human wants to accept the fact that they can be manipulated by an unknown force whom they have no clue exists. The alien presence would also have space-time mastery, meaning that they could travel to other parts of the galaxy and beyond. Dolan also made other observations they were important; he suggested that they appear emotionless and the question of "do they look like us or not" scenario.

When we look at the oldest piece of human history in this sequential time era, we must look to the Sumerian tablets. According to the tablets, we were created by the *Annunkai*, a race of beings from a world called *Nibiru* who discovered this backwater planet to mine gold for their own world [41]. They needed manual labor like any enterprise, so they created humans to do their manual labor through genetic manipulation. If this was the case, they have been on this planet before us for an undetermined amount of sequential time. Dolan's question then remains most pertinent, since we must investigate if they were already part of this planet or not. He even furthered the thought that they could be from other dimensions, or another time. The situation is more complex than we can fathom resulting in our current predicament.

Are we really ready for a *full* disclosure? Do we have the mental and spiritual prowess to understand even the minute details that we are receiving in the present time? Can they be trusted? Are they truthful or not? Did they create us, enhance us, and are we they property or investment? If so, how long do they plan on keeping us? These important questions are the reason Dolan is truly a pioneer in discovering the alien agenda. This eliminates the illusion that all entities are benevolent; for we need to see who is here in our best interests. One cannot blindly accept propaganda or an illusion of a utopian principle if an investigation is not part of this acceptance.

Organized religion has blinded us for more than two millennia with the promise of everlasting paradise without examples or proof. These alien beings have the capabilities of showing us many things with their knowledge and technology. It would be easier to sway the simple minded in believing anything with actions instead of false promises. The author suggests this could be our weakness and could lead to our extinction if not careful. Will these aliens baptize us into their beliefs or practices? Have they already done so using our world leaders as slaves to do so? Will they eliminate us due to our fragile nature? Dolan discussed two major fallacies that he believed could be dangerous if misinterpreted.

Firstly, we would assume that since they are so technologically advanced, this would mean that they have solved all of their major social, economic, and political problems correct? Dolan doesn't believe so, and stated "not necessarily." Since we are assuming, why would we think that they would contain the same world model as we do? Since we are stuck in the concept of time, we would not be aware of how long it took this advance civilization to reach its current state; everything works in balance and causality.

Secondly, since they arrive here to "help" us as Dean and Dr. Greer presume, that means that they are ready to welcome us into the cosmic family paradigm. The arrival of super intelligent beings does not constitute harmony or a better future for humanity. It would not make sense for the entire universe to be benevolent in nature because then the balance would not be maintained. Chaos begets creation and vice versa. Not everyone can be friendly; this would be ridiculously ignorant to assume this. Unfortunately, there isn't much we can go on when it comes to the "them" category, so this will have to happen as events mold our future (both force by the hand of men and nature). One can only hope that the few who are actually worthy to be saved do their purpose and give the human creation justice and purpose before we are essentially altered.

In conclusion, Dolan tried his best (as humanly possible) to attempt to awaken the public in order to give our species a broader look into our own known universe. For his finale, he ended with the inevitable notion that disclosure would be in our near future; exactly ten years by his assumption [42]. He first stated that the concept of disclosure was impossible; however inescapable with six possible outcomes. Firstly, there may be confrontations with "them." As we have discussed, many people will either fear them or initially try to attack them due to their lack of understanding. Secondly, the government will eventually have to form some sort of public relations explaining the illegal structure of secrecy.

Trust would be undermined in the government and people will finally expose the government(s) for what it really is. Next, there would have to be an answer for what the "secret plan" was all about and why it took so long to expose. After this, we the people would have to now understand them with no other option (sort of a forced "peace ambassador" for these unannounced guests). Along with this impromptu relationship, we would also have to try to understand their interest in us. Finally, all we know and have thought was our reality concerning the structure of power, politics, industry, legal, finance, and elite control would be forever changed indefinitely.

Dolan pushed the idea that we are in the process of a dramatic transformation and called it "the greatest show in the quadrant." It doesn't seem clear what he meant; however, it should be pretty interesting to debate in the coming years. Along with this forced change, we will be leaping into their world completely as we have been doing slowly for the last one hundred years or so. Dolan forces us to analyze the current situation and pushes humans to attempt to utilize the few brain cells we have left. During the last hundred years or so, the greatest technological advances have been horse and carriage (even the transcontinental railroad) to transport goods and services. One hundred years later, we now have personal computers that will very soon match human intelligence (even surpass it!) [43].

How did humanity in just a century jump from something simple to a more complex reality that will eventually eliminate the need for human judgment or error? Dolan suggested that they have been here all along carrying us, watching us, and helping us the "few" while the rest remain asleep. Dolan then exclaimed that when this disclosure happens, the obvious conclusions would be the following: the obvious challenges to the structure of power. Who is in control now? Do we even bother to listen anymore to public servants, the army, or the U.N? How does the government undo a lie this big? Obviously they cannot tell us "by the way, we forgot to tell you," that wouldn't be sufficient. Just imagine the cultural stress it would have worldwide.

Modernists versus Traditionalists

Dolan believes that there would be two groups who split into *modernists* and *traditionalists*. We also have to think about riots, vigilantism, and some sort of armed revolt like *V's Fifth Column* (an attack on the uninvited alien visitors). The economic/financial disruption in greater detail will affect petroleum, steel, and other alternative methods that supersede our current technology. Dolan even suggested that free energy might finally be available to the public, however, stated if we do receive this power, can we be trusted with it?

Can the human power structure survive this disclosure? Dolan also pointed out that many people would probably be angry and not understanding at all, with possible lawsuits to put the national debt as mere change. Finally, will the elite be forced to institute more repressive methods when this disclosure occurs? The major reality is that the world would spin out of control, and there would be what Dolan described as "spiral of reformation." Someone would have to explain sixty years of lies with unlimited possibilities of an end result. Disclosure will happen nonetheless and we must deal with whatever comes.

The pace of change will may be too rapid with an era of great instability, something unexpected would occur, and a sort of spin control would be attempted. There will be mistakes (with any plan done by humans), the plan will probably not succeed, and there may be more than one "enemy." Dolan finally ended with the goal of his agenda; it is the human's job to ensure this plan doesn't transpire. We need to learn what is going on, and must be vigilant on a variety of fronts. He described both our weakness as a species: hope and fear. Fear causes humans to act irrationally and cause even more chaos. Hope deludes us and diverts us from reality and we become un-alert. To be "awake" and aware requires a higher consciousness and to accept reality using spiritual, mental and physical power. Dolan was sincere; however he may be expecting too much from human beings albeit our capabilities.

Dr. Greer's Disclosure Project

Dr. Steven Greer is another speaker for Exopolitics that has a different point of view concerning alien agendas and their reason for being amongst us. Greer is physician and Ufologist who established a view that aliens are here to help us ascend; so that we can one day visit other planets like ours and give the same aid [44]. Robert Dean mentioned him as one of the "three Steve's of the apocalypse" concerning end times and disclosure. Greer was responsible for the creation of the *Orion Project* and the *Disclosure Project* to help uniformed people reach out to our galactic neighbors. The Disclosure Project that started in 1992, dealt with government agencies covering up sensitive information concerning UFOs and their presence here on Earth. His main philosophy was that intelligent beings were piloting the spacecraft and that the U.S. government was hiding this fact from the people of Earth [45]. The project also concerned the fact that the government had obtained highly exotic technology that they were keeping from the public. He stressed that this reason was for the push by special interest groups to continue supporting the oil industry and the like.

Dr. Greer has traveled to Washington D.C. in order to appeal these claims to push for a disclosure of the free energy for the public in need. He also attributed his claims to military personnel who have documents and personal history within the black budget programs [46]. His take on the *Orion Project* and his philosophy was intended for Earth to use clean energy sources for the twenty-first century and beyond. Although his intentions seem positive not only for the environment and all of the species as well, we have to revisit Dolan's concern on the capability on our claim to maintain a peaceful environment if we ever acquire this technology. The idea of a super civilization where technology and clean sources available to everyone sounds like an ideal utopia; however will corporate interests just disappear and agree to this idea? It seems unless there is profit to be made, it doesn't seem logical that the free energy sources would be released anytime soon (if it can be helped).

Dr. Greer seems too idealistic in his push for this type of disclosure, especially if the uniformed citizens of Earth are not able to make a distinction on what is beneficial and what is detrimental. Through environmental studies, *MDCs* (more developed countries) and *LDCs* (lower developed countries) either consume too many resources producing too much waste or sinks, or misuse nature's resources simply because they have no other choice to survive. The education just on the use of fossil fuels is still being taught to poorer countries as of late to usher them into the next industrial wave of development [47]. This might take a considerable amount time to wean them off this easily acquired energy (i.e. coal, natural gas, etc . . .) and introduce them to a "cleaner" source that Dr. Greer claims will be available.

Back in 2009, Dr. Greer attended and was a guest speaker at an *exopolitical* summit in Barcelona Spain for his new program *Project Starlight*; which aided in the disclosure and contact process for alien presence here on Earth dealing with government cover-ups. The program itself was present for the people to understand and learn three major things: to help each other and understand what was going on right now, that aliens were here and are from other star systems, and that we will never be alone and were never alone. His philosophy stemmed from his belief that his life changed due to an event when he was seventeen years old. He described himself having a near death experience. He ascended into space as a consciousness and discovered what he believed humans were here to do: wonderful things [48].

He did not explain what those things were, but as he spoke, the excitement was felt in his words as the audience displayed their interest. The idea that humans are here to do positive things is little if at all evident. The reality we can deal with is that few people have feelings, spiritual understanding, and the mental capacity to change their barbaric behavior without tying to harm other organisms on this planet. The group of people we have representing us do not care about anything but profit and the need for power. These two concepts should be separate; however they are not. Power can be used for good things as well; the difference is who wields it and what their intentions are.

As Dr. Greer followed up on his experience, he set up *CSETI* (Center for the Study of Extraterrestrial Intelligence) in the 1990s as they became more profound. This program was set to train people to become diplomats and ambassadors to the alien presence. He also added this as a protocol for making contact with them. It seems that he is here to make a positive effort; however Dolan's views about the negative effects of this idea seem to diminish any positive connotations on the subject. We have already pointed out that humans have little or no idea what we are dealing with here due to the lack of information. How are we to know exactly whom we are communicating with for this "contact?" What happens if we communicate with the wrong entities? We could easily give ourselves up and surrender without them having to move a finger. The idea doesn't seem like the right method to apply when dealing with unknown entities in general.

Planetary Unification

Dr. Greer then extended his idea to help out the president of the United States, believing that he was not informed and denied access to this secret information by a secret cabal known as Majestic 12. His main statement was "secrecy is killing the life on this planet" which is not untrue. Since 1993, Greer has believed that the world has been ready for alien contact, and that they are ready to answer our call. The question now is what exactly do we want from them? Are we that dependent and weak that we cannot handle our own affairs? It is asinine to assume they will carry us and "save" us every time we make a catastrophic mistake. The law of the universe doesn't work that way as Green has explained. We have to evolve on our own; and cannot be helped even for the simplest tasks. If we are helped every step of the way, we would become inadequate and for that reason should not be allowed to continue rising up the evolutionary ladder. A newer creation of humanity should be created, making them *more* independent than the original host.

Greer also stressed the notion of "course correction" which implied a sort of planetary unification that would have to take place in order to put the planet on the right course. He went as far as to say "the leaders will follow the people" and we would ascend into greatness. This notion is far too illusionary and abstract. The idea is noble but impossible in the current human state of mind. The people do not know how to lead, nor do they display a capacity for greatness; they seem foolishly dependent on their governments whom they surrender their freedom to and hope that they will *save* them from *themselves*. How can the children lead the parents if they are not trained to do so? There is no way that the elite will follow or surrender their power for the greater good as the idea is counterproductive to their agendas! The people are their commodity strictly for profit purposes. Such a plan would destroy the market and eliminate control, power and revenue.

Greer also talked about rising up in peace because it is our "human sacred obligation" due to time being short. This concept of sequential time is correct on his part that we have already made the decisions or have allowed them to come into existence. In this instance, we cannot change anything to save ourselves as the damage has already been done. It is possible that a few anomalies could be spared due to their capacity to think, act, and be something wonderful however;

maybe they cannot stop the decay of the world around them without the means. The Earth itself is running out of patience and Mother Nature will probably not be able to distinguish who aided in the change and who did not. Greer believes that the alien visitors or what he calls "guardians" will not allow men to destroy the biosphere because this planet is here to give birth to intelligent life and intelligent civilizations [49]. It could be speculated that the concept of intelligence died along with Atlantis and the ancients [50].

Greer stated that a new civilization is among us and no force on Earth can change this from occurring. The truth is yes we are changing, and this new civilization will probably be engineered to eliminate any more mistakes that have been previously done. The question is who from this time period will be allowed to take part in the change. Only the elite, secret societies that have served their masters over the last millennia or humans with souls (or developing a soul) could be candidates. Maybe the few, who are really concerned for their actions and really desire to make a difference, could without the presence of fear and false hope. This way the result would be a new world of unknown promise for the future of all organisms.

The ideals that Dr. Greer preached in his sermon-like address drove the point on the importance of tuning the brink of human extinction. The idea of a fossil fuel free society and economic slavery would give the common person enormous power. Just imagine if all people around the world would join in the effort to bring the cell around us down. We would finally be free from mental, physical and economic anguish. Would we know what freedom is? If you let a canary out of its cage, would it fly away or would it stay after being accustomed to its environment? Greer assured that the aliens would help us and they are not hostile in nature. This was his idea into reality with the Project Starlight agenda. With his plan, Greer and his team have explained going to Washington D.C. and talking with the CIA and president Clinton in 1994 [51]. Dolan mentioned this as a fiasco earlier and totally disagreed with this move. Greer believed that the executive branch was cut off from the "secret military complex" and according to him, Clinton was supportive of the idea (however was afraid of being assassinated like JFK) but decided to abandon the idea and backed down.

There was even an attempt to release files according to the New York Sun in November of 2007, however, Greer still remains optimistic due to the large amount of documents being released from the national archive [52]. All he desired was peaceful contact, however only humans could help with a specific stipulation. If the executive branch would not extend its aid because of fear, what then is the pubic to do? It is obvious that telling the truth is not healthy for someone who plans on living for a long time. Somehow choosing the path of truth telling brings sudden serious "complications" causing an early leave of absence from life.

UFO Contact & Technology

Dr. Greer discussed the *USAP* (Unacknowledged Special Access Programs) and their secretive projects that have neither constitutional oversight nor presidential decisions. He estimated their annual budget at about \$100-\$200 billion a year which is more than the defense budget of the entire world [53]. Greer also believed that the current situation had to be balanced. How do start in achieving that balance? Who do we turn to in terms of seeking the right organizations to help rebalance the world? So far Greer did not offer any suggestions; just exposing them was all he was attempted to do. He repeatedly mentioned the Majestic 12 group and their plans for world domination along with the elimination of seventy-five percent of the global population. Greer described the group as being a threat to "Earth humans" (with the examples of new technology and the slow attempt of disclosure) he then pushed further for his illusionary dream that the people of the world must teach the leaders, offer our "prayers," and tell them how to lead. The whole concept of this dream is completely far from realistic goals and/or human progress. In fact, this hinders any sort of positive change for humans in general.

Being the "small voice of the many," one does not trust the leaders because of their unwillingness to share anything that benefits all citizens and their ability to lie immensely. If Greer pushes for new leadership (which he will indefinitely do), how are the people able to distinguish of this new leader "for the people of Earth" will actually do their job? Is it just another political game where this galactic politician would just sell us another lie with fancy syntax and a big smile? Will Greer take this position? He seems to try to sell an idea so hard, that there must be another hidden agenda behind it.

He is too eager to teach people how to contact these aliens in order for help and surrender themselves to a new world. This is not a bad concept, but we are too ignorant to make a distinction about what is good for us? In 1998, the United States and U.N. or any other governments were not planning to follow Greer's illusionary dream or suggestions [54]. Due to the disdain for disclosure according to Greer, his group was founded to counteract this issue. As of now, France and the United Kingdom are disclosing documents although the United States is still not involved [55][56]. It seems that the program (that will eventually cause trouble for him in the U.S.)

was not a good idea for alerting the executive branch, who is probably very aware of the situation at hand.

Greer had another issue with the fact that the energy from other worlds was not being shared with the public and fell into the category which he described as *WSFM* (weird science and freaking magic). All technology was labeled as *trans-dimensional physics*; which included the concept beyond electrons, the speed of photons, and resonation beyond the speed of light. Greer described his idea of trans-dimensional as consciousness which blended the idea of coherent thought with the human being and not the speed of light [57]. One's thoughts, awareness, consciousness, and thought all play a part in developing power. The human body is something extraordinary created for a greater purpose by whoever made us. Our thoughts are able to transmit frequencies into the universe and vice versa. We act as a sort of portal or station where energy can be harnessed and used for whatever purposes.

Greer added that the lucid dream state was a way to activate this to make contact. He also added three important details: firstly, there aren't any more private conversations. Secondly, anything and everything we can imagine or have seen on sci-fi shows has been done at *Skunk Works* at *Lockheed* in California. Lastly, we have the technology to travel to the stars (as he mentioned Ben Rich and his final statement before his death) [58]. If these three allegations are true, that means that Greer's idea of the guardians prohibiting us from destroying this planet might not work at all.

If we can match their power and technology, which meant that we have been to other planets in this solar system, established a sort of social structure elsewhere on these planets, and have set up a sort of galactic trade system with other beings. Greer described interstellar travel as "strange" and if it did not appear strange to the person, it was probably man made. He also stated that we would be able to identify seams and rivets that were designed by Lockheed, *SAIC* (Science Application International Corporation; a fortune 500® company) or another corporate interest. He also pointed out that we as humans carry a universal communicator (our thoughts) and we must use this as a group mind in order to be successful.

It seems that a one world mind is the agenda of Greer which doesn't seem at all different from the Majestic 12 or the Masonic orders. What separates him from them? Could it be the fact that he tried to disclose to the world secrets and technology that we could never understand or have access to? He had videos from CSETI showing him establish contact with some entities using his "techniques" (which included Zen meditation and mantra), and a laser pointer to alert them of his location [59]. He distinguished the entities from the range of fully materialized to one-dimensional, and then as plasma at any level (meaning transparent or invisible). He attributed this to the universal field and common life, to make us "awaken from our slumber." We must be vigilant as Dolan reminded us to make sure our "universal communicator" doesn't pick up the wrong signal.

Final Warnings

All of the exopolitical community agree on the fact that the United States started contact after Roswell with the first president Eisenhower as our human representative in 1954. Greer warned us that the Majestic 12 group was against the alien presence and were at war with them. He group was simulating events to mimic alien contact starting in the 1950s, turning themselves into the nexus of fear. There would be interplanetary war which would definitely cost a lot of lives. If he is correct, they would stage a hoax using *ARV* (alien reproduction vehicles), man-made antigravity crafts, and psychotropic weapons systems with electromagnetic devices involved (using this to covertly deceive people, as this is a mind affecting device).

He also warned us of *PLF* entities or programmed life forms (which look like Grey, Reptilian [Draco] look-alikes) to appear as invading entities from space. He assured us that they were not from space, but man made here on Earth by a special team with alien interests. They are used as abduction agents from either the NSA or alien groups that the governments work for. The problem now that Greer had was he stated why his belief that no alien civilization from space was hostile. If this speculation was correct, we would not be able to breathe air. He added the idea that we had weapons in space since the 1960s using electromagnetic scalar weapons. One documented example was made by a statement by former *Soviet First Secretary* (1953-54) and *Chairman on the Council of Ministers* (1958-1964) Nikita Khrushchev:

> *"We have a new weapon, just within the portfolio of our scientists, so to speak, which is so powerful that, if unrestrainedly used, it could wipe out all life on earth. It is a fantastic weapon." (Khrushchev to the Presidium, January 1960)*

Another expert in this new science of scalar electromagnetism Dr. Thomas E. Bearden who published some interesting facts of exactly what can be done with this sort of weapon:

> *"In short, Russell, the Secretary of Defense of the United States confirmed that there are indeed novel kinds of EM weapons, right now and have been for some time, which have been and are being used to (1) initiate earthquakes, (2) engineer the weather and climate, and (3) initiate the eruption of volcanoes. We wrote about those exact uses of the weaponry decades ago. Several nations now have such weapons. Three of them (two on one side and the other on a hostile side) are even firing practice shots into Western Australia, as a convenient test range." (www.earthchangetv.com/ufo/0209gander.htm)*

Could this be the result of all the earthquakes done to Christchurch, Fukushima, and Chile within the last two years? Also, Greer stated that the government also had their hands on a Neutrino Light detector which can track ships before materialization. There happens to be one known observatory that has this weapon in Sudbury, Ontario Canada called *Sudbury Neutrino Observatory*. It contains a twelve meter sphere filled with water that is surrounded by light detectors and is located two thousand meters below the ground. According to the observatory, the sole purpose of this device is only a "physical apparatus" designed to study neutrinos. Another location is under the Antarctic ice that costs up to $271 billion including a telescope. With this neutrino device, they plan to unearth dark matter and the size of this object is immense (being taller than three of the largest skyscrapers in the world). Their supposed goal is to find and study neutrinos for a single purpose:

> *"IceCube is operated by the University of Wisconsin-Madison and the National Science Foundation, with funding provided by the United States, Belgium, Germany, and Sweden. Researchers from Barbados, Canada, Japan, New Zealand, Switzerland, and the United Kingdom are also involved in this project. For IceCube, construction at the South Pole all came down to their scientific goals. The observatory is designed to find extremely high energy neutrinos— tiny subatomic particles—originating from supernova explosions, gamma-ray bursts and black holes, with an emphasis on expanding humankind's knowledge of dark matter. . . ." (Neal Ungerleider, Fast Company December 21, 2010)*

The article itself was very informative and discussed using this energy to better understand the universe, however, as a weapon could spell doom to the entire world if misused improperly. Greer ended his lecture describing to the people the need to stop using weapons to solve the problems of the world and left us with this statement: "free nonpolluting energy will evolve the planet in intelligence, and the 500,000 year cycle will result in us traveling to other worlds. It is our obligation to turn this planet or Gaia in the right direction." He insisted that we as humans would survive this interplanetary war and 2012 to live on and become a perfect society as we travel to the starts to find other planets in need of "help" like we do. It seems he forgets that we still adolescent in nature and in the understanding of how the universe works. It might be a long time before we even reach a level where other primitive civilizations might learn from our example.

As we close this discussion of Project Starlight and Dolan's investigative materials to better understand our history, we must look at this issue from many sides. As far as Dolan goes, he gave us insight and the need to be more investigative to use our power of the mass to demand the history of the last sixty years revealed. He believed that if we remember our history, then we can move forward as responsible human beings. This is very true as we must break the mold of our current human cultures in order to get anywhere. For Dr. Greer, his illusionary dream of the entire utopian paradise to travel to the stars has many faults, and will not be successful in his current mind state. He forgets that all of our destructive cultures and the way we treat each other in all parts of the world inhibit any spiritual, mental, or positive results. He did agree that we do not have the time, but still he remained foolishly hopeful. Dolan's idea of our enemies of hope and fear play a part here in deciding if we have what it takes to move ahead and fix our problems. This must be solved before we have illusions of grandeur about a galactic ascension.

If the UFO presence does decide to help us we must as least grow individually in nature; for not everyone can be saved. We must potentially "hear the call" as the movie *Knowing* (*2009*) has showed us. Maybe they do select a certain few to continue the human experiment in the stars. We must have the power within us that a religion could never give us, culture can never give us, or a group mind. Until this realization is achieved, we will not have the means to travel anywhere to help others, for we will only destroy them as we are doing now to ourselves. Even now, Greer and Bassett tried to force the Obama administration to come clean with the UFO disclosure idea. Much to their disappointment, the government continues to deny the truth about UFO activities [59]. Simply demanding the elite to come clean with signatures is not enough for them to tell us what we want to hear. Can we handle the truth?

End Notes

[1] Richard M. Dolan. *UFOs and the National Security State: Chronology of a Cover-up 1941-1973.* Charlottesville, VA: Hampton Roads Publishing INC. (2002; p. 478).

[2] Ibid 1.

[3] Deuteronomy 13: 6-10.

[4] *Keyholepublishing*.com

[5] Sean Rayment. "Invisible tanks could be on battlefield within five years." *The Telegraph U.K.* (January 2011).

[6] Project Camelot. "Richard Dolan at the Awake and Aware Conference." Los Angeles, CA (September 2009). Projectcamleot.org.

[7] Alexander Hamilton; letter to John Jay (November 26th, 1775)

[8] Plato and B Jowett. *Plato's Republic.* New York: The Modern Library (1983).

[9] tavis-walton.com/ordinary.html.

[10] Don Ecker. "DSP Satellite spots UFOs" *UFO Magazine Vol.9 Issue 39* (January/February 1994).

[11] Ibid 1.

[12] Travis Walton. *Fire in the Sky: The Walton Experience.* Marlowe and Company 3rd Ed. (August 1997).

[13] ufocasebook.com/Walton_gilson.html.

[14] Philip J. Klass. *UFOs: The Public Deceived.* Prometheus Books (1983).

[15] Geoff Price "The Travis Walton UFO Abduction Case." *Cohenufo.org.*

[16] Stephanie Dearing. "UK farmers blame UFOs for sheep mutilation." *Digital Journal* (April 2010).
[17] Paul Geraghty. "Human Mutilations." *UFO Encounters U.K.* (December 2010).
[18] Erich Von Daniken. *Chariots of the Gods: Unsolved Mysteries of the Past.* Berkley Books (January 1999)
[19] Tim Stouse. "Nazca Lines." *Timstouse.com* (December 2010).
[20] Ibid 1.
[21] planetinfowars.com/uncategorized/bildeberg-2012-6.
[22] Ibid 1.
[23] Ibid 1.
[24] David Axe. "Russian Navy Declassifies Cold War Close Encounter." *Wired.com* (July 2009).
[25] Eric Schultz. "Who is really in charge of the United States?" *NBC News* (May 2011).
[26] Ibid 1.
[27] fordlibrarymusuem.gov/library/speeches/740001.asp.
[28] Ibid 1.
[29] Ibid 1.
[30] Ibid 1.
[31] Richard M. Dolan. *The Cover-up Exposed, 1973-1991: (UFOs and the National Security State, Vol. 2)* Keyhole Publishing Company (September 2009).
[32] Craig Hight and Jane Roscoe. *Faking It: Mockery Documentary and the Subversion of Factuality.* Manchester University Press (February 2002).
[33] Richard Dolan "Steven Greer and the Disclosure Project." *Hostcentric.com* (2001).
[34] rosewellfiles.com/articles/theGAOreport.htm.
[35] Ibid 1.
[36] Ibid 1.
[37] Ibid 1.

[38] Ibid 1.
[39] Ibid 1.
[40] Ibid 1.
[41] Zecharia Sitchin. *Genesis Revisited.* Avon (October 1990).
[42] Richard Dolan and Bryce Zabel. *A.D. After Disclosure: When the Government Finally Reveals the Truth About Alien Contact.* New Page Books (May 2012).
[43] Don Mowbray. "Computer intelligence will surpass human intelligence this year." *BBspot.com* (August 2011).
[44] Dr. Steven Greer. "The Unknown Agenda." Exopolitical Summit, Barcelona Spain (July 2009).
[45] Ibid 44.
[46] Ibid 44.
[47] Charles L. Harper. *Environment and Society: Human Perspectives on Environmental Issues.* Prentice Hall 5TH Ed. (July 2011).
[48] Ibid 44.
[49] Ibid 44.
[50] Virginia Essene and Sheldon Nidel. *You Are Becoming A Galactic Human.* Spiritual Education Endeavors (April 1994).
[51] disclosureproject.org/projectstarlightClinton.shtml.
[52] Josh Gerstein. "Clinton Library Releases Files on UFOs." *New York Sun* (November 2007).
[53] Ibid 44.
[54] Ibid 44.
[55] L. Vincent Poupard. "French Government Releases UFO Files." *Yahoo.com* (March 2007).
[56] Graham Tibbetts. "British Government Releases UFO Files." *The Telegraph U.K.* (May 2008).
[57] Ibid 44.
[58] Ibid 44.
[59] disclopsureproject.org/docs/Obama/index.shtml.

"Surely the ass who invented the first religion
ought to be the first damned."
-Mark Twain

"This world holds two classes of
men—intelligent men without religion and
religious men without intelligence."
-Abu Ala Al-Maari

V

Jordan Maxwell: Alien Symbolism and the Human Connection

Symbolism is a part of our human cultures around the world and embedded in our daily lives. One can go anywhere and find humans adhering or using a symbol to guide and dictate their lives. All organized religions seemingly use them to control the mass and provide those means to escape the harsh reality [1]. Where did the idea of symbols stem from and why are they so powerful over humans? The answer is different in every culture; however, there is no definitive answer universally. All of the interpretation on symbolism that will be covered depends on one's upbringing, points of view fed by peers, parents, educational institutions, religious leaders, and mass media outlets. The idea we need in order to quest for some sort of understanding in general, is to try to steer away from the previous groups that project these beliefs subliminally every day.

Instead, one has to gather this understanding from our DNA or "gut feeling;" where the possible truth lies. Finding a way to tap into one's internal power can almost be impossible since we do not give ourselves sufficient sequential time in our daily lives to do so without the means. Humans are too busy trying to survive rather than to discover, which could be done purposefully in order to halt/extract our ability to ascend/surpass the mental and spiritual prison that we have been living our whole lives. Although most humans share this physical life with others one must work individually to find "the way" out of this predicament.

Somehow, we were thrown into this world alone making this an unfortunate lone journey. This does not mean that humans cannot share their experiences with those that they feel connected to; this way one can learn from the other and vice versa. Humans must be careful with whom their share their lives with. The other companion may destroy one's chances of ever discovering oneself; putting humans in a difficult decision in choosing the "right" human companion. Humans may be able to have an easier journey so to speak, if we understand the history of symbols and what they were really meant to accomplish in human beings based on the original concept lost in translation.

Ancient Symbols Lost in Translation

Symbols and their meanings hold water in every human's existence. What do they mean in terms of alien and spiritual representation? All of the symbols come from an ancient past full of mystery and intense magic. The majority of humans use them without fully knowing their origin. Jordan Maxwell is an individual who defines symbols as a necessity and researches them to find their true origins [2]. Maxwell has over forty years of personal research and tries to help humans who are interested in finding their true origin. As opposed to the dogmatic view humans have now, Maxwell attributes the knowledge he has received not from "Jesus" "Yahweh," or some religious cult figure, rather *aliens* [3]. The only problem with this revelation is that most of established science and academia discredit this notion immediately. This argument could go against religious beliefs that border psychotic when a human believes/claims to have seen the "Virgin Mary" in their grilled cheese sandwich, Jesus' eyes on their bathroom door, or even worse Jesus' image in their cat scan [4][5].

In times of desperation, people will believe whatever they want to believe in order to make sense of things. The door seems to swing both ways here when one has to choose a side to explain the unexplainable. The symbols they represent whether they are plagiarized or not, must come from somewhere not of this world. They could be connected; however, with the symbols going beyond human affairs and meanings. Maxwell presents us with information that many will not believe because they cannot. Those who will venture beyond this illusionary mind block will be able to view an old perspective in a different light. We as responsible humans must operate this way, otherwise we stop learning and our journey ends without new present knowledge.

Maxwell was also one of the speakers at the *Awake and Aware* conference presented by *Project Camelot* back in 2009. His presentation did not last as long as the other speakers; however, the information he had concerning UFOs, symbols, and human beings was more detailed (almost as much as Dolan) [6]. The people who were entertained seemed interested in new leadership to govern their personal lives. The knowledge presented went beyond the realm of religious understanding, spiritual advice, or gratification. With this outlook, would it be in the people's best interest to trade one master for another? The most positive message that Maxwell presents is that he does not claim to be a *messiah*, nor is it his mission to *save* any humans as well. Maxwell did not want to change anyone's belief system; rather, to present the information based on his findings and research to have people see the world in a different light. This is a very positive approach simply because of the many reasons that complete this agenda: no salvation, no judgment, and no blackballing anyone from expressing their own opinion (more than 99% of these "opinions" are not original) unlike the organized religious agenda [7].

Maxwell also did not claim to have answers as well, he simply presented the facts and we have to judge what to believe or not. He mentions this ideology with an interesting point: *people will believe/support what they want to hear and will not support what they do not want to hear.* The common example would be a religious fanatic who does not want to hear that the idea of a spiritual father figure is mere fantasy. This reality would shatter their fantasy world that a protector is there safeguarding their every decision. The existence of other entities not only discredits the impossible "one god scenario," but also destroys the concept of heaven and hell suggesting new alternative routes may be available depending on what alien culture believes is their afterlife.

Maxwell described his interest in theology not for learning, rather learning about it to see how the government adheres to the same construct of control. Within the constructs of this ideology stems the subject of the *occult.* What exactly does occult mean, and why is it so important to human lives? *Occult* according to Maxwell means the government, banks, educational institutions, and maritime commerce (court system) [8]. He even goes as far as to discuss the word *court* and what it symbolizes. A court is seen in sports events and almost any game; however, we also have a "court system" that decides laws and regulations as well. They are both related in that they are games merely to entertain us and drive us away from the reality of the human condition. Maxwell describes the lawyer as the greatest sports player in our time. The lawyer will play on a court just like a tennis player or basketball player would, except the stakes are higher and the skill must be top notch at all times.

Engaged in a court of law (the game), the prosecutor is on one side of the playing field, with the defense lawyer in on the "opposing team." The judge acts merely as a referee (who really is not concerned with the winner because they are paid regardless). The jury of course, would represent the crowd who is given the illusion that they are somehow in charge of the situation and given the ability to "judge" another human's life [9]. As they throw the "ball" (prosecuted individual) back and forth, the severity of the problem lies in the fact that the game piece is most times a poor individual dependent on his "game player" who isn't interested in the idea of justice or law, rather only interested in making profit and winning victories. An ambitious lawyer loses the sense of justice which is separate from the concept of winning; only business matters. We as humans need to look at the situation for what it really is. Law is nothing but another sport bent on the manipulation of the individual for the means of control and profit. It is another glorified sport under the guise of suits and ancient law practices hidden in obscurity.

When we look at the players involved more closely, Maxwell entertains us with another question: why do priests, judges, rabbis, students, or religious figures wear black robes? Why is black a prominent color for most institutions or practices? Ancient symbolism, civilizations, and research brings us to the fact that all of this ties into something bigger than we are made to think. Black, presents the planet *Saturn* (also known as the "Lord of the Rings") and all of the ideas of the color with everything associated with it comes from this planet [10]. Why do we wear earrings as many humans building fascinations with them? Is this for fashion, gothic appeal? What is the real significance where some people go as far as to pierce their entire bodies? Women in ancient times would *listen* to their gods by wearing earrings which was an instrument to connect her to the divine by establishing a connection for ascension [11]. The god Saturn it seems appealed to men as well, as now both sexes wear them. Why was this symbol prominent to females more than males? Did this signify that females played a more important role than men in ancient times? What is the significance of humans consummating their marriage by placing a ring on each other?

In modern times, the majority completes this task in the presence of the Jewish god Yahweh; however, in ancient times this was done in the presence of Saturn. Interestingly enough, Saturn himself is a Middle Eastern god that the Hebrew has fashioned to create one of the many personalities of present day Yahweh. The Phoenicians also, worshipped this deity before the modern concept of "god." Since the Hebrew were nomadic tribes at the time, they would have traveled to these locations adapting and coveting this information and using it for their own religious practices. The Phoenician word for Saturn was *Shabath* [12]. With striking similarities to the Hebrew word *Sabbath*, the Hebrews altered the original symbol, having omitted an *H* replacing it with another *B* forming the word *Sabbath*. Finding the origin of the ancient symbol, we now know that the Hebrews could in fact be paying homage to the Phoenician adaptation of the god Saturn or *Shabath*.

Maxwell evens pointed out that another interesting symbol; the *star of Saturn* was also copied and adapted by the Hebrew to create their "star of David" symbol displayed on their flag. Both stars have six points and are hexagonal in nature with the obvious older symbol being that of Saturn [13]. *Dagon*, an ancient fish deity was also worshipped in ancient times having a crown with the presentation of six points just like the star itself. The Hebrew themselves worshipped

Dagon as Noah (the mythical Hebrew male was adapted from the Babylonian account of Gilgamesh) although their bible stated he was a Philistine god [14]. The Christian/Catholic faith today represents him and worships him as well using the crown for their demigod the Pope [15]. Using the ancient fish god's staff and crown, why do humans so ignorant and needy, not question any of the origins of these symbolic meanings? According to the Universal Jewish Encyclopedia, the star itself was not theirs as it belonged to the ancient Egyptians:

> *"Acts 7:37-43 this is that Moses . . . to whom our fathers would not obey, but thrust him from them, and IN THEIR HEARTS TURNED BACK AGAIN INTO EGYPT . . . And they made a calf in those days, and offered sacrifices unto the idol, and rejoiced in the works of their own hands. Then God turned, and gave them up to worship the HOST OF HEAVEN: as it is written in the book of prophets, O ye house of Israel, have ye offered Me slain beasts and sacrifices by the space of FORTY YEARS IN THE WILDERNESS? Yea, ye took up the tabernacle of Moloch, and the STAR OF YOUR GOD REMPHAN, figures which ye made to worship them: and I will carry you away beyond Babylon."*

Using the Old Testament itself to describe the plagiarism of ancient ideas would be the best way to discredit the entire religion in its whole form:

> *"Amos 5:26-27 But ye have born the tabernacle of your Moloch and Chiun (Remphan) your images, the STAR OF YOUR GOD, which ye made to yourselves.*

Therefore, will I cause you to go into captivity beyond Damascus, saith the Lord."

The majority of the Hebrew religion through extensive research either originated from Sumer, Egypt, Babylon or Phoenicia [16]. Does the meaning of the symbol change with each culture? In the ancient cultures, the symbol somewhat unanimously represented Saturn with different names. In the Judeo-Christian religion, the meaning has changed into a darker, evil, or "satanic" view although they followed similar protocol of the original religions. This confusing idea not only makes the religion invalid, it also makes the religion shameful. The symbols themselves once changed lose their worth and become lost in history along with the truth behind it. Humans must stop erasing our history and allowing these organized religions to replace it with fabricated and invalid versions that we have now for the past two thousand five hundred years. Maxwell further clarifies the idea that churches themselves are disgraces founded on lies; mimicking moneymaking corporations based on *maritime admiralty law* [17].

He does an exceptional job exposing the lies and deceit that organized religions have done to the world concerning the nature of the true symbolic meanings. The idea that the Hebrew religion is a BCE religion is not accurate as well as the idea of an "ancient Israel." Moses never existed at the time the Hebrews claimed (only the Babylonian *Mises* that was a completely separate Syrian legend) along with the other two inventions of "David" and "Solomon" [18]. *Judaism* itself according to research was invented in the 8th century CE by Jesuits who have rewoven the ancient past according to their asinine ideals and beliefs [19]. Two Jewish archeologists by the names of Silberman and Finklestein have done their own research concluding in their book The Bible Unearthed, that ancient relics discovered in Iraq obliterate the ideas of the bible and the entire history. With the obvious facts dismantling the entire religious structure, an obscure plethora of symbolism is left with confusing details.

Mentioning the invention of the character Solomon is a more complex idea and symbol than we as humans could have expected. At first through research, it was not surprising to find out that this iconic Hebrew forgery was in fact not even Jewish at all, rather a myth based on the sorcerer pharaoh *Nectanebus* from Egypt who was said to be the father Alexander the Great [20]. Maxwell however, imposed a new outlook on the situation. It seems that the name is in actuality a mere symbol representing another enigmatic ancient meaning. Maxwell split the name into three different sections describing them as three different entities. "*SOL*" for instance, was synonymous with the sun from ancient times as it still bears that name today. The "*OM*" or (*Aum*) meant the "creative force" pertaining to esoteric languages and meanings. In such religions as Buddhism and Hinduism, this was a most sacred symbol and was also known as the "symbol of the absolute." The "*ON*" was the most curious with the results again being of non-Hebrew origin. The name stood for an ancient Egyptian location hat represented the "City of the Sun" or what the Greeks called *Heliopolis*.

As a result, we can now see that the name itself represents not a man as we have been deceived to believe, rather symbols representing the sun and other mystic powers. This power stems from an ancient past which now has been altered and represented a completely different meaning. The question now becomes the true agenda of the organized religious cults by altering the significance of the actual symbol(s). It is obvious that with symbols comes power. With this *power*, any structure can be threaten or even destroyed *especially* a false concept such as the current theological thought. Whatever the reason for this deception points at controlling the mass. Does this concept go beyond just control? Is it some other elusive force from the stars that has confused the mental and spiritual powers of human beings? Does this explain our current spiritual state, and the reason why we lack knowledge of the symbols for what they really are? Most people cling to symbols and wear them without knowing their past and true meaning. All we do is blindly believe what our "spiritual advisors" suggest what they mean without research. One must investigate thoroughly and question before considering it "gospel." Maxwell not only helps destroy the false concept, but instead gives us an idea of *the possibility* of where they derive their meaning from and their foundation/origin derived from the stars.

The Symbolic Meaning of "Tinsel Town"

Another iconic symbol and name that most people do not even question or identify as esoteric with a shadowy past would be *Hollywood.* When we think of Hollywood, immediately rushing to our thoughts are movies, entertainment, stars, and the iconic name "tinsel town." Another way of looking at this iconic location with Maxwell's research provides us with a deeper examination of *why* the name Hollywood is given and what it represents. There is a reason why "entertainment" is so coveted and successful: the symbol it presents now is *power.* Maxwell's research dictates a different story of its origins going all the way back to the Druids [21]. The Druids themselves are an ancient priesthood that many people know little about. The main belief that Stonehenge was crafted and created by the Druids is really the only piece of knowledge that the majority receive. The Druid priesthood has darker connections that still exist today in our century and according to experts had nothing to do with the creation of Stonehenge [22]. Their system of ideals and meaning of power are evident with the two countries that follow "*Druidian law*:" the United States and Canada. Most attorneys, politicians and the elite adhere to the practices of this ancient priesthood.

Their symbol of representation was the *magic wand*, and magic wands at the time were made of a specific wood. Normal wood was never used, and they only selected a special type of wood called *holly* originating from the holly tree. When we separate the name into two different parts "holly" and "wood," we then find the media entertainment giant uses an ancient symbol to represent their practice and beliefs [23]. What if the movies produce an elaborate message through the guise of entertainment to grasp those who can identify the symbols? One example of this theory is Maxwell's interpretation of *The Matrix* (1999). When this movie was produced and developed by the Wachowski brothers, it introduced a concept that tantalized humans with an artificially induced computer world for the human mass. This world was made to subjugate humans and keep them from the *truth* that they were slaves used for their BTU body heat, and used as batteries to power the machines. Was this the message that the movie was trying to give us about the current situation?

The refusal to see reality could be why most people survive. Humans must be entertained through the eyes and ears, in turn we process the information that our brain receives through these two outputs. After the information is obtained, humans (based on cultural, religion, fears, and personal experiences) use this information for positive or negative effects. When humans are entertained certain messages, sounds, or waves are transmitted (alpha, beta or theta) that affect us unconsciously [24]. Even though we are enjoying the movie (or not), we are receiving transmissions that could be whatever the producers/creators want us to know or display. Could they be numbing humans down and lowering our intelligence in the name of entertainment? Or could they in fact try to "save us" the only way we seem to focus through movies, television, music, etc . . .? Neo's character (religious concept/symbol), was an anomaly who did not follow the protocols of the system program and in turn became a threat. Not having to follow the laws of the system meant he could experience and produce miraculous events (flying, dodging bullets, and eventually stopping them with his mind).

Maxwell it seems was able to find other symbols making this move more than just an action sci-fi thriller. A hidden code of sorts depicting the date of 09/11/01 was in fact evident within the film two years before the event transpired. After personal research in this claim, the result held water. When Neo was interrogated by the sentient program Smith, the files that contained his "two lives" actually had more documents that were briefly shown. Neo's driver license can be seen with the expiration date of *September 11, 2001* with the place of origin being Century City (another name for New York). Is this a message of the attack that took place two years later or is it just a coincidence? In order to really study the scene, the movie must be paused. Only for a brief instance, the license is displayed.

Even more bizarre, was the series created by Chris Carter two years later (the creator of the *X-Files*). The show called *The Lone Gunman* aired in February/March of 2001. The first pilot episode dealt with certain factions of the government and terrorists working together flying a plane into the World Trade Center *on purpose*! The event took place eight months before the real event, which might have explained the short run. When asked why the antagonists performed this action, the response was "we need to control the Middle East," "oil control," and "war for business." How should we respond to this, as simple entertainment, coincidence, or something bigger? Is Chris Carter trying to tell us sensitive information behind closed doors at government proceedings? Another quaint but interesting fact that must be investigated: *GE* (General Electric now owned by Comcast) three or four years before 2001 released a refrigerator with the emblem containing two jets flying into the World Trade Center. This appliance unfortunately was not sold in the United States; it was only sold in Italy [25].

ABC's "Visitors"

These perceptions only offer one suggestion: "Hollywood" may be trying to subconsciously influence the general population through movies and innovative shows. Those are only a few examples; however, they could change the way we see television and movies in general. In 2009, Maxwell discussed the emergence of what was then a new show on ABC (Disney owned) called *V*. The show was already created in 1984; however, was redone to fit our time now that contains many possible symbolic meanings. The pilot episode dealt a post 9/11 scenario of a worldwide appearance of alien ships over twenty-nine major cities. The beings inhabiting these ships, presented themselves as very attractive looking humanoids who displayed feelings of *peace* and *happiness.*

These *Visitors* reminded the humans that there was nothing to fear, and that they were lost in search of "help" in returning to their home planet. When the aliens obtained the necessary supplies, they would leave the human race behind leaving advancements in technology for our benefit. Maxwell focuses on the pamphlet that the Visitors hand out to the humans within a sort of "*peace ambassador program.*" The citation on the pamphlet states "dawn of a new day" which hinted at the poem the *Aeneid* created by Virgil, the classic Roman poet. This poem dealt with his vision of a new world order emerging with the presence of a "*Sun King*" leading the world from the throne of Cesar. Could this mean that human-like hybrid aliens will emerge from the stars to lure humans into a false sense of security and dominate us?

Maxwell strongly believes that the *Reptilian agenda* exists and seemed to dominate the heart of exopolitical discussion these days [26]. Maxwell also believes that humans are going to awaken sometime in 2012 and realize that they have been deceived about spiritual ascension that automatically happens within our brains. This does not fall under the Judeo-Christian concept of "revelation;" although churches and religious institutions will try to market this idea. This ascension process stems from a deeper, ancient meaning that could be embedded in our human DNA from past lives.

The major concept of using the phrase "dawn of a new day" has been utilized in ancient times signifying the symbol of change. The "war for our souls" as Maxwell describes it, is due to the beings that created us who have powerful enemies. This is why he believes the world military presence is at maximum. The show *V* itself was interesting, displaying concepts/symbols that targeted the Reptilian/Draco agenda. One episode called "Laid Bare" dealt with the Visitor Queen Anna, displaying to her daughter Lisa how to extract a human soul using a device that in turn destroyed the human in the process. This could be hinting at the possibility of a forced colonization and occupation that is already ongoing *now* in our lifetime.

Symbolic Meaning in Everyday Life

Maxwell introduces us to other areas of our human lives that contain symbols overlooked and continue to go unnoticed; the two concepts of *land* and *water*. In ancient times, especially with Native Americans tribes, the land meant a sacred symbol of *Mother Earth/Gaia* which was intended for all living things to share for prosperity while giving back. The water symbol was the bringer of life and was held sacred as well as properly maintained and protected for the welfare of all species alike.

Unfortunately, the ancient meanings of these two symbols are long gone, and new meanings have emerged: *law, profit,* and *power*. The first law (obviously being the *law of the land* or law of the people) states that all humans that live in certain areas of land, have laws they must follow. Depending where you live on the globe, the laws change and have different meanings (this law is very clear cut with no mystery, puzzle or dilemma: it just is). The ancient idea of sharing is now eliminated and replaced by "landowners" that have control and divide among themselves with the poor "renting space" on their property.

The poor must bring profit as they till the land or labor as they are charged to live, breathe, and exist there living the illusion of owning property. The more land one controls, the more power one has and in turn, does whatever they please. As we have seen through sequential historical time, the idea of *sharing the land* was never popular in the thoughts of religious colonists and imperialists [27]. The law of *water* as we have discussed, is the symbol of life. Through changes in its meaning now, we have a different reason for it. The idea of life still stands; however, the purpose now is to control who receives this life and how to distribute it according to the controller's desire. The original idea of life for all now changes into a selective process. Is this how a business person views the symbol of water? For the corporate interest, water represents the *law of money* or *profit* which includes cash flow and liquid assets [28].

An example that Maxwell offers is the idea of ships and their cargo. Ships arrive in a harbor and bring products to produce commerce. All of the ships are female (*Demeter*, *Santa María*, *Niña*, *Pinta* etc . . .) and the "female" produces a *product* like the human female produces a child. On a ship, one receives a *certificate of manifest*, while the child receives a *certificate of birth*. The ship pulls into a dock, while human children are delivered by a "doc" as well. Are these two systems related or do they have two separate symbolic meanings? Are we humans just commerce just as Maxwell, and the movie the Matrix displays? Could we be financial security on the New York stock exchange?

Maxwell believes in this idea of *human commerce* with many key examples and symbols within our own society and cultural background. When we are born in the United States, we obtain a social security card that is issued with a number for our identification in society. On the back of the card, there are red numbers in a series that represent us and our physical bodies on the stock exchange. Realistically, without this identification, one could not do the following: take out loans, open bank accounts, buy/rent houses, work, live, collect income tax, or partake in an of society's basic functions.

The result seems that we cannot not exist or have any of retirement or amenities that humans are required to have. We in fact need this number to identify us in order to get "paid" or make any sort of living. Maxwell may be showing us a bleak reality that we in fact are only numbers to be traded away on the exchange for what we are worth. He hinted at us about this by exposing that on every Federal Reserve Note, there are a series of numbers that indicate the series of bills produced. According to his research, these numbers line up to the numbers in red on a social security card [29].

We can imagine that about six billion bills are circulating worldwide which means someone is buying and selling our personal body ("numbers"). Who would benefit from a scheme such as this and most of all, whom are we collateral for? Is this just corporate interest or is something bigger at play here? The sad truth is that the banking system is based on this practice and those who run the banks are none other than international bankers and special interest groups. It seems that governments themselves and banks are indeed following the same guidelines as religion. Isn't there supposed to be a separation of church and state in this country?

It would apparently be an illusionary idea or contrivance to lure us into believing false ideals. Religion as it seems, never fails to surprise, upset, destroy and delude humans from the ultimate goal of ascended consciousness. We cannot go anywhere in the world without hearing someone's interpretation of this fabled, forged, and nonsensical copy of tall tales. We cannot escape the vice grip it holds upon us and for a good reason. Religion is not in plain sight, and is the foundation of our educational system. This dangerous and ignorant idea is secretly fed into our daily lives through not only places of worship, but schools as well [30].

Maxwell tells us of the *Knights Templar*, (a secret society) who are the founding fathers of the banking system and still run the institution today. Their ideals based on the ancient Greek phrase: *in hoc signo vinces*, is roughly translated to "in this sign you will conquer." Does this translation bring the grim reality that indeed religion will consume the human race and conquer its soul, mind, and body? The secret society here in the United States employs a different slogan using biblical quotes from Psalms 115; basically stating "not unto us O Lord, not unto us, but unto thy Name give the praise." In the King James Version however; the last sentence replaces *praise* with *glory.* These two words have about the same meaning basically admiring and worshipping a deity. Although the very idea that this phrase represents humility and thanks, it was the staple of the crusade's ideology of conquering and slaughtering the enemy against the Judeo-Christian god.

Perhaps they need to rethink the definition more clearly based on their violent history including Cashmere, the Inquisitions, the Crusades, and the conquest of the New World. The Protestants also believed in this ideology when they journeyed to the New World in search of religious freedom. It seems however, that their "freedom" meant displacing and evicting the Native Americans whom already lived there (and did not fit into their biblical beliefs) in the false name of "thanks" and "humility" [31]. The universities of prestige such as the "top ten" or ivy league schools are run by the Roman Masonic Order. Through research, Maxwell has found that the *Kippah* or special hat worn by the Hebrews is not theirs by origin. The hat was issued by the Vatican who forced their brethren to wear it to show subjugation to the Roman Catholic Church and to Rome itself [32].

The Christ Myth

The Jesus character myth considered to be a Hebrew male, could in fact be merely a symbol according to Maxwell and not to be taken literally. Although most Christians ignorantly belief the Christ myth to be original, over 35 other messiahs were crucified long before the invention of Christianity [33]. Although many experts claim that they have undeniable proof that a man named Jesus existed, all ancient religions (Cambodia, ancient China, Egypt, Sumer, Babylon, Phoenicia) prior to this Christian myth, had their own messiahs who were treated in the exact same way in the context of experiencing crucifixion, rising from the dead, curing the sick, walking on water, twelve disciples, etc . . . [34]

Maxwell presented another way of looking at this myth in the form of symbols to possibly clear any foolish ideas people still may have. In the first place, this Christian myth was fashioned and forged due to the fact that by the end of the Old Testament's rewoven tale, no savior or messiah ever presented itself in actuality. After the Council of Nicea reached a decision in 325 CE on the status of inventing a messiah, Constantine combined all different religious beliefs into one entity so that everyone could easily subscribe to it [35]. Truthfully, the entire myth was fashioned after Pagan sun cults and symbols. The Christians and Jesuits have believed this symbol to be the son of Yahweh; however, in reality "Jesus" was the sun (sol) itself [36].

Many "god-child saviors" were represented as personifications of this star (we call the sun) that provided all the ancients with life and amenities that we still have today (food, water, vegetation, etc . . .). Sun worship is based on astrology and the twelve signs of the Zodiac. The majority of its creation was fashioned from older ancient pagan beliefs. The *twelve disciples* as Maxwell points out are just the twelve signs of the Zodiac that were eliminated as symbols and fashioned as real people [37]. To elaborate further, Judas (another fictional character), according to Matthew 26:49-50, is said to have kissed Jesus on the cheek. Ancient stories tell of the "kiss of death," but the culprit happens to be a *scorpion*. When a scorpion stings a human, the marks represent human lips (both cuts). This makes the story we are interpreting the twelve signs of the Zodiac using *Scorpio* (Judas), the *sun* (Jesus), and the *Virgo* constellation (also known as the "virgin").

On December 22nd, (the exact date of the winter solstice) the sun rises up every day on the same degree for three days. When December 25th commences, the sun rises one degree north of the original position while the *passing* of the sun happens over the equator on the vernal equinox. The Hebrew belief of "*Passover*" pertains to the sun ritual of the sun passing over the equator and nothing more. Their Christian counterparts, however, dealt with the "resurrection" of the sun creating "*Easter*" when the sun rises over the equator on the vernal equinox. Due to two opposing Hebrew beliefs, one had to differ from the other (since the existence of a messiah did not emerge yet). They did not worship the same holiday and the Christians decided on Easter due to the rising of their iconic god-child after three days. The true fact here is that *both tribes* merely engaged in sun worship, which existed long before the creation of either religious thought [38].

Ancient Symbols Transformed

Mises (or what the Hebrew called Moses) was another symbol adapted by Hebrews, became the leader of the moon (lunar) cult [39]. The Hebrews, during their nomadic journeys adhered or attracted themselves more to Moon worship. Moon worship itself had been practiced long before the Hebrews by the Vikings, Native Americans, Sumerians, and Egyptians. In fact, almost all of the Hebrew beliefs concerning Moon worship come from Egypt or Sumer with the iconic figure itself taken from Syrian legends [40]. The moon's lower quarter is represented by horns in the Syrian account. Mises had these horns fashioned above his head on the top of the mount where he received his "commandments by his god." Early Hebrew copies of this story had begun changing the name to "Moses," however, still kept the horns until they fashioned a *halo* instead later through the centuries. The symbol of the horns originally represented divinity, intelligence and holiness. Now, the idea has changed into a darker meaning of demonic principles and negative forces.

The name *Sinai* that the Hebrew hold dear and mention in their Old Testament was in fact not originally theirs as well. Separating the words, we now witness another symbol that meant something completely different than we were made to realize. Instead of the proposed belief of a location, Maxwell was able to separate the words into two different symbols from the one word. "*SIN*," a word originating from ancient Arabia before Islam, was the name of the moon god. "*AI*" was a word in ancient Egyptian that meant *mountain*. Ancient Egyptian themselves, believed that the moon god lived in the mountains due to the fact that the moon rose from behind the mountains every night hence the name "*SIN AI*" ("*the moon god of the mountain*") [41]. Were these changes deliberately done to hide some unknown, mysterious, or truthful answer(s) that could explain some of missing pieces? Why have religious interests changed important symbols into meaningless religious jargon to fool us?

Another example of changes are the famous "breaking the bread," "drinking the wine," and "eating the body" of their suppose savior. This is being a symbol of cannibalism, could in fact represent more than the obvious implication. Maxwell believes so, as he discovers that there is in fact a deeper meaning than we were originally led to understand. Wine usually derives from red grapes for this type of ceremony, and *these specific grapes signify red blood;* which is another word for *atonement* or blood sacrifice. In ancient times, grapes were considered *divine* because ironically, they grew on vines. Maxwell has pointed out that since the beginning of the new age of religion in the eighth century; Europe has dominated everything from the Caesars of Rome to the Roman Catholic Church [42].

Through Maxwell and his research, his conclusions included the fabled concepts concerning "holy" Israel, Salt Lake City, and the Holy Father, had no *divine* meaning whatsoever [43]. He stated that the masters (whomever they are) set up institutions (schools of thought, universities, academia, etc . . .) to govern and run the lives of humans. In order to be anyone in society, it seems that we need to graduate from a (distinguished) university or school of thought that presents us with a certificate of proof that we are educated in their eyes and society's as well. We must follow their guidelines as they fashion us from the age of five on how to think, what to do, and what they decide is the most important position of power and respect. Maybe Maxwell isn't being eccentric or irrational when it comes to his claims, maybe he has a point.

We must remember when we play a part in a game small, large, on the side, or directly in the middle, we are essentially part of the design. One is still as responsible as the original game player who orchestrated the plan. Coupled together, organized religion seems to be a direct threat to the human race in terms of hindering thought, logic, rationality, common sense, creativity/imagination and spiritual ascension/ consciousness. He has extensive research on Masonic orders and their hidden agendas, which could be due to his own quest for the enlightenment. By exposing them to the few of humans who are aware, one can view who is exactly running our lives, what symbols are being used against us, and what power they hold.

The Vatican/Masonic Orders Connection

Propaganda Due; a shadowy mysterious Masonic order controls most of our human daily lives. This order is a combination of memberships within the groups *Knights of Malta*, *Opus Dei*, and the *Jesuits*. The result of this union makes them a sort of *grand council* dealing with worldly affairs. Together they form what Maxwell describes as, a "crime syndicate" dealing in human trafficking, drugs, and violence [44]. Maxwell also specifies that America and the ideas of pseudo-liberty, pseudo-justice, etc . . . will not be saved, and the human race in general will not be saved. Many religious interests and professionals alike will criticize and ridicule responses and claims such as these claiming there are too extravagant, foolish, and wrapped up in conspiracy. Even Project Camelot, who conducted the interview, could not believe such a powerful reality due to their belief that humans will all rise above this outcome. The others would cling to the old phrases of "I don't believe you," "you are a conspiracy theorist," or "all you need is Jesus/Yahweh" premise; however this maybe a serious case of denial and delusion.

Why do the religious devotees bow to the Pope and kiss his ring? What is this symbolic representation describing about human behavior? Through this act, we are seemly signifying his "divine right" to rule humans through our submission. Why should we as humans bow to another when he is equal to us? Is he even human, or is he wearing cloned human flesh to disguise his real appearance of a reptilian entity like David Icke suggests [45]? *Leo Lyon Zagami*, a former Mason and still a Jesuit Co-Adjutor who is now supposedly against the idea of Masonic orders, claims to be a witness that visited the Vatican itself. He also claims to have seen an underground base stationed at the base structure as a foundation of sorts. This also meant that the Vatican was built upon this base of operations. Zagami claimed to have discovered chambers that contain infinite knowledge of the past, but it is known that those who enter may never leave. It seems his agenda is to cause an uprising within the Vatican to change the current belief system for his own purposes or the group he is working for [46].

By exposing the Vatican, there seems to be a deeper religious/political reason for his disobedience and betrayal. Should we believe Zagami, or is he part of another group trying to lead humans into ignorance? Through research, Zagami is said to have ties with the CIA as a disinformation agent, and believes in the idea of the North American union superhighway which feeds directly into the one world government mindset of unity under one rule [47]. In one way he is pro-*illuminati* and on the other side, he preaches against the religious faction. It seems that this "illuminati whistleblower" is working both sides of the field, which means it may not be a good idea to trust him. To further implicate the findings of how mysterious the Vatican is, two movies were created as an in depth look on the organization.

The Davinci Code (2006) and *Angles and Demons* (2009) were supposedly created to expose the Vatican as Tom Hanks took us along a dangerous journey to expose the truth. We are made to believe that Dan Brown created and orchestrated the whole idea on his own; however, this is far from the truth. Brown coincidently plagiarized the work of three distinguished

British authors who wrote the book *Holy Blood, Holy Grail.* Maxwell further clarifies that Brown was just taking credit for something he did not write; however, had to present it in a way that his "masters" wanted to display it to the public. This way, the Masonic order laid the building blocks for a new world order [48]. The three authors *Henry Lincoln, Richard Leigh, and Michael Baigent* outlined the *Knights Templar* and the whole concept of Masonic secret societies further back in 1983.

The Symbolic Meaning of Sex in Subcultures

Another symbol grossly misinterpreted is *sex.* This symbol happens to be overlooked, abused, and controlled by the power elite. Maxwell displays to us that sex is everywhere and into everything. The black robe and its symbolic meaning are not of masculine origin. The female priestess in ancient times, wore this as a staple and representation of feminine sexuality and essence. The *cross* before the Christian religion ever acquired it, was a sexual symbol as well in many cultures [49]. The Egyptian obelisk itself, represents the male erection and solar worship that is seen in many locations such as Washington D.C, the Vatican, New York, etc . . . Most of the national monuments that we encounter and sometimes jokingly reference to the male phallus, female breasts or any sexual connotation could in fact be accurate. Why do most humans view the symbol of sex taboo, negative, and even let it control the very fabric of our humanity through society's influence? Before in ancient times, sexual gratification was honored and necessary as part of discovering oneself.

The symbol was something positive in nature, as it was considered paradise with orgies; sometimes with the same sex (ancient Rome and Greece). Of course the world was never perfect, but the symbol has change severely since ancient times into a method of control and shunned by religious dogma. A woman for instance, cannot explore herself without being labeled derogatory statements such as "prostitute, whore, harlot, slut, etc . . ." by Judeo-Christian or Islamic principle. Because of this "principle," the female's need for sexual gratification is more focused on a male driven agenda. The essence of the female is completely destroyed in most cultures that follow organized religion (Christianity, Islam, and Judaism) and some are more dangerous than others. Subcultures in Latin America abuse the woman and use the bible as an excuse to dominate them, rape them, and keep them spiritually and physically incarcerated by the father, husband, or even brothers.

In turn, we find most Hispanic women very defeated spiritually and unaware of their true bodily function sexually, unless used for propaganda by networks and cultural means as a product/marketing proposition. The ridiculous and archaic concept of *virginity* still holds water before marriage and the woman must never engage in sexual activities before marriage lest she be scorned as "sexually immoral" [50]. The woman truly unaware of her sexual spirituality and body, consummates with a man ignorantly and is forced to bend at the will of this new "master."

Women are left void of the knowledge of *sexual healing* and *gratification* due to these preconceptions based on religious dogma. Those who do break free of this mold, either go too far and exploit themselves for the misunderstood concept of "sexual freedom" or seek the same sex for answers that their partner could not give them. There must be a balance if humans are to ever understand each other as opposite sexes. The saying "sex sells" is completely evident as we see most propaganda and commercials using the female body as an idea or attracting the male audience for their profit. For many Hispanic subcultures, it is alcohol/dancing, soccer (*futbol*) games with attractive females in sports jerseys, or automobiles where beautiful women are dressed revealing mostly all of their bodies in order to appeal to the sexual weakness of the Hispanic male.

The Symbolism of Women in Islam

The symbol of *sex* is used in this society as a marketing strategy and controlling the main consumer: *the human male*. Unfortunately, the original meaning has undergone a severe metamorphosis into a dangerous weapon. Many Hispanic subcultures are not the only destructive results, all over the world women are objectified, used physically and spiritually in order to control the male interest. In Islam, the father, husband, and brother all have dominion over their daughters, wives and sisters [51]. Using religion, they justify their actions and subject women to cover themselves in order to hide their "beauty" which is considered "sacred." The Islamic faith in general teaches utter disrespect for women as mere possessions [52]. In most extreme cases, if one Muslim woman is raped and plans to accuse her attacker, Pakistani law mandates that four men must witness the event to testify for her [53]. As sickening as the religion is, most women sadly defend it with their lives ignorantly and naively demeaning themselves. In some places such as Saudi Arabia, Iran and Sudan, the raped woman can be incarcerated or executed if they fail to meet Islamic law's "high standard of proof."

It is a sort of reverse psychology when it comes to Muslim women as they are told that their beauty is *sacred* and too great for other men to see. This way, they must remain in the company of their husband only. As we have seen, women defend this idea destroying themselves in the process void of a soul or feelings. They become ignorant in the idea of orgasms, freedom of the body, and the exploration of themselves in order to make a stronger connection with the opposite sex. This vicious cycle continues as female children are considered only property and male children are preferred. If the daughter never marries, she is controlled and passed into the control of the brothers for the rest of their lives. The symbolic example is more destructive than the western version that gives the illusion that women have the freedom of choice. Changes are transpiring in the Middle East; however, they are done as a result of anger and repression. Women are now turning against their established order while fighting back [54].

Are they equipped to do so? Has the last two thousand years crippled them spiritually and mentally that they are not ready to lead us as they have done in the past? "Violence solves nothing" they say, and patriarchal societies may have destroyed the female essence completely. Of course there are some anomalies such as my mother who has suffered the grotesqueries of the Hispanic rural subculture. She evolved protecting her body from harm, mind, and spirit and emerging into a woman of extreme caliber. These examples must be cherished and protected for they are precious and rare becoming extinct. There is also a balance that must be made, and it is not suggested that women use their bodies to control men for all of the destruction that the gender has inflicted. This in turn, would be destructive and would not solve the problem. The problem is in *culture/ subculture* and *religion*. As long as we have them in their current state, things will never change and more humans will be destroyed over a symbols/meanings that we humans have little understanding of.

The Symbolism of Democracy

Do humans *really* know how the world works? This question is not to be answered with the concept of one's own fantasy world, or perception of the world around them. Maxwell believes that mankind cannot handle the truth. The way humans run the world today as irresponsible individuals, seems that we are not *getting it*. Maxwell stressed that current governments work in a mob or gang mentality like the Bloods or Crips. Maxwell also alerted humans to the reality that both parties that we elect as our representation for leadership work for two main parties: *arms* ("the military party") and *petroleum* ("the oil party") who own both sides of the playing field [55]. Whoever becomes the next "president" in 2012 will help decide how long this game will continue.

Do they then use these ancient symbols in modern times hidden in plain sight? Is this really just a business venture? The pseudo-democratic order that we live in now simply does not work. Human believe in the concept of *democracy* and fight for it to the death. Do we really know what *democracy* means? What is the true symbol of its meaning and origin? Two symbols can be identified as we separate the word in two entities. Humans are lead to believe that the meaning stands "*for the people*" however; we must identify what "*people*" are being referred to.

The word is Greek in origin and the translation of *demo* which means "mob," and *ocracy* which means "the rule." The true meaning of *democracy* would mean "*the rule of the mob,*" not the power of the people. Since Maxwell described the leaders of the country using a "mob mentality," it is no surprise that this country is run by a mob of corporate interest and government agencies [56]. The original concept of the founding fathers is completely destroyed as the original goal, was a *constitutional republic* [57]. The purpose of this idea was to prevent and protect the people from the mob mentality or the law. It could be safe to say that Jefferson, Washington, or Madison would not be pleased as the symbol that they stood and fought for, changed into something else entirely today. Maxwell expresses his sadness about the current state of this nation which he believe stood for freedom, rational thought, and the separation of church and state as the *Treaty of Tripoli* in 1797 signifies. Specifically, *Article 11* states the following fact that most people are ignorant about specifying that the U.S was *not* founding as a Christian nation:

> *"As the Government of the United States is not, in any sense, founded on the Christian religion; as it has in itself no character or enmity against the laws, religion, or tranquility, of Mussulmen; and, as the said States never entered into any war, or act or hostility against any Mahometan nation, it is declared by the parties, no pretext arising from religious opinions, shall ever produce an interruption of the harmony existing between the two countries."*

America now, is not a country of laws although people still want to view it as so, rather it is a mere shadow of the past in control of industrial and banking interests laid down by Teddy Roosevelt and his pact with corporations during the 1900s. The court system which places the judge as the deciding factor of whatever he/she believes, changing the law according to their belief system, preconceived ideas and/

or biases. In this case, humans must investigate on how many different "opinions" we have offered. Maxwell describes the answer pure and simple: "it is whatever the *boss* says." The plain and honest truth is that one cannot win in a court of law based solely on facts. As we remember, this is a game and a winner must be decided regardless.

The idea of lawless structure runs into religion as well. Maxwell points out that the Mormons, and Jehovah's witnesses (the down syndrome sects of Christianity), change their laws frequently depending on who is in charge of the church or organization [58]. With each sect or group, the priest or leader decides what goes and end up arguing amongst themselves on who is the better expert of Yahweh's "wisdom." The Mormons are the same sect that also believes that "magic undergarments" are impervious to bullets and other threats against them (this being just one example of the extent of their madness). So as a result, the symbols of freedom and law are changed into games as the symbol of spiritual, metaphysical and magical beliefs have been transformed into present day religion. Both symbols have been destroyed and have completely lost their true meaning, manipulated to control the human rather than assist them in finding their purpose and self-worth.

The Symbolic Meaning of Colors

Colors themselves play an important role in symbolism of not only religion, but government. Maxwell had discussed black as an important role in religion; however, two other colors play a part in all of our daily lives being red and white. He attributes all three colors to the Reptilian Illuminati Agenda. These colors together represent what have been called "death head colors" that are prominent in Hollywood and from the Nazi groups such as the *SS* and the *Gestapo*. The two special Nazi groups were considered the *Order of the Death Head* and carried a skull and bones symbol.

Could this also be the symbol for the infamous Skull and Bones society? Why are these specific colors always prominent and continue to be so in our modern day history? In movies, Maxwell pointed out that when someone died or was going to be killed, these three colors were always present as if they were trying to symbolize something [59]. Do they symbolize the darkest of darkness or the essence of evil as Maxwell states? Or do these colors point at something else that coincides with our humanity as a missing piece? Maxwell also mentioned that DNA contains special colors themselves; probably hinting a deeper meaning beyond human understanding.

The meaning of colors are everywhere and do not stop just as these two important places. Masonic orders, even gangs here in the United States (Mexican and black) use different Masonic symbols of opposing forces. Through these colors and symbolism, Maxwell believes that U.S gangs are funded and orchestrated by European masons that wish to destroy American culture and the country [60]. The idea may not be so far-fetched, and could be researched with very compelling data and results. Is there a reason that gangs are allowed to wreak havoc and cause destruction? The American colonies themselves were founded as a privately owned corporation by the Bank of England that forced colonists to use valid British currency as opposed to colonial paper money [61].

The Illuminati Symbolic Premise

We have discussed how the Masonic orders run the world through institutions and the latter, but where does the *Illuminati* come from? Why does the group come up in social circles, however, still dismissed as a false pretense or even conspiracy? When we usually hear about the subject, Alex Jones (who considers himself as a *paleoconservative*) screams and rants his ideals on his syndicated public radio show bashing them, and accusing them for all misdoings in the world and the downfall of the United States [62]. However at most times, he really does not attribute the atrocities of the Zionist Jews and their followers, rather blaming Chinese, American, Arab freedom fighters, and even England. Whether this man can be taken seriously by advocating against this group while working for them, take serious consideration and research. Does this group represent something more than the ranting and ravings of this glorified radio show host? Where do they originate from? Maxwell provides to us a detailed history of the order, and we find that their beginnings stem from Europe.

This ancient order was founded in Spain, later organizing themselves into present day Jesuits. The Vatican itself, according to Maxwell, is another sinister group who work with the Jesuits forming an "evil organization" that run the planet. Maxwell through research believes that the Vatican is the bone work of another sinister group known as the *Knights of Malta* [63]. This order consists of six members that also have strong ties to the CIA and happen to be catholic as well. This does not bide well when humans are faced with two major problems: *firstly*, belonging to a religious organization that has killed more people in the world throughout history than anyone else [64]. Belonging to a clandestine operative group that works beyond the law of human rights has either taken part in creating a dictatorship or destroying a republic through assassination. Could this be where the Spanish conquistadors received their "training" as they destroyed, raped, ravaged and robbed the ancient Aztec, Inca and other native tribes in Latin America?

There is probably a strong connection here on how they operated in the past, and how they still operate today: nothing has changed except the weapons we use. As mentioned before, the Knights of Malta also took part in the banking system, and own many of the banking fraternities. *Bank of America, Union Bank of California, and Chase Bank* are just a few examples of their interests in the general population [65]. Most of the general population has bank accounts in these locations. Does this mean that we are indirectly financing terrorism all over the globe in the name of a religious authority? Vatican Rome has dominated the globe for more than two thousand years by the "divine right" of Kings. The Pope himself as we have discussed, is a representation of the divine that could be considered a king within the construct of how the organization is run. The symbols he wears, the *challis* (which represents the "holy grail" so to speak) all point to symbols that place him above the rest of humanity as some sort of "pharaonic entity." In all fairness, it is safe to assume that he is the present king of the planet Earth. Do the people have the option of voting for this illustrious title? It seems that the "divine right" is selected by those in power and the idea of the "people," is completely delusional as the concept of freedom is nonexistent.

The Concept Of "Paradise"

Maxwell gave a personal interview concerning symbols to Project Camelot besides lecturing for their conference back in 2009. In this interview, Maxwell presented a more in depth view of his personal beliefs, how he acquired his knowledge, and what he believes about the UFO agenda in relation to where human beings are headed. He also maintains the importance of symbols in human culture and life; through the use of ideas and physical representations. The same symbols we use for protection and spiritual advancement could also destroy us in the process, since we are using them incorrectly. Maxwell warns of an emergence of world leader to dominate all life on this planet. The leader will not be human as he has mentioned and goes under the title of *Sun King*. This odd but interesting revelation seems like a sci-fi movie, where the end of the world is a result of an alien force wiping out humanity as shown in *Skyline* (2010), *Battle Los Angeles* (2011) and Spielberg's new show *Falling Skies (*2011*)* where humanity is fighting to survive after six months of an alien invasion.

His outlook on this Sun King is that the result will be a negative impact on humanity. Maxwell attributes the three major cults of Christianity, Islam, and Judaism; along with their perspective sub sects (*Jehovah witnesses*, the *World Wide Church of God*, *Mormons* etc . . .) are playing part in some new world movement [66]. This movement is taking place mostly here in the western world and according to Maxwell, sadly "people have bought into it." What have these religious scam artists tried to shove into our faces besides the pseudo concept of self-sacrifice that we must follow in order to be "saved?" After this obvious waste of time, we then are allowed to ascend into a glorious afterlife where we meet our ancestors (which may not like us or vice versa). This heaven premise depends on what fantasy you choose to buy into/ believe in.

Muslim men for instance, (women are not part of this plan; neither animals) ascend to a rich paradise with Allah with the "promised reward" of seventy-two virgins. This of course is due to their undying loyalty to their god, and following orders here on Earth (meaning killing all infidels, and setting themselves as human bombs destroying the "enemies" of Islam). In this male dominated society, as a man the best choice would be Islamic paradise instead of "walking with Jesus all day" until the end of time. In the author's opinion, the concept seems utterly boring and pointless since eventually there is nothing more he can tell or show you. We must ask logical and rational questions that always seem to destroy these religious fantasies: why do we need seventy-two virgins? Why that specific number? Is this something that men really want to relive again in paradise? The idea after death is that we materialize into spiritual beings void of physical properties and desires. How can sprits have sex if we no longer have the means to do so?

Back on Earth, was as men had to remember the experience and the difficulty to woo a female into exploring the sexual adventure. As we can see plainly in nature, not everyone is a winner when it comes to expressing male dominance. If we ever succeed in getting the female to notice us, it is more stressful to perform something that we have watched on television that would result in the same "perfect experience." Most teenage boys either panic or prematurely ejaculated before the girls reach a sense of arousal. The story doesn't get better as men reach their 50s either. Will this problem arise again in paradise, or will it finally be addressed and resolved by Allah? Are there unlimited resources of *Cialis* and *Viagra* in the Islamic paradise? Can we really forget about all of our problems and everything will be perfect?

Imagine for a moment, that you meet the same woman again, do you think she would remember you and your failed attempt at sexual arousal? If so, then we as men can kiss our chances goodbye with the other seventy-one! Obviously, women share their experiences with each other bad or good.

As males, we engage in the same activity, however fabricate certain events lest we be ridiculed by our male peers or acquaintances. Do we have to meet the parents of each single virgin as we previously did here on Earth and do we have to have the essential "pep talk" with the father of each one? Can we really do this seventy-two times, or does Allah understand this human practice and excuse us from it? Do you think Allah himself is ready for this complexity? How do we as men know that we will receive seventy-two beautiful women? What transpires when we receive a physically unattractive woman or one that is mentally affected? Can one trade them like baseball cards or does Allah say "all sales are final?"

When these fools invented this idea of paradise, did they think these things through before jotting them down? What happens if you're a gay Muslim? Most homosexual Arab men due to their culture rarely would admit it. If they do, they must flee otherwise suffer their fate of being stoned to death or worse. They do have families not because of personal desire; rather they do not want to die. We must understand that survival exceeds the need of desire when it needs to be programmed somewhere in the human brain. So theoretically, when this homosexual Muslim man dies, what does he do with seventy-two female virgins? This whole idea is confusing and hasn't been well thought out. As we have studied, the foolish concept of faith lacks sense and rationality as its inception lacks the very basic nature of what human should have.

In this case, Maxwell may be accurate in his assumption that human beings are "bought." The issue is deeper than we are led to believe and on top of this stipulation, it is all done on a personal and individual level. In any case, anyone's fantasy can be viewed as correct considering that the plans, rules, and rewards are carefully thought out and processed realistically.

The Emergence Of The Sun King

This idea of a new world order stems from older sources that have been orchestrating plans from the beginning of its creation. Maxwell points to the Japanese flag as one of the implications. Interestingly enough, Japan has always been known as the land of the rising sun, although the flag has changed since the Axis power days of WWII. Even with the rays being eliminated, the flag itself still represents the red sun. In ancient Roman times, poets were a very important part of society especially for Cesar. As the known ruler of the world, the poet was hand selected to write poetry for him. This poet had to produce an immaculate and artistically perfect piece, displaying the glorification of the king himself. As noted before, the Roman poet Virgil (*Publuis Virgilius Maro*), created a very special poem for the Cesar known as the *Aeneid* (*Aenes* in Latin). The poem dated to be about first century (between 19-29 BCE) and entailed the life of a Trojan called *Aeneas* and his journeys. More importantly, a special grouping of words "*novus ordo seclorum*" (which specified a time when a great ruler would emerge in the seat of Cesar) foretold that "an awesome ruler greater than any man" would emerge before us. When this ruler came, the sun would arise and it would emerge. Is Maxwell implying that a non-human would rule humanity under the Japanese banner?

Japan has emerged as one of the world's leaders in technology and commerce. Although they have suffered many past obstacles such as the bombing of Hiroshima and Nagasaki by the United States, the forced imprisonment of Japanese Americans in concentration camps during the war, and the strange and/or enigmatic earthquake on March 3rd, 2011, they still managed to salvage themselves proficiently despite the chaos. Was this earthquake a marker for things to come in the near future?

The symbols that are being represented here are right in plain sight in front of our noses. The same grouping of words ironically enough, are located on the back of the one dollar bill along with the Egyptian god *Horus'* (*Heru*) "all seeing eye." Is this coincidental or is there another message of Virgil's *Sun King* prediction? Could Japan be the new nation to emerge as the new model of this order coming to spell doom for us? The current train of thought is crippling the environment, our health is affected, the use of pesticides/herbicides, investment in monocultures, GMO in our food supply, hormones in our dairy products, fluoride and chlorine in our water, etc . . . When do we draw the limit in deciding when we have had enough? What will it take to halt the process of our own neurological and spiritual degeneration?

As we have an idea now of this future ruler of humanity, what exactly will this new Solar ruler do to the human race upon his arrival? Maxwell suggests that this king will dominate humanity for a single purpose: to control the human family and to mutate the human race [67]. What can we expect from this mutation, and what does that mean exactly? Could it be the transfer to a scientific facility undergoing tests with various chemicals to transform humans into hideous monsters, zombies, or hybrids? According to Maxwell this doesn't look like the case entirely. It seems that this agenda is not based on eugenics or evolution, rather the ancient process redone to formulate a new "change" for humans. He believed that these changes entail the shaping of a human being into something else, making us essentially non-human.

The six main points he clarifies as negative changes are the following: firstly, our entire "humanity" will be affected. Secondly, our feelings, cares, concept of love, and kindness will change for the worse. Next, our emotions will also be eliminated, possibly replaced with robotic programming. After, the "American" system of freedom, liberty, and justice will be nonexistent. Then, the concept of family that we all hold dear will be changed forever, although we have to admit, this concept is nonexistent already (we all have our ideas based on cultural upbringings; however the initial model is never followed). Lastly, genetic modification will be done in order to make us more submissive.

All of these points are very important and bring us to a horrifying thought: can we imagine a human being with no cares, feelings, emotions or freedom eventually becoming a mindless zombie? Don't we display these actions now? Our corporate masters already keep us fashioned only to the idea of consumption with no desire for thought, other than obey without question. The only thing that matters is profit and consumer diligence. What happens to the planet when too many of these mindless humans overrun it and deplete the resources? Is this why the Majestic 12 insists on this apparent human genocide for the planet's benefit or their own? How far can we go with this idea of genetic modification anyway? The answer is so vague that one can ponder this on all levels. Is it the process of extracting DNA/RNA, altering the nervous system (endocrine), or curing common sicknesses in order to create a new type of humanoid more subservient to the original host?

UFO Contact in Ancient Times

In explaining the UFO concept in Maxwell's eyes, one unfortunately has to look at the religious symbols in order to understand that most of our beliefs stem from an extraterrestrial source from eons ago. All ancient beliefs considered "myths" by the modern world, are in fact the original accounts of ancient stories of UFO contact. Slowly more and more rational humans are discovering the plagiarism, manipulation of ancient knowledge, and the complete confusion that the Judeo-Christian and Islamic cults offer the common populace. Maxwell as we remember, does not expect religion to offer us any insight that could ascend us; rather to learn from its imperfection to realize that events, our humanity, and the world is more complicated than what the Torah, Koran, and bible myths have to offer. In one example, Maxwell covers the creation of man in the Genesis account pointing out that the language used is not to be taken literally. In Genesis 18, we can examine the following passage:

> *"18:1 And the Lord appeared to him by the oaks of Mamre, as he sat at the door of his tent in the heat of the day. 2 He lifted up his eyes and looked, and behold, three men were standing in front of him. When he saw them, he ran from the tent door to meet them and bowed himself to the earth 3 and said, "O Lord, if I have found favor in your sight, do not pass by your servant. 4 Let a little water be brought, and we wash your feet, and rest yourselves under the tree, 5 while I bring a morsel of bread, that you may refresh yourselves, and after that you may pass on—since you have come to your servant." so they said, "Do as you have said." 6 And Abraham went quickly into the tent to Sarah and said, "Quick! Three seahs of fine flour! Knead it, and make cakes." 7 And Abraham ran to the herd and took a calf, tender and good, and gave it to young man, who prepared it quickly. 8 Then he took curds*

> *and milk and the calf that they had prepared, and set it before them. And he stood by them under the tree while they ate. 9 They said to him, "Where is Sarah your wife?"* . . . .

The rest of the passage explains how Sarah did not believe Yahweh when he claimed she would have a son and even the subject of fear and doubt entered her mind as Yahweh claimed a son the very next year. There are certain discrepancies here that almost all the versions seem to omit. Sarah it seems is fixing dinner at the demand of her husband for three men whom were greeted by Abraham. Loosely translated, it seems three strange men passed by the camp of the Hebrews stationed in the wilderness were invited to eat, and offered to be cleansed by Abraham and his wife. When we study the actuality of a god, their bodies do not work the way that humans do. The need for a food offering suggests that these are in fact humans or humanoids far superior to Hebrew nomads, however still required food for their existence.

These three men denied the offer at first; however after Abraham insisted, they decided to join them both (the King James Version states this passage differently). All five of them ate dinner under the tree and after finishing two of the three men left and went about their "business." What this business was at the time unknown was later altered to fit the rest of the story in the next chapter. Who were these so called men, and why they left the third man behind solo? The passage states that both men traveled to the mythical cities of Sodom and Gomorrah; however, doesn't explain what they planned to do yet. Were the agendas different, or did the third man intentionally stay as if to do something with the couple? He explained that the third man happened to be a "creator god" who gave prophecies to the Abraham and then simply left. Although the passage calls the third man "lord," the true origin and name was *Annunaki*; which was the oldest Sumerian creator race that created humans living in the Indus Valley (the oldest human in recorded history). As we go further, Genesis 19 and the meaning of the passage shares the following confusing language:

> *"1 And there came two angles to Sodom at even; and Lot sat in the gate of Sodom; and Lot seeing them rose up to meet them; and he bowed himself with face toward the ground; 2 And he said, "Behold now; my lords, turn in, I pray you, into your servants house, and tarry all night, and wash your feet, and ye shall rise up early, and go on your ways. And they said, "Nay; but we will abide in the street all night. 3 And he pressed upon them greatly; and they turned in unto him, and entered his house; and he made them a feast, and did bake unleavened bread, and they eat. 4 But before they lay down, the men of the city, even the men of Sodom, compassed the house round, both old and young, all the people from every quarter: 5And they called unto Lot, and said unto him "Where are the men which came in to thee this night? Bring them unto us, that we may know them." 6 And Lot went out at the door unto them, and shut the door after him, 7 And said, "I pray you, brethren, do not so wickedly.*
>
> *8 Behold now, I have two daughters which have not known men; let me, I pray you, bring them unto you, and do ye to them as is good in your eyes; only unto these men do nothing: for there came they in to sojourn of my roof." 9 And they said, "Stand back." And they said again, "this one fellow came*

> *in to sojourn, and he will needs be a judge: now will we deal worse with thee, than with them." And they pressed sore upon the man, even Lot, and came near to break the door. 10 But the men put forth their hand, and pulled Lot into the house to them, and shut the door. 11 And they smote the men that were at the door of the house with blindness, both small and great: so that they wearied themselves to find themselves the door. 12 And the men said unto Lot, "Hast thou here any besides? son in law, and thy sons, thy daughters, and whatsoever thou hast in the city. Bring them out of this place: 13 For we will destroy this place, because the cry of them is waxen great before the face of the Lord; and the Lord hath sent us to destroy it." 14 And Lot went out, and spake unto his sons in law, which married his daughters and said "Up, get you out of this place; for the Lord will destroy this city. But it seemed as the one that mocked unto his sons in law . . . .*

The rest just describes so many discrepancies concerning the whole ordeal. The two "men" that were present in the previous chapter are now angels as described by the Hebrews. Apparently, Lot knew that they were coming as he waited by the gates of the city. They first refused his offer of lodging and food as they previously did to Abraham before; with their only interest being the streets at night for reasons unknown. It seems that they have no interest in talking to their "servants" unless they forced them by pleading. Again they ate like humans and washed themselves as of course Lot offered. It seemed he had to really "press against them greatly" as it described in verse three to force them to come into his house. By this time, the men of the city knew they were present also as they visited Lot's house to meet them.

Here is where things become unclear. It stated that men came from the "city" as well as Sodom, meaning there could be multiple cities around besides Gomorrah which they did not mention at all. First they introduced the men and then other "people," who came to look upon these humanoids that were obviously not like them. Not only did Lot call them lords, but they had power to subdue the people trying to attack Lot, after he refused entry into his house. Lot was willing to sacrifice his daughters whom he claimed were virgins in verse eight for the people to do as they saw fit; however, they were more interested in these male humanoids that were extremely attractive.

The problem here is that later as he was warned about the impending attack on the city, he acquired son in laws that somehow appeared in verse twelve. This is confusing, because if the daughters were virgins, that means they weren't married or sexually active. Either Lot was lying, or too many stories were mixed confusing the plot even more. Lot supposedly closed the door behind him to talk to the people in verse six; there is no mention of the door being opened after. In verse nine however, the people only mention one man besides Lot that needed to be judged, even attacking him and Lot. Why did they only mention one? What happened to the other man? When during this time did they leave the house to confront the people? In verse ten, after being attacked, both men appear again to save Lot from the people and in turn shut the door. This is when they blinded all men trying to enter the house; who after disappear out of the story. When they tell Lot that they were sent by "the lord" to destroy this city, they tell him to take his sons, daughters, son in laws, wife, and escape the city.

Now Lot having sons adds other family members not mentioned before. If the townspeople were indeed homosexual as they hinted, why didn't Lot offer his sons or sons in law? Why not himself or his wife? It was clear that these humanoid beings could defend themselves, so why this elaborate confrontation at his house? The story takes another strange turn later in verse sixteen, as only Lot, his wife and his two daughters are allowed to leave holding hands of these two men. What happened to the sons and the sons in law? Did they change their minds, or were they rejected at the last moment? The whole story as we see, is not well put together with many loopholes and mistaken identities making it a very confusing fairytale.

Towards the ending verse thirty-six, Lot even sleeps with his daughters placing the concept of incest into the story. The daughters fed him wine just as Noah's story went. With the concept of the two men, why were the townspeople so attracted to them? The obvious result was because they were handsome, and we can assume that the third man is of the same quality. Another loophole in religious law is that no man is to "see god" under any circumstances as stated in the beginning of the book (except for symbols such as the burning bush or other illusions). So why is Yahweh changing the rules now? What happened to secrecy? Why would this god commit such an act against his own rules; would that not make him inconsequential and irresponsible? Why did he want to share secrets with man, after all the mistakes they made? Could it be that these two alien humanoids traveled to cities of men to expose their obscure and crude nature?

These alien beings were obviously not monsters, as the homosexual men were interested in the two strangers. As a result, the obvious facts suggest that the third man and his companions were all similar in nature of an unknown race of beings. Maxwell adds to this by stating that man was already here, and the previous prototype of human beings did not reflect on our current physical quality; we were transformed and mutated [68]. The *Annunaki,* as we know from the beginning of the original creation story cause a genetic manipulation of more than one race to create another new being: humans. By creating us in their image, resulted in humans adhering their physical qualities and possibly some super mental intelligence.

With this process, a reformation of sorts genetically transpired for humans to fit their physical constructs and their behavioral patterns (i.e. jealousy, anger, murder, and other events in the Old Testament by Yahweh). This then makes the entire story based on human feelings which the gods do not obviously share. Since this mutation already occurred once, this new change that we can expect might change us into what? Could our physical bodies undergo new transformations into something more complex, even grotesque? Maxwell has added that these entities also have a caste system of social classes as humans have. Will we finally acquire some sort of status in their eyes after this new change? Will we become more subservient than we already are making humans a new breed of slaves?

"Angels" Versus "Sons of the Gods"

Going further into the subject of gods and angels, there is a significant difference between the "sons of the gods" and angels. The sons of the gods, (Horus, Hercules, Pluto, Buddha, Condom, Thor, Loki, etc . . .) are entities with physical bodies that we are fashioned to look like; however come from a non-terrestrial location. This location was not earthbound, meaning that they could be from any number of races existing within the universe. An angel on the other hand, is a spiritual entity (not pertaining to any Judeo-Christian belief) belonging to the race of *etheric* beings making them more powerful than the physical sons. Since all three men "walked together," this signifies that they were all of equal power, and the two others were not just subordinates of the third man. The Hebrew version twisted this idea of a special symbol of significance as to hide the truth of the origin of human creation. This union of sorts was more equal than we are led to believe making the symbol now worthless in the ancient sense.

Lucifer, the archenemy of *Yahweh*, (*Thor* vs. *Loki*, *Ahura Mazda* against his own shadow, *Amun-Ra* vs. *Apep* [*Apophis*], *Enki* vs. *Enlil*, etc . . .) was supposedly the first creation of the angels. This meant that he belonged to an entire different race of beings than the Hebrew creator god. When they first created humans, they seemed to be allies as they "created" the idea of paradise. Are we then led to believe that they are enemies, or could they in actuality have some sort of alliance against man? As we look through the Hebrew Old Testament, we see that both parties enjoy torturing man at some level whether it's proving one's loyalty, or making bets to see if the human's "faith" is extinguished as they did with Job [69]. How then we to decide which one represent the benevolent one and which is the "satan" (enemy)? This suggests that taking the bible seriously in any shape or form, is not an option since it distorts all concepts using poetic banter. Should we as humans view this as a campaign for a new candidate? We have to return to the original premise of the creation of humans by "Yahweh" and his anonymous guests, which now we know as an entire different race of aliens or etheric beings.

Between the *Annunaki* and this spiritual elemental race, they created a new hybrid race of man. With the original

Sumerian account, we find this creation to be a negative result for humans as we were designed for slave labor and the mining of gold [70]. Somehow, we were also embedded with special mental gifts and a soul entity residing in our physical bodies. For what reason do we receive these gifts from the gods? Do we humans believe we were created to destroy? Is this why the gods "leave us behind" as we see from Egyptian, Sumerian, and other ancient texts?

We are on our own, and we must rectify the situation without looking up at the heavens and begging for forgiveness. The answer may lay inside of us that were placed there for humans to discover who is fighting for us, and who is fighting against us. The sons of the gods as we may understand, were the ones who resulted in the mating of human women and powerful gods (*Zeus* morphed into a swan to seduce *Hera* with the result of creating *Hercules*, just as the Christian copy of Yahweh transforming into a dove to seduce Mary for Jesus). In order for a woman to be attracted to a man, the obvious stipulation remains in the physical. It would be highly unlikely that a woman would fall in love with a horrid beast-like creature (no matter how intoxicated she is!).

This "man" had to be sexually appealing with the result of their consummation creating the half-god/half-human hybrids that are still among us according to Maxwell [71]. These new creations as he furthers states, are "running the show" today in our time. Can they be trusted? Are they the result of our current situation and result of the events transpiring today? If this is the case, it would seem logically safe to assume that humans are not in their best interests (poverty, chaos, war, death, madness, ignorance, religious dogmatic mind control, etc . . .). Are these ancient legends of the past creating this end world scenario to appease their original alien forefathers? If they are in fact here as Maxwell believes, we as humans must consider the next ruler of our personal lives. Is the Sun King going to replace them, or is this another trick to force humans into deeper submission?

History of the Titans

Another entity that Maxwell presents us with was the giants or the *Titans* (the Hebrew refer to them as the *nephilim).* One specific Titan that Maxwell refered to originated from the Hebrew plagiarized account of the Babylonian/Sumerian flood story (the fragmented tablet excavated in Nippur; specifically the Utnapishtim episode in the Epic of Gilgamesh) called *Og of Basham* (or "king of the giants"). Legend spoke of one giant who survived the flood and was able reproduce more like himself. Apparently, they resembled humanoid form, just bigger in size. There have been mentions of giant-sized people living in *Tierra del Fuego,* Argentina referred to as the *Patagones* (which roughly translated as "big feet" signifying that the size of the individual was enormous in nature) during the time of the conquest by the Spaniards and the discovering of new lands by Magellan.

The region was later named Patagonia due to the fact the explorers came into contact with some of these individuals, and the large footprints that they left were too large to be categorized as normal human size [72]. Argentina was not the only place that we find these large skeletons of giant men and women. The United States (Minnesota, Pennsylvania, New York, Wisconsin, Ohio, and Nevada) contained skeletons of an enormous nature within underground Indian mounds with the shortest being only eight feet tall. The Pennsylvanian mound discovery was one of the greatest examples found that proved to display ancient giants roaming the lands of the American continent long ago:

> *"A large Indian mound near the town of Gasterville, Pa., has recently been opened and examined by a committee of scientists sent out from the Smithsonian Institute. At some depth from the surface a kind of vault was found in which was discovered the skeleton of a giant measuring seven feet two inches. His hair was coarse and jet black, and hung to the waist, the brow being ornamented with a copper crown. The skeleton was remarkably well preserved. Near it were also found the bodies of several children of various sizes, the remains being covered with beads made of bone of some kind. Upon removing these, the bodies were seen to be enclosed in a net—work of straw or reeds, and beneath this was a covering of the skin of some animal . . . . The relics have been carefully packed and forwarded to the Smithsonian Institute, and they are said to be the most interesting collection ever found in the United States. The explorers are now at work on another mound in Barton County, Pa . . . ." (From Ancient Man; A Handbook of Puzzling Artifacts. William R. Corliss, Sourcebook Project, 1978 American Antiquarian, 7:52, 1885)*

What does this tell us about these wondrous giants roaming our world in different locations around the globe? The bible only mentions them for one paragraph as if by mistake; however, the *Greek* and *Babylonian* account give us more explanations making it enough to question their existence as more than a hoax. The simple biblical explanation does not serve its purpose as authentic, which most religious scholars will claim. This goes beyond simple plagiarized scriptures; as we must investigate why they have disappeared, how they viewed us as humans, and if there are any live remnants left around the world. Maxwell makes an interesting point that "we look like them; they do not look like us." If this is reality, it is safe to say that more than one color of entities exist that have created the four original races we have seen. If we are a mere replica, how do we investigate our origins? We as humans, seem to set the standard on which race is superior to the other.

Coupled with the Hebrew Old Testament myth blacks, whites and Asians are mentioned only in this peace omitting the Native Americans. Was it the fact that Noah forgot to mention to his Caucasian wife that he also slept with a native woman? Did he leave her and her son to die along with all the other mystical and factual creatures never mentioned (dinosaurs, centaurs, dragons, pixies, unicorns, medusa/snake people, and the latter)? Did the seven authors that copied and pieced this asinine story together from other sources agree on the stipulations, or did they just butcher each other's work? Whatever really transpired, is now unknown and we are left with just the three races. The fourth one popped out of nowhere when the English, Dutch, Spanish, and the Vikings went out into the New World, gracing the ancient world with a "warm welcome" to the Native Americans. Through genocide and religious reformation (due to this story), most of the red skin is all but extinguished. Why do all the races hate each other on some level or another? Did our alien creators leave with us their disgust for their other enemies? Why do we hate to an extreme level that we try killing each other off? When they genetically bonded us with the beast to create "man," was this hate also part of the protocol? Is this a part of their DNA, or did we develop this character trait along the way?

Sun King Symbolism

The importance of the symbolic meaning of the Sun King is prevalent throughout the discussion. It must be investigated why this concept is a mystery with only a handful of chosen members of "special people" aware of its existence. The group mainly responsible according to Maxwell is the Illuminati along with the ancient symbols they use. Maxwell's research states that this king is to rule humans between two mountains of the east [73]. The significance of two or twin symbols plays a big part in this meaning and prophecy. These twin entities whether they are twin towers, obelisks (or any other Egyptian temples, symbols etc . . .) carry an ancient meaning now void from our present knowledge. As Sir Francis Bacon reminds us, "knowledge is power" making the secret societies one step ahead or more than the regular citizen.

What exactly are the two mountains they mention, and where are they located? Where do we look to the east, and at what vantage point? Anywhere where we stand in any part of the world, one can view the east having a different location due to the planet being a sphere. For Spain, the west is the United States, as for China the United States would be east. The origin of this location poses difficultly in where the location of the Sun King's emergence would take place. Could it be the location of the Indus Valley civilization? Is this why the United States continues to fight their "war" against the terrorists that threaten our "national security" in the Middle East? Is this also the reason why the self-proclaimed state of Israel is centered right near the location of the *Annunaki* return?

Could this be more complicated than a few Arab freedom fighters who want the black gold themselves, and the destruction of their Jewish foes? Interestingly enough, the Mesopotamian god *Shamash* (that the Hebrews also adapted to make Yahweh) happens to be the Sumerian/Babylonian sun god. From the tablet, we can see his emblem is a sun shining as he sits on his throne. He is also known as the god depicted from the Sumerian clay tablets as the "one who rises through the mountains." Could it be that the god Shamash is to return to rule again after much time away from his human slaves? Why does the Pope fashion himself as a representation of the god as to sit and utilize the ancient symbols for his own purpose [74]? Does the Christian demigod serve the ancient Sumerian sun god? The obvious signs display the Judeo-Christian interest worshipping and using ancient symbols not pertaining to their culture, and paying homage to an older civilization. This could explain why the orthodox Jews have the illusion that they are the "chosen ones." Will this misinterpretation and the robbing of ancient cultures, lead to our doom simply because we really have no idea who or what we are worshipping?

Our cultures that we learn from are obvious symbols or representations of our many creators from the stars. They have damaged us thorough history with examples of poverty, war, famine, disease, and the superiority complex that we have over each other. With this result, it seems that we may not be able to deny our fate: the human race will be scientifically altered from human beings into a subservient, obedient creature. Maxwell is just pointing out our fate as we have discussed, and this is something that people do not want to believe or hear because it threatens all of their simple existence. Life is a cycle, and since the *Annunaki* have completed this genetic project before, it is time again to alter our conscious and behavioral patterns. The Christians refer to this as the "second coming" myth along with the prediction of revelation. We must view how our current situation has left the world in a state of disarray. The people do not seem to care about each other anymore, rather just on consumption and technology. Organized religion has further enslaved us as we adhere to the victim consciousness whenever we are faced with a problem.

The pharmaceutical companies force us to rely on them for "health solutions" meanwhile they take all holistic, botanical and natural approaches for the elite as the poor suffer the experimental damage. Our rainforests contain plants and other cures for many ailments/diseases on the planet earth man made or not [75]. The idea of profit has festered within them as they use the mass to give themselves power and control. Our food is controlled and given chemicals to destroy the only muscle we need to utilize to free us from submission: our brain.

Artificial sweeteners (aspartame, acesulfame potassium, and sucralose), high fructose corn syrup, sodium benzoate and other forms of MSG constantly enter our bodies and systematically destroy us mentally and physically. After our physical bodies take the toll, then the "healthcare" system comes to our rescue to cure the symptoms, but not the disease. We have allowed them to poison us, to damage our DNA and our nervous system as to dumb us down for reformation. They promise us that they are interested in our well-being; however, they seem more interested in our spiritual being and destroying it. After we are transformed into a new genetic culture, will our spiritual essence still be in tact? Will all cultures be affected or just the slave class we now have?

Maxwell describes the word culture as another symbol we can utilize. The human culture is similar to a culture viewed by scientists under a microscope. We were fashioned by a group of galactic scientists under their "microscope" to allow us to develop, and then watched us emerge into what we represent today. We could be compared to a bacteria or disease festering and destroying everything around us. Could reducing our number cause us to become less harmful in the eyes of our new masters? Humans have been following this protocol throughout history in reducing the numbers of a certain group in order to achieve a goal. The English experimented with the Natives, Hitler experimented with the Jews, Stalin and the poor, etc . . . In fact, Hitler was trying to formulate a new example of a perfect human for the future. Where did we as humans get these ideas? Maxwell states that the ancient knowledge from Egypt and Sumer helped these groups in their quest for altering humanity [76].

The English have focused on Egypt as we have seen from their museums. The capital of Egypt; Cairo is the symbol for Mars. Maxwell has shown that the *Annunaki* have a direct correlation with Mars and the ideas of pyramids. The Egyptians themselves do not realize, but they have Mars as their capital here on planet Earth. This could hint at the possibility that some of the entities among us, are still here in Egypt walking around in humanoid form. With the discoveries by Hoagland displaying the pyramids of the exact same design on Mars and the Moon, the ridiculous story of any humans or even more absurdly building the pyramids, is asinine [77].

All historic and ancient monuments that we see standing today that survived the passage of time clearly indicate that humans had no part in the design. What exactly do they represent and mean? These alien symbols possess a far deeper meaning than we are led to believe. The pyramids of Giza are lined perfectly with the Orion-Osiris belt, and they are able to position the pyramids with one hundred percent accuracy as they follow the star's path. Although there are quarryman's inscriptions of Khufu (Cheops) found within the great pyramid, is questionable at least. There seem to be no other markings beside it, and no carbon ash left by torches, that would obviously be used to construct the inner chambers that need illumination to see.

Maxwell himself in the 1980s spoke to an ex-CIA agent called Virgil Armstrong (also known as the "hero of Sedona, AZ") who discussed the reality of people actually living on Mars since the mid-80s [78]. As we remember as well, the movie *Total Recall* (1990) tells us of Schwarzenegger's journey and experiences of Mars in the future. Although the movie was based on the original story by Phillip K. Dick's We Can Remember It For You Wholesale, the Martian concept was added by story creators to maybe hint at us possible government activities? Maxwell also discusses the man called *Henry Deacon* (a pseudonym; not to be confused with the sci-fi character on the show *Eureka*) who happened to be a Livermore physicist, really went to Mars using a "jump gate" to go between planets [79]. He also stated that the U.S. government has had many bases there since the 1960s. This idea would be equivalent to the movie *DOOM* (2004) where the space marines actually used a teleportation device, to navigate them from Nevada to the Martian base Olduvai within mere seconds.

Are these symbols just the imagination of a science fiction mind? Are we so boring and convoluted with such fear as to step outside the realm of our benign social constructs, and usher ourselves into a new world that has been there all along? Germany on the other hand focused on Babylon and Sumer. Many of the symbols Germany used and now the United States use are taken from these civilizations. Maxwell points out that the United States is currently using symbols from Phoenicia, Syria, Ancient Rome, and Britannia. Whatever the symbols we view today, have a darker and deeper history unknown to us.

As we entertained the idea of U.S occupation of the Middle East, Maxwell discusses the possible reasons why the United States would never leave. Despite all of the political jargon and religious nonsense, we find the idea of *stargates.* William Henry, a researcher interested in Tarot and the inner spirit, stated that there is in fact a stargate in the heart of Iraq where ancient Sumer resided [80]. The stargate itself is where the ancient gods of old emerged from as they journeyed from earth to other distant planets. The idea was entertained in Hollywood through the sci-fi franchise created by Ronald Emmerich and Dean Devlin called *Stargate* (1994).

The movie itself is entertaining and full of adventure based on true facts of the gods represented by RA (ree-hu), who descended on Earth during its primitive state to encounter humans in their raw form. He then enslaves them and uses these created stargates to transport humans all around the universe to other planets for mining of a certain special element. The impossibilities that we deem as "entertainment," may reflect our past history and our future. Maxwell points out that Hussein himself, with the occupation of Iraq before the Gulf War, had to do with a device that was called a stargate [81]. Where he acquired it from or if it was even real remains in question. We are told by the mass media that Kuwait, a "helpless nation," was occupied for their oil and that we as the "big brother" of the planet should not allow tyranny against democracy. Hussein supposedly knew of this stargate and planned to use it for his own purposes. What were the purposes of Hussein in terms of using this stargate?

Task Force 20, a task force designator assigned to the United States Second Fleet in the Atlantic, was in charge of routing out HVTs (high value targets) such as Hussein, before he could utilize this weapon. What are the purposes of the United States and its occupation of the territory for the last eleven years? Why did the U.S build an embassy the size of one hundred four acres, almost the same size as the Vatican (one hundred and nine acres)? Henry Deacon tells us of a man made stargate in Los Alamos California, created by the same technology that was "given" to us [82]. Could these stargates also be utilized by the alien visitors as well, or do we humans occupy it only? Maxwell believes that the United States feared the coming of this alien group and do not know what to expect. Will the date be 12/21/2012? We are being led to believe certain ideas may go "viral" in a very short time; however by the time people know it is an actuality it would be too late.

The Philadelphia Experiment

Another interesting group of ideas that Maxwell covered concerned the *Philadelphia experiment* and the concept of time travel. Preston Nichols and Al Bielek both offered us ideas that stem beyond fantasy and enter the realm of reality. As far as the Philadelphia experiment goes, the U.S government has made it their main goal to discredit any information of these events as realistic. Also known as the *secrets of the Montauk* or *Project Rainbow*, certain events transpired that could not be labeled as fantasy. During WWII, the United States had plans to defeat the Axis powers using a technology that could make ships disappear and reappear wherever the controller desired.

They also wanted to create a ship capable of being undetected by magnetic mines and/or radar [83]. Initiating the planned attack on Pearl Harbor in 1941, the United States could now apply Einstein's Unified Field Theory that the U.S navy believed to be unfinished. The U.S.S Eldridge was the supposed boat that completed the task of this theory, which caused the lives of the crew, imbedding them within the ship's hull after complete time displacement. Many witnesses including Bielek himself as well as *Carlos Miguel Allende* (Marine Corps 1943) had many bizarre details concerning evidence that described the boat traveling from one place to another in mere seconds:

> *"The worse side effects of the experiment occurred when men became "stuck" or "locked into" what seems to be another dimensional space. Getting stuck consisted of becoming invisible and being unable to move, speak, or interact with other people for a period of time. Allende told about these events in his letters to Dr. Jessup. The ship's crew members identified the occurrence of "getting stick" as "Hell incorporated" . . . . The fires could not be stopped, despite multiple attempts to quench the flames. Needless to stay, the laying of hands was discontinued from that point on. Then, men started going into the "deep freeze," when a man would be frozen for several days to several months. During this time, the man is completely aware of others and their actions but was unable to communicate to them or interact with them . . . . The man who was stuck for 6 months went completely insane by the*

> *time he got out. Carlos Allende wrote: "Usually a deep freeze man goes mad, stark raving, gibbering, running mad, if his freeze is far more than a day in our time." (The Philadelphia Experiment, p. 42-44)*

Maxwell added that upon these experiments using recently acquired alien technology, "open doors" were created in order to alter us. What the ramifications are exactly, Maxwell does not go into detail, but as Bielek: "the Philadelphia Experiment was a key part of American history because it demonstrates what a government is willing to do to have an advantage in a war." He makes a point in terms of the uncaring results that may occur when tampering with technology that we have no idea about. Humans will do anything for the opportunity to rise above all others to claim the glory and benefits.

While this door remained open, Maxwell states that certain unknown races have traveled through this window of opportunity to do a "job." What kind of job are they here to accomplish? It is for our benefit, or will it destroy us? Did some of us have the privilege to pass through this door to the other side? What mysteries lay waiting on the other side of the door: another dimension, planetary body, or alternate reality? If the government causes more damage than good, discover new places, or destroy and create enemies, are they really the ones to represent as humans? Do we want those making decisions for us while we pay the price for their mistakes? Whatever they do and have done, reflect on all of us as a race, henceforth fulfilling the term: the fate of many in the hands of the few.

Why do we as humans have the illusion for change and a better future? The only time we ever work together is in the face of danger; however, the true intentions of every single individual remain hidden under the guise of false faces and agendas. We have to look at the facts about ourselves; we all want certain things in life and will do anything to get it. We really do not worry about conscience, unless we fall too deep as gain is the goal. We seem to use whoever is around us to get what we want. With this bizarre human behavior, how can we really trust each other?

Can we really go the distance for someone we do not know and rely on that same person in the process? The aftermath of the future events will tell us if we will change or forever remain the same. Maxwell believes that the U.S government is in league with UFOs of a negative nature [84]. We have to analyze who really is the threat here. Humans will fear anything that we do not understand. A new force change will emerge upon us and Maxwell suggests we must counteract this movement in order to reestablish (or attempt) humanity because we are losing it. Maxwell does not remain optimistic about our future, but he shares what he can to inform humans about this situation.

We are creatures of habit no doubt, so changing into something entirely different overnight seems impractical. Even in the years to come, there is no denying the mark we have left here on this planet due to our ignorance, foolishness, and uncaring attitude towards each other and all organisms. We are a competitive species that cares not about how to get to the top, rather just arriving there victorious. Later, when we have reached our zenith, some begin to have a conscience about things as we fill ourselves with guilt, pity, anger, or pride (others simply are void of any soul or feelings as it has been eliminated). Everything has a price as we have been told, and Maxwell believes this price will allow the enemies of our creators to use the sole agenda of domination of our species. Maxwell adds that his mission is to alert humanity to put a halt to this enemy from engaging in genetic mutation that they have in store for us [85].

He may be sincere; however he is not stressing the fact that humans are also losing our intellectual freedom due to our current train of thought. We as a society are not as intellectual as before because of the digital age along with AI, are doing all the thinking for us. Being lazy is our new freedom; surrendering away our only gift that would save us if we know how to use it properly . . . . our minds. As humans need help in order to figure certain things out, where we gather information from is vital in our investigation.

Maxwell like all of us noted this as a fact and gives credit where credit is due. Most of his research originates from an individual called *Manly Palmer Hall*. Born March 18, 1901, Hall was an educator, author and mystic from Canada. According to Maxwell, he was an educator who never promoted anything negative although belonging to a Masonic order. Upon his death on August 29, 1990, he bestowed upon Maxwell all of his research journals (which Maxwell considered to be a monumental gift) which contained about eighty books of esoteric material, six ninety minute lectures, and forty-six subjects and rarities that many of us would like to know [86]. Maxwell did not plan to share any of the volumes or any other information concerning Hall's findings, because the information was not intended for public view.

Why would Hall as an accomplished author, educator, mason, and esoteric master need to share his information with Maxwell (who was clearly against all Masonic orders)? Did he regret what he discovered? Did he believe certain humans had a right to know what was going on? Did he believe in the greater human good? The only topic Maxwell mentioned about the research was that the Obama administration is run by many negative powers who mean humans harm with the possibility of WWIII. This hidden knowledge leaves the rest of humanity in the dark as to what is happening; however the U.S government we can assume is not out for the greater good of mankind.

As we close this discussion, we must ponder many questions. Maxwell offers us his insight on a twisted, complex, and secretive world that seems void of hope and a future for human beings. He states that the Illuminati will bring down the United States very soon. He also states that they cannot be stopped and that there is no reasonable evidence for America or the world for that matter, to last any longer. The awaited light that we are graciously waiting for at the end of the tunnel is really a train coming our way at full speed.

According to Maxwell, people are too stupid, unread, ignorant, greedy, and misinformed with the bottom line being that they just do not care. According to Ludwig von Hessen, "people have always supported a dictator, and they always will." This statement is true because there has never been an instance in recent history of a real uprising against a dictatorship from freedom except for the American Revolution. The sad part is that only three percent of the population of the colonies took arms against their British masters. Maxwell assures that this monocle of freedom will never happen again. Why are we so accustomed to be ruled this way? Is it in our nature to allow control over what to eat, how to think, feel, when to sleep, and what we should dedicate our lives to? Why are we not sincere with ourselves? Why do we allow culture to develop and mold our minds into savage slaves of our corporate masters only looking for profit on their behalf? Maxwell tells us the obvious truth through symbols and their meanings; however it is up to us to figure out what those symbols represent on an individual level. Many things have been done that cannot be redeemed, as it is painfully obvious we are on a one track mind heading to our demise. As demonstrated by the natural cycle, all organisms eventually come to an end. Is this the example we want to leave as we disappear into the primordial ooze of creation?

Kerry Cassidy decided to comment on Maxwell's views and ask him why he was so pessimistic (in a passive way, without being direct). She strongly believed that there were some races here willing to "save us" and that we have a chance as people to rise up and become one to ascend to the greater meaning of life together. Maxwell already stated the painful truth, and Cassidy was reluctant to hear it; however she is not alone in this.

Humans all do this as we have to invent a fantasy world in order to escape the harshness of reality. The problem lies in the seriousness of trying to return to the surface from our fantasy into the realistic world. Those who control our destiny are aware of our weakness and have supported us in destroying ourselves with little effort. Cassidy views Maxwell as a messenger to save us, as her preconceived ideas got the best of her. We are all responsible for creating an impenetrable shield of fear and lies around us. We are also responsible for our own demise and the misrepresentation of symbols that we have used to drive us into the deep end of the sea of our own creation. All we seem to have now is borrowed time.

End Notes

[1] Karl Marx. *Critique of Hegel's Philosophy of Right*. Cambridge University Press: Joseph O'Malley (1970).

[2] Project Camelot. "Jordan Maxwell at the Awake and Aware Conference." Los Angeles, California (September 2009).

[3] Ibid 2.

[4] Associated Press "Virgin Mary grilled cheese sandwich sells for $28,000." *MSNBC News* (November 2004).

[5] Daily Mail Reporter. "Jesus really does exist inside us: woman claims to see the image of Christ in her chest x-ray." *Daily Mail U.K.* (December 2010).

[6] Ibid 2.

[7] Ibid 2.

[8] Jordan Maxwell. *Matrix of Power: How the World Has Been Controlled by Powerful People Without Your Knowledge*. The Book Tree (May 2003).

[9] Ibid 2.

[10] Jordan Maxwell and Ernest Busenbark. *Symbols, Sex, and the Stars*. The Book Tree (January 2010).

[11] Ibid 10.

[12] Jordan Maxwell. *That Old-Time Religion: The Story of Religious Foundations*. The Book Tree (May 2003).

[13] Ibid 2.

[14] Joseph Fontenrose. "Dagon and El" *Oriens 10.2*: pp.277-279 (December 1957).

[15]religionstinks.xanga.com/669573192/item/

[16] Lloyd M. Graham. *Deceptions and Myths of the Bible*. Citadel Press (June 2000).

[17] Ibid 2.

[18] Ibid 16.

[19] Ibid 12.

[20] Geoffrey Dennis. "Solomon the Sorcerer." *Jewish Myth, Magic, and Mysticism* (January 2009).

[21] Ibid 2.

[22] Geoffrey Ashe. *Stonehenge: The Arthurian Encyclopedia*. Peter Bedrick Books: New York (1986).

[23] Ibid 2.

[24] "Subliminal messages in Hollywood movies." *Subconscious-mind.org*.

[25] Ibid 2.
[26] Ibid 2.
[27] Associated Press. "Protestant Church Apologizes for Massacring Native Americans." *Fox News* (November 2009).
[28] Ibid 2.
[29] Ibid 2.
[30] Ibid 2.
[31] Ibid 27.
[32] Ibid 2.
[33] Kersey Graves. *The World's Sixteen Crucified Saviors or Christianity before Christ.* Truth Seeker Co. Inc.; 6th Rev and En Edition (June 1960).
[34] Ibid 33.
[35] Richard E. Rubenstein. *When Jesus Became God: The Struggle to Define Christianity During the Last Days of Rome.* Mariner Books (July 2000).
[36] Acharya S. *The Christ Conspiracy: The Greatest Story Ever Sold.* Adventures Unlimited Press. (July 1999).
[37] Ibid 2.
[38] Ibid 36.
[39] Ibid 16.
[40] Ibid 16.
[41] Ibid 12.
[42] Ibid 2.
[43] Ibid 2.
[44] Ibid 2.
[45] Michael Shore. "Do Illuminati Lizards Rule?—David Icke's Case." *Rense.com* (August 2004).
[46] "Project Camelot Interviews Leo Zagami" Oslo, Norway (February 2008).
[47] "Leo Zagami exposed by Greg Szymanski and Slats Grobnick." *Investigative Journal*; Libertyradiolive.com (May 2008).
[48] Ibid 2.

[49] Ibid 10.

[50] 1 Corinthians 7:2.

[51] Quran 2:228, Quran 2:223.

[52] Acharya S. "Pakistani Muslim Rapist Admits Women Have No Rights or Opinions in Islam." *Free Thought Nation* (May 2011).

[53] Associated Press. "Islam and Rape." *Wall Street Journal* (August 2006).

[54] Austin Cline. "Malaysia: Muslim Women Fighting Back for Equal Rights." *About.com* (June 2005).

[55] Ibid 2.

[56] Ibid 2.

[57] Ayn Rand. "United States was found as a Constitutional Republic and not a Democracy." *The Market Oracle U.K.* (November 2008).

[58] Ibid 2.

[59] Ibid 2.

[60] Project Camelot. "Jordan Maxwell: The Take Over of Planet Earth." Los Angeles California (September 2008).

[61] S.G. Wood. *The American Revolution: A History*. Modern Library (2002).

[62] Info wars. "In your face: the Globalists' language is hidden in plain view." *Infowars.com* (April 2004).

[63] Ibid 60.

[64] Rit Nosotro. "Christianity's Bloody History." *Hyperhistory.net* (2000, 2010).

[65] Ibid 2.

[66] Ibid 60.

[67] Ibid 60.

[68] Ibid 60.

[69] Job 1: 1-12.

[70] Estelle Nora Amrani. "The Annunaki" *vibrani.com* (January 1999).

[71] Ibid 60.
[72] Jorge Fondebrider. *Versiones de Patagonia*. Buenos Aires Argentina: Emece Editores S.A. (2003).
[73] Ibid 60.
[74] aloha.net/~mikesch/verita.htm.
[75] Tony Medley. "The Rainforest." *Tonymedley.com* (1995, 2009).
[76] Ibid 60.
[77] Richard C. Hoagland and Mike Bara. *Dark Mission—Book One: The Secret History of the National Aeronautics and Space Administration*. Feral House Books (2007).
[78] Ibid 60.
[79] Project Camelot. "An interview with 'Henry Deacon,' a Livermore Physicist." *Projectcamelot.org* (October 2006).
[80] Chad Stuemke. "Stargates hidden in plain sight." *Unknown Country* (February 2011).
[81] Ibid 60.
[82] Ibid 79.
[83] William Moore and Charles Berlitz. *The Philadelphia Experiment: Project Invisibility*. Fawcett (March 1995).
[84] Ibid 60.
[85] Ibid 60.
[86] Ibid 60.

The possibility of reduced-time interstellar travel, either by advanced extraterrestrial civilizations at present or ourselves in the future, is not fundamentally constrained by physical principles.

–Dr. Harold Puthoff

VI

Dan Burisch: "Majestic" Interactions of a Futuristic UFO Paradox vs. John Titor: The Human or Computer Program from the Future?

The idea of time travel is apparent in our pop culture as well as our entertainment venues since the 1950s. Sci-fi shows such as the *Twilight Zone* and the *Outer Limits*, have tantalized us with the possibility of going back or forward in time to either experience our life in a new light, or change the mistakes of the past. Dan Burisch, who actually claims to have been associated with the legendary Majestic 12 group, has a speculative view of the government at work on some of the subjects that are considered just myths or nonsense.

He discusses his role within the government dealing with alien groups that he believes are actually future versions of the human race from the range of forty-five and fifty-two thousands years in our future; from two different potential time lines [1]. Our job now is to investigate these claims from an individual concerning our future, past, and what possibilities await us due to our behavior in multiple time lines of a clouded vision. Are these aliens whom we have glorified, worshipped, and feared really future versions of "us" so to speak? Does Burisch point out that there are no other types of races in this universe? Could we in fact, be alone only keeping company with our versions of a past, present, and future?

Burisch considers himself a microbiologist and a scientist trying to help out mankind from destroying themselves. He also claims to be a twenty year member of the infamous group Majestic 12 since the year 1986 [2]. He then worked on and developed programs such as *Project Lotus*, *Project Aquarius*, interacted with aliens that he nicknamed "j-rod," and lived in a secret government facility known as *S-4* near Area 51 first made public by Bob Lazar [3]. Through research however, Burisch may be fabricating his story to a high degree. It seems that he has two other aliases; one being *Catselas*, and the other being *Crain*. Why would he need to announce himself as three different people? Although his birth certificate states his name as "Danny Benjamin Crain," he later had it changed to Burisch for reasons unknown. Many believe he has started a cult, giving people the idea that he has worked with aliens stored in the infamous Area 51 base located in Nevada.

Channel 8 news in Las Vegas put their lead investigative reporter *George Knapp* to help clear this misunderstanding of a man who had such bold claims. Through his investigation, Knapp had discovered as well, three different names for a man who called himself doctor, scientist, and secret operative. Knapp also found that Burisch himself back in 1994 was only a volunteer teach at the *Boys&Girls* club as Dan Crain [4]. Knapp pointed bizarre behavior concerning Burisch as he claimed to have spoken with "angels" that spoke Hebrew located within the base. Angels as we have learned are an elemental race completely separated from humans or physical alien types. The idea that Hebrew was the language they spoke would be speculative, simply because he was attributing to the Hebrew myths. The oldest languages recorded are Sanskrit (circa five thousand years) or Tamil (circa 10,000 years) [5].

His wife Deborah Burisch seems to be his only strong supporter except for his mother Dodie Crain (who seems to doubt her son and has not seen him in over twelve years) in his belief that he discovered the "first seed of life" on Frenchman's mountain located east of Las Vegas [6]. Along with his colleague Marcia McDowell, they claim to be secretive operatives of the government which further complicates the story in general. Do we trust the corporate agenda new station that may be purposefully damaging Burisch's credentials in order to hide reality of secret government's plans? Or are they exposing a delusional man's fantasy about working for the government and being friends with a future humanoid alien? The situation seems ambiguous by changing his name, falsifying that he received degrees from universities that do not have records of him attending there, and claiming to have worked with people within the government that do not know him:

> *"This is the biggest bullshit story I have ever heard in my life. Anybody that actually believes this guy should be ashamed of themselves. I have never worked at Tonopah. I have never met this knucklehead." (Bob Lazar; Channel 8 news, Las Vegas Nevada, 2000)*

Another retired military general Colonel John Alexander, also reported the views of Burisch's claims as "highly improbable" [7]. Knapp has found that Burisch has never served in the military although they have a sticker of Nellis AFB allowing access and have worn military fatigues with no record in the military whatsoever. Stony Brook University in New York states he never attended as a student there. He claims that they have erased his records; however, this is something that cannot be proven so it his word against theirs [8]. Knapp had also discovered that when he claimed to be in New York earning his degree, he had a full time job in Las Vegas as a parole officer. Burisch changed his story claiming he flew back and forth to New York on weekends. He also met his wife working together as officer he claims; however, the state of Nevada displays she was an actual prisoner there on drug charges [9]. He did however; receive a B.A in psychology at the University of Las Vegas. As far as the PhD claim from Stony Brook, the university stated that it does not verify someone's post graduate credentials, meaning that anyone could put whatever they deemed appropriate for their future professional profile. This is not unheard of since recently, MIT suffered a blow to its institution as Marilee Jones falsified her PhD and was forced to resign [10].

The Three Races

In 2006, Project Camelot had a chance to interview Burisch and his associate in a location located in Las Vegas concerning his involvement with black projects, the idea of future technology concerning stargates and a device called the "Looking Glass" (which allowed an individual to view future prospects within certain timelines). Burisch considered Project Lotus to be an "accessory project" with funding that was not of a critical nature. Ironically, he introduced this project as an "earthshaking experience" at what he called the TAU-IX Conference [11].

He described this secret conference as the push for the preservation of humanity. It is not known by most of the public, and it is renewed every nine years with the belief that the number nine is sacred to the Zeta Reticulum factions of alien groups involved with the government. The treaty according to Burisch, was originally established in 1958 and renewed four times within our current history in 1967, 1976, 1985, and 1994. The final treaty before its closure originally set for

2003. "Negotiations" and unknown reason pushed for a 2005 date. His only response concerning this was that there was a breakup of the original MJ-12 (Majestic 12) and the Illuminati factions to form a new group: the CotM (Committee of the Majority) [12]. Others experts disagree and push the original date to 1955; however this detail is argued only among those who claim to know about this conference.

According to Burisch, the current human representation at this conference is two groups known as the Magi and the Illuminati (with a few members of the UN present). There are also three main groups of nonhuman origin as well: one being from the *Republic Society of Zetan* (what Burisch calls "j-rods"), the *Rogue Zetans* (also known as "j-rods"), and finally the *Orion "Talls"* or *Nordics.* He gave a brief history on each group in order for the "uninformed" to have a better idea on just whom we were dealing with. The Republic Society is the alleged descendants of the human survivors that fled underground when a catastrophe affected the whole Earth causing billions of deaths. He added that the survivors sought refuge in the shelters built by the Majestic 12 back in the 1950s, preparing for this sort of future event considering the Nibiru "winged planet" scenario proposed by the ancient Sumerians.

Eventually as they recovered from this event, they moved off planet from Earth to Zeta Reticuli *in* the future splitting into another group of individuals. This other group of individuals was the Rogues, whom Burisch described as those controlled now by the Illuminati and were forty-five thousand years from the future on our current lifetime (also called P45). The Republic Society according to Burisch, was fifty-two thousand years ahead in our timeline (P52). The last group called the *Orion "Talls"* (which Burisch also mentions were P52), were descendants of the human survivors above the surface of the planet Earth during this event. They eventually find their way to the star system Orion [13].

If this was to be true, then the previous statement of these beings being "nonhuman entities" was not accurate seeing that they come from the human survivors of the past. This also could hint that these beings may have traveled back in time to accomplish an agenda of sorts. These "treaties" were established for a purpose and negotiations supposedly took place in New Mexico for the last time in 2005. Burisch considered them time travelers and that they were not able to sustain themselves in our current environment. He stated that they needed some sort of artificial dome or protective environment to communicate with humans. The reason was due to the fact that they could only expose themselves to their own environment in the future timeline. Existing in our standard pressure and temperature was not possible so they were given "special units" to sustain their life intact at these meetings, so that were easily able to move. Burisch called this device a "stroller system" that was encapsulated on wheels that might resemble a carriage of sorts [14].

The project called *Lotus* was discussed at this conference and the P45 group wanted this project implemented in the treaty with humans. This was done because the P45 group needed to ameliorate their personal neuropathies. This was considered crucial and the project in their eyes and had a potential value, since they were suffering from a condition. Burisch claimed that he argued this move and did not want them to allow this technology, since it was not part of the "natural process" of a creator system in this universe (not controllable by humankind, aliens, or humanoids; only an invisible deity). This concept seemed asinine, since the future human factions have already broken the natural system by manipulating time and venturing in the past for their own agendas. Logic and common sense were void, as his explanations unfolded into failure. If these humanoid factions have indeed disturbed the natural order, they could easily change their current predicament in order to repair their physical and mental deficiencies that Burisch claimed them to have.

As we have mentioned earlier, the aliens represented three human lineages that exist simultaneously in our current timeline in two different points in time (with a separation of about seven thousand years). He described these timelines as branching into two outcomes where the P45 (what he also called Greys, besides "j-rods") came from "timeline 2" and the P52 (Nordics) come from "timeline 1." The *Republic Society* (also P52) is never mentioned again as they disappear into obscurity. The concept itself was confusing, as Burisch changed his description every time the events manifested another possibility.

In order to grasp this concept, we must first investigate what timeline we are currently headed in and research whether there was only two timelines to begin with. The concept of time travel is more complicated than just two simple outcomes, and it may have many branches of possibilities resembling a tree branch structure. Kerry Cassidy during the interview asked him a question about the infamous Reptilian groups and their agendas. Burisch stated that the term "reptilian" was a misnomer and that the proper terminology was "j-rod," which he also considered a Grey. He attributed the misnomer to the fact that according to him, they appeared to change their skin which made them appear reptilian in nature (what he called "praying mantis") [15].

They appeared to lurch forward due to their sicknesses and syndromes that he claimed they were trying to eliminate. While personifying the "praying mantis," in fact could change their appearance as he suggested. Burisch tried to remain inclusive, but stated that it was hard to believe that most witnesses have seen "reptiles." He appeared to give a more scientific approach in describing them based on their pathophysiological and biological constructions. He stated that people without a scientific background, would not be able to determine these key factors and would use the term "reptilian" to describe them as a common mistake. Burisch himself did not have any scientific background although he claimed to be a microbiologist. Nevertheless, Cassidy pushed for an answer determined that there were Reptilian Illuminati factions within alien groups; however, he denied knowledge of any of her claims and stated he was never briefed on "Reptilian-Draco" phenomenon [16].

The Ascension from Childhood

In order to understand where Burisch conjured the belief that he was interacting with UFO interests and/or supernatural forces, we need to view his experiences as a child in his perception. In turn, we may be able to distinguish if he is telling a sort of truth, or is completely delusional and immersed in his fantasy world of "extraterrestrial excitement." He described his life changing event in the summer of 1973, where his grandfather took him to the park located somewhere in southern California. They engaged in a game of baseball that he described was one of his favorite activities. At this time, he was nine years old and witnessed a strange occurrence with the grass at his feet eventually growing a black shadow. The shadow formed a triangular shape covering the sun in his location. After, Burisch stated there was a flash of light and he felt time had passed without him knowing. His grandfather had what he stated as a "terrified" look about him; however refused to discuss the transpiring event with him or anybody. Due to this incident, Burisch explained this incident for the grandparents moving out of his home (due to the difficulty between his parents as the relationship went downhill from there) [17].

From this moment on, Burisch began to have dreams where he supposedly walked to his bathroom opening this door, then becoming unaware of anything else after that (everything else went blank). He did however; add that he encountered an entity that he called "Harry" which he also described as his "little friend." He then contradicted the story by stating that he had no visual memory. He added the fact that his parents naturally did not believe him, but it seems that he was also unsure of his story as he hesitated and refused eye contact with Cassidy during this point in the interview.

Using the excuse that he was adolescent at the time, he could not distinguish what was real and what was not. Incidentally, he changed the story at the baseball park describing a "tall" person now standing next to his grandfather (this later piece of information only took place as he got older). Another interesting fact was that Burisch did not know whether or not these were his real parents as he describes them as "mom" and "dad" growing up. Could this be the reason for his changed name from Crain to Burisch? His mother stated that Burisch's birth certificate had the name "Crain," so where did the name *Catselas* emerge from? Why the elaborate mess of last names as to confuse not only the people trying to understand is story, but himself as well?

Another alien entity that he called *Chi'el'ah* (pronounced kai-el-la), later displayed to him what happened at his childhood in 1973 at a later date. According to his claim, Burisch was able to view his younger self "pulled" at the chest and brought upward into a chevron (triangular) craft. He also mentioned that he viewed this event at the S-4 facility, where he also saw his grandfather panicking and crying near the tree. After these events, he was laid upon a table next to other children, especially next to one "special child" that he called the son of MJ-1. This child was supposedly the son of the Majestic One representative that interacted with these aliens since the 1950s. One of the twelve members, number one was the leader of the entire group.

Why his son was on board this craft posed a lot of questions as to why this happened, why this was allowed, and where they were taking these supposed "experimental children." Burisch stated that the son died of complications due to the sort of experiments that were done to the children. Before this boy died, he was fastened with what he described as "probes" and "neurological devices." The aliens tried to save the child; however, even with their advanced technology they did not and the boy died. They did however; store his "essence" or soul within these devices as information. The P45 *Rogue* group according to Burisch, only viewed humans as mere "storage capsules" or "containers" of electromagnetic material. The aliens at this point then proceeded to store the deceased boy's information within him, so that their minds connected together.

With the result of this union, Burisch then claimed his intellect was heightened and his whole life changed as he went in a different direction. He could not distinguish whether it was maturity or the union of the boy's energy with his own. With this fabricated solution, he can cover all the bases as to what one can believe or not based on evidence. He called this procedure a "soul transfer" and that the Majestic group was aware of what transpired. Why would MJ-1 allow his son to die if the group knew of the experimentation? Did they anticipate that Burisch would replace him and he would become the new "son?" Clearly, there is a huge hole as far as an explanation goes whether this could be believable or not. Due to his explanation, Cassidy then assumed that Burisch was "chosen" for some reason to save humanity from an oncoming threat (he denies this course).

Investigation Revealed

Burisch amazingly described himself as a "random sample" of the population and that his mentor Dr. Jim Reynolds along with certain others, were placed in his life to "train him to become what he is." As he grew up, he stated that MJ-1 had kept an eye on him and his progress into a new person. MJ-1 supposedly met Burisch at the age of thirteen when he also claimed to belong to the *Los Angeles Microscopical Society* (now called the MSSC or Microscopical Society of Southern California). A few years after he became "interested" in science, he was involved with protozoologist Dr. John DeHass; whom according to him was an assistant professor at the time in the University of Southern California. DeHass also later became an accomplished scientist at UCLA becoming the seventh president of the MSSC in 1971 [18]. The rare opportunity to question the current president Mr. James Solliday about Burisch's claim of belonging to the society at a young age arose and presented the following:

> *Dear Mr. Astrada, 05/01/11*
> *"In the early 1970s, we had a young man about the age of 15 regularly attending the meetings. At the time, we gathered at the George Page Museum off Wilshire Blvd. However, his name was* Henry

> VenDuren. *Henry was a great student and learned much which he applied in his work later in life. Now there was another young man who also attended about the age of 13 or 14, if it helps he was at one point sponsored for a trip and stay in England. At the time he was also considered to have a lot of potential. After his stay in England, he was not as active or perhaps discontinued his association. At the time, he was looked after by the President Gil Mellé. I don't remember his name, but if Dan Catselas claims to have been sent to England, then it might be the same. The name does sound familiar, at least the "Dan" part. Wish I could be more helpful, but this should give you something to work with."*
> *Sincerely,*
> *James Solliday, Pres. MSSC.*

It is clear through this brief email, that Burisch may be taking the credit for another man's accomplishments. *Gil Mellé* was president in 1974, making him ten at the time. If this childhood event happened in 1973 as he claimed being the age of nine, he would still be too young to fit into the timeline of his proposed admittance into the society. Since DeHass was the sixth president, Burisch was placing himself in a different timeline than the actual current president stated. At no time did he ever mention Mellé as a protector or at all involved with him during his interview with Project Camelot. For him to be fourteen, the event would have happen earlier unless he could somehow extract himself from one timeline to another (this idea he did not mention, therefore we have to rule it out). Another strange fact that surfaced was at no time in the email to president Solliday did the name Catselas arise for inquiry. Why did the president give a different name when the investigation called for "Burisch?" A few days later, another email from president Solliday was received with a note attached concerning new information about Burisch. The note came from Mellé's wife stating her possible encounter with someone called "Danny:"

> *Dear J. Astrada: 05/03/11*
> *"I have received more information for you, this should be helpful indeed. The following is the reply received from Gil Mellé's wife, she remembered "Danny" and provided the following information:*
> *"Hi Jim,*
> *Yes, I believe you are thinking of the same kid, Danny. Our friend, the late John Bunyan, who came to a couple of our LAMS meetings when he was visiting the States, and who I'm sure you will remember, was so impressed with Danny when he came to one of those meetings, that he arranged for a special scholarship to Oxford University as Danny was only around 13 or 14 at the time. John let Danny stay with him in England while he studied for the entrance exam. Then we started hearing stories from John about Danny's odd behavior, and things went south after that. Danny came back to L.A. suddenly and we never heard from him or his family again. I know they moved to Las Vegas. John Bunyan was very upset about the whole episode, and for a good reason. But I see no reason for James Astrada not to mention him, as Danny was the youngest member we ever had. I remember he dissected a frog and brought it to one of our meetings, and spoke quite eloquently about how he went about preparing it.*

> *We were all so impressed at the time. We really did have high hopes for Danny."*
> *Denny (May 2, 2011)*
> *P.S John Bunyan was a well-known microscopist living in the U.K. He had a very wonderful collection of antique microscopes and slides.*

* * *

> *Now for the most important line in your research, I have corresponded with Alan DeHass and he does indeed wish to talk with you. He will be your best source of information and was there for the establishment of the LAMS. The following is his email and phone number . . ."*

Could this be another paradox, or is Burisch trying too hard to belong to a fantastic event completely fabricated by his own mind while inserting himself in another individual's position? Even though Mrs. Mellé gave a fantastic description of a young individual and his accomplishments, Burisch never mentioned anyone by the name of Bunyan, traveling to England, or even dissecting frog for the society in the interview. All of these important details were needed by Burisch to make him fit the description, which he failed to do. Only later does Project Camelot at the request of Marci McDowell (his closest supporter and partner) conveniently add information tying Burisch with Dr. John Bunyan in September 2006 [19]. This "Danny" could be someone else that he was trying to impersonate, as both could be from Las Vegas.

As far as Alan DeHass goes, an attempted contact by email and phone concerning the investigation was initiated; however neither response nor a follow up from Mr. Solliday was given. The only response received was a secretary informing that the first initial email on the investigation would be forwarded to the current president.

What sort of "odd behavior" was he displaying? Could it be the experience on the ship which caused the society to dismiss him? Why didn't Burisch mention these facts when conducting his interview if he was being honest? Was he embarrassed that he lost a lifetime opportunity, or was it simply just an invention of the mind? Despite all of the facts here, Burisch still insisted that his story held water. Nevertheless, his supposed interaction with MJ-1 was brief and from a distance. According to Burisch, he was like a "son" probably due to the union of what he thought transpired beforehand. Chi'el'ah eventually befriended Burisch and became his connection to the alien groups for years to come.

According to his new found friend, the aliens did travel back to 1973 to work with Burisch. At the exact same time these aliens traveled back to 1953 to experience a crash that took place. The crash would be the Roswell incident; however original records show that two possible crashes actually taking place in 1947 [20]. He then explained that this was a paradox; where the aliens visited both time frames at the same exact time simultaneously experiencing both the "abduction" of Burisch, and the supposed 1953 S-4 facility event. There is a mass confusion of details that create more obscurity for the entire story. Is he in fact telling the truth about his new friend (that now has a different name from the original "Harry" creation from his childhood) about the Roswell crashes? The dates are incorrect, the facts prove otherwise, and the lack of honesty is destroying any credibility.

Chi'el'ah and Area 51

Chi'el'ah, whom Burisch referred to as a "j-rod," usually communicated with him through telepathy. In 1993, he claimed to have made direct contact with his new friend, opening a new frontier for human/alien interactions. Burisch also believed that something was amiss with the j-rod as he was "off shifted." There was matter there; however he described it as a "ghost with a body" that did not belong [21]. He stated that the communication was acoustic in nature and that a sort of "thumping" occurred until the waves lined up within the brain. Dolphins also communicate with the same type of method. Cetacean intelligence allowed the dolphins and other cetaceans such as whales, orcas, etc . . . to emit two distinct kinds of acoustic signals called "whistles" and "clicks [22]." The clicks are described as quick burst pulses used for echolocation (bio-sonar) either for communication or in some cases, a lower frequency for non-communicative purposes. These clicks are emitted in intervals of approximately 35-50 milliseconds. The whistles are narrow band frequency modulated (FM) signals used for contact or "calls" to other family members [23].

With this understanding, Burisch's aliens could also have used this type of communication as an entrainment for a connection of the human host and their alien companion. The experience was described as being "pulled in" and acquiring a sort of theta state where he was told by the j-rod: "I'm not going to hurt you." Burisch exclaimed that he did not trust him at first and naturally became scared. He also described the j-rod as three feet tall with a change of stance, wobbly, weak and sickly looking. He also stated that the j-rod had a name for him as well as he was called "beeany" (beanie) [24].

This was done telepathically with the location of this event transpiring in what he called a "clean sphere," where he belonged to a "B-unit" that was only there to assist the scientists. Coincidentally, he also became "promoted" due to the j-rod's wish to use him as the communicative human. Burisch seemed to add to the story a more fantastic sense of Cassidy's wish for a savior of humanity. He contradicted his idea of the "random sample" theory as he is becoming the central theme in his UFO/human adventure.

The process of the event as Burisch went into greater detail, further slandered his professional career. He was first flooded with what he called a "natural opiate" for the communication process to transpire peacefully. He stated that these aliens were considered a threat, therefore the scientists did not allow communication to take place outside a controlled environment. He believed that these aliens were trying to reverse their condition or illness by stripping the exterior cytoplasm of certain cells and produce cells that would function independently [25]. He did not go into detail on what sort of cells they were, what human cells would be utilized, and which group was involved out of the potential three. He explained that one would need to understand the alien entities biochemically, and genetically to create a graph in destroying or resolving their physical problems.

Burisch seemed to have extensive knowledge of these alien groups (that would be our future relatives) beyond the scientists that worked with him. In the clean sphere, he claimed that the event did not happen on Earth; rather thousands of miles away where the person would potentially be alone with the aliens even with radio communication. Precautionary measures were taken and the volunteer would have to come in terms with the idea that death was a possibility. If a leak or danger occurred (where the sphere was compromised or the facility itself), all of the individuals located on that level were sealed off from the rest and scheduled for a decontamination process. Why would other employees be affected if Burisch claimed to be thousands of miles away from Earth when communicating? He attributed his "profound knowledge" to the study of biochemistry for his rather calm attitude during the meetings with the j-rod or what he identified as now a P52 "human."

This now changed the story again as the "friend" instead of being a j-rod (P45 as we have been told), is now from the Nordic side of the three groups changing the entity entirely. Also another stipulation in his story mentioned before was that the P45 groups were the ones with physical conditions that needed to be resolved, not the P52 Nordics. His friendship (or what he also calls kinship) with this now P52 was acquired instantly we he remembered his childhood "park incident." Over time, his trust grew with his new alien contact attributing to his strange sense of humor that for some reason, only the alien could understand. He explained that he had trouble identifying the emotional state of this alien, due to the physical state that Burisch thought he was in.

He either guessed that the alien was in pain, or complete anguish due to the facial expressions. In order to better understand the emotional state, he had to be told telepathically. If Burisch had such a strong connection, why go through the trouble of guessing? If he first described that he only communicated through telepathy, what was the need to study the physical mannerisms of the alien? Where was the confusion coming from about his emotional state? As they became more connected, Burisch expressed his desire to continue communicating with this alien, and did not want to lose its friendship. For this reason, he claimed that during the many sessions they established, he lied to the viewing controllers concerning the facial expressions when Burisch displayed his emotions.

This alien Chi'el'ah, was a captive in his eyes as he also felt captive within the Majestic group. It seems very odd that Burisch would be able to fool scientists whom have had extensive communication with these beings over sixty years. Most scientists have inquisitive minds and through research and study, are able to determine anomalies, deficiencies, or other processes of the human being and their ability to be dishonest. If they were in fact fooled by Burisch and his alien contact, what would be the need to continue the sessions if not for research? Why would he be the only human there with that ability to mask his emotions? Certainly his "B-unit" also had the same qualities he displayed, who could easily identify fabrications and illusions that a regular human would try to concoct. The story seems to invent itself as time passes.

Firmly believing in captivity, Burisch felt that they were both "prisoners in their own right" and concerned with the treatment his alien friend received (as he considered him a human being). He seemed to casually throw around the terms *human* and *alien* as he interchanged them carelessly. He doesn't seem to make up his mind on what exactly these groups are: future potential versions of ourselves who are returning to the past to understand their mistakes, as they watch us go through the process of destruction and chaos? Or were they aliens from another time or civilization interacting with present day humanity?

By labeling these ideas "paradoxes," he eliminated the need to explain himself or his ridiculous speculations. Because of the treatment of the alien, he became upset as he was told telepathically that the use of needles for experimentation was frequent. To add to this intense story, Burisch was warned that if he didn't cooperate, they would change the pressure in the sphere with the result of physical damage to the alien. If this was the case, the scientists seemed to notice that he was lying otherwise there would be no need for threats. Because the alien had lesser density (or physical weight per volume), the bone structure was less dense with the result being intense pain.

He now adapted the role of a liaison to the alien, as he claimed to fight the group's torture methodology against Chi'el'ah. This way according to his beliefs, gave them a more immediate connection. Only Burisch in the Majestic group seems to believe that these aliens were future human beings. If the group truly knew that they were dealing with future humanoid versions from a potential future time, they would try to learn from them to avoid the same mistakes. It seemed to logically prevent a disaster that would ruin the elite, financial situations, and the power structure, they would need to inquire from these so called "distant relatives," methods to keep the current situation flowing for a successful future.

As far as Burisch goes, he stated that he did not stop communicating telepathically with his alien friend, even though Chi'el'ah journeyed back to his home in the Reticulum star system (as far as he was aware). If indeed Chi'el'ah was a P52 humanoid, he would then be from the Orion star system as we have been told. Further adding another tale of excitement, Burisch claimed in 2003 that he helped the alien escape the clutches of the Majestic group by pushing him into a stargate upon the alien's request [26]. This action supposedly ended the relationship with the group, Burisch, and the alien. Adding more last minute details, this event supposedly transpired in Egypt due to the alien's desire to see his son whom he missed immensely. Burisch also mentioned that within the whole Majestic group, he was the only one who could communicate with this alien to help him "relax" (his reason was that he considered him human and that they both experienced childhood relations to each other).

Burisch clearly fabricating this whole event centered himself as the main character. He has now morphed from a random sample, into a human representative bent on saving a future version of humanity, whom he can only communicate with, understand, and help. He added a more emotional state to this friend of his that seemly became less alien, and more human. Majestic, which he believed thought they were more superior to this alien, were more inclined to strengthen their ties with the P45 Rogue group. It seems that the older P52 group was considered inferior to the past version of themselves.

He felt honesty with his close alien friend describing the event as an "inconsequential future," or subsequent event across a future timeline. He disagreed with the idea of taking polygraph tests (of course!) because he believed that they "didn't work." He believed that all beings would be judged by their honesty, spirit, mind, and heart. Are humans in a position to judge at all? Do we have the right tools equipped to make a decision of that magnitude? The way we are currently living on this planet, and the way we treat it, displays that we do not know what judgment is or the purpose it serves. Burisch added that he viewed from his alien friend's memory, a "child and mother connection," as a more humanistic trait. He believed that this was a common theme in the alien group based on one friend. Do we judge all the aliens based on one's actions? Are we not doing the same bias that we put upon ourselves making it irresponsible? This was Burisch's justification as he pushed the alien into the stargate at the time to "save" him from the human masters.

Illuminati versus Majestic 12

Due to his actions, he claimed that he was arrested for violating protocol after helping the alien. Supposedly, Majestic was furious and imprisoned him as a "level 3 demotion" at the S-4 facility. In his "B-unit," he stated that they were only allowed the basic amenities and no freedom. According to Burisch, this was "torture" along with what he called "unkindness," physical harm, psychological interrogation by operatives of the Majestic group (not the *J* members) [27]. These operatives according to his statement, fell under different leadership separate from the government since the 1940s. After the physical treatment within the group, the experience has left him not well. After 2003, the Majestic 12 disbanded, forming a new body with two secret societies that have been placed in control to his knowledge to change leadership roles. Claiming that Majestic was as important as the Freemasons; there was a struggle for power.

Why would the operatives allow photographs of their own handiwork as to incriminate them? Wouldn't this move be sloppy on their part? Giving his insight on how the group split into two different ideologies: the first group was obviously the York and Scottish rite adhering to the Luciferian concept of rule and prophecy. Burisch foolishly described this as the train of thought pertaining to "satanic," materialistic, willing to give their lives, families, and honor to create a new order under the rule of a new god as the leader. This idea could relate to Virgil's idea of the Sun King as mentioned before. However, the actual definition of a Luciferian principle pertains to the planet Venus when it rises ahead of the star sol (sun) of our solar system [28].

It is argued among experts that the belief system has a more positive light rather than a dark satanic meaning as Burisch likes to believe. The entire ideology is fashioned from ancient civilizations such as Rome, Egypt, Greece; then later changed by western Occultism and Gnosticism [29]. It does suggest that Burisch is applying religious dogmatic thought to his belief system of the group's collaboration with the devil himself, adding religious fantasy to his story. He then added that the P45 Rogues were also are against humans, and that this group wanted to join the Illuminati making this a double team effort. Why would the elite human construct want to join a future version of humans that would eventually eliminate them in the process? If the P45 group disliked all humans in general, that would mean even the elite would suffer as well (unless they have special access to be classified as more than human).

The other part of the group, Majestic was what he called the "enlightened ones" and shared much in common with his belief. Burisch took sides with the same group that supposedly beat him unmercifully making the whole story confusing. He added that Majestic was "god fearing," which he believed was a positive idea. Overall, the main idea that Burisch pushed for was that a secret war between the "unholy alliance" of the P45/Illuminati faction, and the Majestic/P52 Nordics (pro-human) existed. This P52 group still has the Luciferian principle in hand; however according to Burisch, wanted to help and do noble things for mankind. The new group called the Committee of the Majority spelled doom as it was considered a "bad element" bent on destroying humankind.

Two Timelines and 2012

The concept of 2012 has been the focus on what could actually happen to Earth this year. In the eyes of Burisch and his paradox timeline theory, there seems to be a more complex view as to what could really happen. In his belief, the year 2012 would fall in timeline 2 of the current path we as human beings are taking. This supposedly would adhere to the P45 Rogue group that is trying to transition to this timeline; in order to fulfill the events that took place resulting in their creation. Another belief was that the Roswell incident took place in timeline 2, which we are now currently making those aliens discovered by the U.S. government *P24's* (past version of the P45 group). This is a mouthful to digest, but Burisch believed this in his mind without a doubt. The aliens that crashed were just trying to find a way home in the same timeline of their future of twenty-four thousand years later from the year 1947 (within the proposed timeline 2 scenario). After this, he then changed his story by stating that we were in fact in timeline 1, and that the catastrophe that the Mayan calendar predicts would not transpire at all [30]. Nibiru, the "winged planet" prophesized by the Sumerians, would not destroy Earth as Burisch reworded his thoughts leaving the question that it might happen.

The weather channel does the same as we can relate to a simpler view of describing this asinine ideology: they might give us the forecast for the week predicting rain or storms with a percentage rate either low or high. If it does happen, then the information they gave to us was "accurate." The opposite result gives us the answer that it was only a "prediction" (where the error is removed from their part). With this excuse, Burisch could make all of the predictions he wanted without worrying about being incorrect, based on these being only his beliefs. Burisch using this ideology exclaimed that an "energetic burst" through the plane of the galaxy would transpire through the use of wormholes (or what the ancient Egyptian called the "Solar boat" and Aztec/Mayans called the "serpent rope"). This burst would then cause a disruption in the Sun, which will in turn provoke a disaster caused by stargates and Burisch's "Looking Glass" (used to see the future) devices that would attract energy to this planet. Much of the planet's energy resides in the crust; therefore the result would a geophysical disaster where approximately four billion people would die.

Burisch did not mention which aliens told him this and if the theory was correct, then the proposed 2000 Global Agenda fulfilled by Majestic would come to fruition. This would be the same Majestic that Burisch believes will benefit mankind. If we are to believe him, we would have to assume that the P45 Rogue group is behind this devious plan to allow the elimination of the majority of the human population. Adding to this story, he stated that he was working with others in an effort to disable and destroy this technology of future viewing, and teleportation to other locations in the known universe. He believed that we as humans will naturally pass through wormholes with the planet along with animal life will naturally change into a "positive perspective [31]." This would result in a rise in spirituality, bright minds, and indigo children (which he considers a rise in consciousness) [32].

The cause of this supposed destruction as we mentioned, would be due to using the technological advances done by alien interests. According to Burisch, these items were given to humans in the 1950s; however does not specify which timeline the transaction occurred. The "Looking Glass" device would display a disaster that due to his belief was 19% probable, then stating that the other 81% was not probable. The Illuminati (not Majestic), was the group who want to provoke this event to take place. He also believed that the P45 *Rogue* groups also wanted this to happen in order to justify their history, and the human followers wanted power control with no intent to share. If the 19% theory works out, then two-thirds of the population will demise into what "are presumed to actually be progenitors of the aliens in the future." If we follow this train of thought, the event supposedly transpired due to the current situation we were in, not due to the desires of an elusive future humanoid race's cause. This is the only way that the three groups would ever be— due to this exact event.

Without it, there would not be any P groups who travel back in time to prevent or provoke this disaster— they would simply not exist. He was certain that the P45 Rogue group was repressed and that the soul did not dissipate; instead returned to the "god source" he believed in. When this event supposedly occurs, the P52 blonde Nordic survivors who do not go underground, become more spiritual in nature, and move off world to find their way to the Osiris-Orion star system. On the other hand, the survivors who do go underground, become "j-rods" and stay for another twenty-four thousand years, until the next transition for them to move off world and find their way to the Zeta Reticuli system.

Stargates and the Future

An "ark" has also been placed on the Moon just in case of this event, where the Nordics will go beforehand, and establish technology for the next several thousand years. The idea may not be as illusionary as the European Space Agency plans to build a "Noah's ark" on the moon before an asteroid hits Earth to end life [33]. By then, a new community will form, and they will then move to Mars creating those monuments that we have seen like the "Face," and the "City" located in the Cydonia Region [34]. Basically, Burisch was claiming that these monuments were created by the Nordics eventually become ruins in the possible future, creating another paradox. With this belief, whenever scientists discover ancient ruins on other planets, they are in fact looking at possible future events that might transpire after the 2012 event.

Maybe this could be the reason that NASA named the Martian surveyor "Viking" due to its connections with the Nordics? All of the structures, whether it is the "scorpion" or Star City on Mars, will disappear if we do not venture into timeline 2. Utilizing the paradox theory, Burisch excuses himself from any of his claims making sense. Since according to him we are looking at possible futures on Mars, every time one goes back in time, a paradox occurs with changes that bring too much energy unnaturally to us. He then claims due to this, there could be infinite timelines or possibilities making the story more fantastic.

Conveniently, Burisch changed his original belief of two definite timelines to an open possibility of many. Although the multiverse theory is in effect a possibility, Burisch did not mention this as part of his paradox theory. Giving credit to the P45 Rogue group for giving humans the "Looking Glass" technology, they deviously planted the device in our past in order to have it now in this day and age. Even in his fantasy world, the events will transpire whether we want them to happen or not. There was cylinder seals kept by the ancient Sumerians that Burisch actually believed were the prototypes of this technology. With this device, one is able to access natural wormholes to allow one to see different aspects of the past. Sumer and Egypt have had these seals and predate them much to be older than their civilizations. Burisch also assured that other countries besides Iraq, Egypt, and India, had these seals (the U.N. and the U.S. government want them for their control).

In 2003, Burisch exclaimed that the Iraqi stargate equipment was given by Hussein to the U.S. government.

Cassidy at this point, wanted to know if we could essentially close the stargates in order to prevent any more damage. Doing this, Burisch responded, would cause more damage to Earth and its inhabitants. His belief stated that they must remain open and whatever transpired cannot be undone. Using this theory, all of his previous statements of "going back into the past to alter certain events," contradict this new ideology. The idea that the human use of the technology for natural wormholes (and of the unnatural effects of enhancing them), causes the damage to our species and the planet. His illusion of "let nature happen and keep our hands off" is a positive idea in its own thought; however looking at our current situation; it is too late to allow the natural process to return (without drastic effects to the ecosystem).

The Men in Black

Another bizarre subject that Burisch discussed was the infamous MIB or Men in Black. They have been a part of our human pop culture for the last forty or fifty years. They are either described as humans or aliens that dress in black suit and tie. They threaten or silenced UFO witnesses about experiences that have been considered top secret [35]. They are also considered to be strange beings working for unknown government agencies that protect "strange activities" or black projects. Hollywood goes as far as to introduce them as humorous characters represented by Will Smith and Tommy Lee Jones who protect the Earth from alien threats; also acknowledge that aliens exist and live among humans unnoticed.

Burisch on the other hand, describes them as psychological operatives that scare people away from knowledge about

UFO phenomena. He stated that they are real and belong to the P45 Rogue group who utilize a sort of biomechanical technology "skin suit" of a dead human as their appearance. He also described them as monotone, bland, and "didn't belong." If he stated that they couldn't exist in our environment before, was this biomechanical suit efficient enough? If they are future versions of humans, what would be the need for such an elaborate mechanism? Nevertheless, Burisch claimed to have met several of them in his life and was very uncomfortable around them. Their tactics were described as brute force, and physical pain to humans without hesitation to get their point across. He does however tell us that "they get confused easily," meaning that they could be avoided with the "right moves."

He doesn't elaborate on what those moves were, just that they can be fooled. His theory also stated that they also have the memories of the dead human skin, and can sometimes lose themselves in the memory of the dead. His description of their appearance was an entity dressed in all black with a preacher's hat resembling a sort of Quaker/Amish individual, which was armed and highly dangerous. He went into detail about one personal experience claiming to have photos during the experiences; however the event transpired at night and the photos were not clear due to the fact that it was a disposable. This whole "experience" could easily be debunked due to lack of evidence.

The Three Particles and Frenchman Mountain

On October 12, 2005, Burisch claimed to have been dismissed from Majestic, and due to this reason he wanted to show the world all of his "experiences." He mentioned that it was disbanded, dismissed, and contained extraneous energy emissions. Now the question remains why Burisch focused on this project whether illusionary or not, what details were so critical in exposing this project to the outside world, and why the P45 Rogue group hasn't acquired this technology yet for their benefit. In May 2001, Burisch claimed to have traveled to Frenchman mountain in Nevada as investigated by Knapp searching for what he called a "bio marker" as a precursor virus prosaic. The P45 group was searching for ways to eliminate their physical anomalies and problems on a cellular level, due to the events that transpired in their past (our future). This project dealt with possibility to cure and eliminate their genetic deficiencies to correct the problem that they had.

During his supposed investigation, he was searching for anomalous (irregular) activity (that could be used as "data sets") attracting electromagnetic energy, and silicon dioxides present in minerals. He also searched for the presence of the emission of electromagnetic bundles to study their nature. He then briefly explained the nature of the cell and other "information" by stating that the activity was associated with cells within the terrestrial environment (earthbound), and somehow modifying the cells to benefit whatever purpose he was looking for.

After, confined subtle matter particles from ancient times (could be fossils or bones of some type) could reflect changes in our environment with his results showing negative at the time. He believed that his purpose was to find during these experimentations, if a living human cell could be affected by what he called "anomalous thermal interruptions" (dealing with thermal conductivity) [36]. To his conclusion, the yeast cells (which he did not mention until the end of this argument) could transform with the right conditions, into animal cells at a high success rate. So in essence, through this experiment, cells that were initially dead could be revived and fully functional. The bacteria called *Deinococcus radiodurans* under extreme conditions could revive itself back to life. In 2006 At Paris University in France, scientists were working on trying to utilize the DNA from this bacterium for potential human applications to revive the dead [37].

This would mean that the P45 group could essentially reverse their condition and return to humanoid form looking like we do. The cell once revived, would not act the same as the functioning precursor, essentially becoming non identifiable. This meant that the cell would change the function of the original purpose to some unknown purpose. Would this not contradict the statement of being fully functional? If the cell was non identifiable, the P45 group would not be able to utilize it for their purpose as it would have become a cell of a different nature. Lastly, he described the process as the cell being repaired by heat and the transformation of the cell with a template or pattern (this template was DNA fitted). Again, he did not go into detail as if the DNA used was human, animal or extraterrestrial.

A "portal" was somehow need as well to undergo the process; with the nature being that of electromagnetic acting as a barrier (but of course mentioned that it was not fully understood yet). He also discussed subjects concerning thermodynamics, biology, bio-molecular study, and the cellular regeneration process. How can we believe his story if it frequently undergoes changes, revisions, and eliminations?

Burisch described three particles that he was somehow able to identify from experimentation with the manipulation of cells. He named them Alpha, Beta, and C-type particles or "Selkies" (this name he credited to Marcia McDowell; his partner who also claims to be a Majestic member) [38]. The alpha particle or what he mentioned as the Ganesh particle was considered the "remover of obstacles." Ganesh or Ganesa, was one of the main deities of the Hindu pantheon. Also known as the "Lord of beginnings, and Lord of obstacles," he also represented art, science, intellect, and wisdom. Since he is synonymous with the first chakra, he is considered to be the foundation, beginning, or "patient zero" (it would be understandable why Burisch would consider this name of the particle) [39].

The Beta particle or "Shiva portals" were considered the emission center for the initial particle. Shiva was also a god from the Hindu pantheon that was revered as a "Supreme God". Shiva was also known as the destroyer, and part of the Hindu trinity as an aspect of the "divine." He is portrayed as a "cosmic dancer" at times displaying the rhythmic movement of the cosmos [40]. He is usually depicted with the third eye signifying the importance of the pineal gland and its spiritual attributes. This could also be the reason why Burisch selected the name since the third eye is the portal to the human soul.

The final particle being the "Selkie" was described as a "crossing guard," that aligned the magnetic peripheries (or boundaries) that acted as guide surrounding the particle. This in turn gives the pathway a "target" or destination (he explained the process dealt with sound, frequency, and science). The acoustic changes affect cell particles, which in turn redirect the position(s) being emitted from the portal or beta location. This then created "micro-size" portals which could range from ten to twenty microns in size. This process can only transpire if using a microscope and the "right conditions" (which he describes as transient in nature). The cells are then deemed delicate with no more propagations or regeneration. Using a quartz crystal for the process, accumulated an unknown substance. He stated that a reproduction of an unknown cell from an origin unknown grew around the crystal. This caused him to halt the experiment due to his belief on "negative consequences." He believed them to be an alien life form that came from "somewhere" and generated spontaneously. This experiment changed the initial belief system of only three known races of life existing in the universe. This mysterious cell originated from another location from a supposed unknown world, using a micro wormhole that was created by his experiment.

He attributed his experiments following the Spallanzani experiment, concerning the use of beef broth in the place of his mysterious cell. *Lazzaro Spallanzani* was one of the first to disprove the belief of spontaneous regeneration. He was an Italian scientist from the year 1767, who proved microorganisms could be killed or destroyed by boiling them [41]. His experiment had four different flasks with four different tests. He wanted to hypothesize whether organisms originate directly from nonliving matter or abiogenesis (non-biological life form without origin). His main concern was what caused microbes to form in the decaying broth he used. He hypothesized that the microbes originated from the air and that boiling water would kill them off. He used the four different tests all using the same method of boiling.

The first flask, he left the open and discovered that microbes emerged and the liquid turned cloudy. The second flask was left sealed with the same result of the liquid turning cloudy and microbes present. The third flasks, was boiled and then left open with yet again, the same result. The last flask had an interesting conclusion: it was first boiled then sealed with the result of the liquid not cloudy and no presence of microbes. It seems that his hypothesis was correct that in a controlled environment, the microbes could not sustain life if exposed to high temperature and the "right conditions."

Did Burisch have the same results in his "experiment" using cells, a quartz crystal, and the microscope? According to Burisch, the cells were "autoclaved" (sterilized) instead of being heated or boiled; with the same setup of an open and closed environment, using electricity and silicon dioxide. Earlier however, he mentioned that the cells were "heat fixed" adding more confusion to the story.

To his conclusion, the closed study contained the growth of cells that appeared to grow and organize themselves in a neural fashion denoting intelligence (an AB, AB pattern). He wasn't able to continue due to the belief of his repercussions. He stated he had "moral" consideration and was very vague in what he actually meant. He then claimed to photograph the cells and killed them immediately to prevent a disaster. There was no evidence of photos, nor evidence of the experiment. After all the ideas and projects he discussed/took part of, where would the consideration of morality enter? According to his story, he took part in the discovery and operation of this elaborate group and its activities. This makes him just as an accomplice as they are. Does he now feel obligated to correct mistakes? Is this a fantasy world in which he cannot snap out of?

The "Looking Glass" Technology

Project Camelot had a chance to interview Burisch again about a year later in July of 2007 in Las Vegas concerning more details about the "Looking Glass" and the stargate phenomena. In this personal interview, Burisch seemed reluctant and vague in describing exactly what these devices were. He started to discuss the "Looking Glass" device and how important it was to the human race. He stated that the device itself showed the possibility of the future or past depending on who was operating it and for what purpose [42]. Another device called the "cube" that he briefly mentioned, (separate from the "Looking Glass") would react to the person who was present in front of the device. Burisch called the cube by another name labeling it the "yellow book" (there was a yellow disk-shaped object on top of the device according to him). He claimed that an elite group has used these devices to view into the future a huge disaster that eventually affected even them. For this reason, Project Lotus was abandoned from the TAU-IX treaty. He went as far to state that each country with elite was allowed use of this cube to choose a better future for each of them to the best of their knowledge. As far as the location of this illustrious cube at the present time, was as he described "taken by someone" and was missing making the whole idea highly improbable. This device described was far from the visual that we could get from the movie *Stargate* (which James Spader and Kurt Russell encountered).

He stated that the device had a barrel component, electromagnetic "rings" and the final piece being something called a projection component. With these parts, the stargate was able to operate at full capacity; however he also stressed that this device was also decommissioned. In order for this device to take hold, a new fourth part he later added called "field posts," had to be positioned around it for the device to activate [43]. These stargates were given to NATO, the U.N. and the European Union, making the three parts into various interests who didn't trust each other. Nothing is told of the mysterious fourth part and who it was given to. Nevertheless, these three formed a group called the "Tri-group." The number he believed of stargates that were made on the planet Earth numbered over fifty. This device accessed portal(s) that drew off from the ERB (Einstein-Rosen Bridge). With this application, interuniverse travel, time travel, and faster-than-light-travel were all possible with the use of the Swartzchild wormhole [44][45][46]. Usually attributed to science fiction, the idea of a wormhole is not taken seriously by modern science and is still considered a theory.

Those who are familiar with the knowledge of metrics can use two equations to decide whether one is dealing with traversable wormholes and non-traversable wormholes [47]. Burisch implied that the "Looking Glass" itself, also worked in tandem with another "Looking Glass" as an acoustic generation was needed (as they were turned on at the same time). For sound to take place two were needed, lest the onlooker would only see a "picture" with no sound.

His belief was that this secondary device from the original "large equipment" originating from the 1960s came from alien origin. The added information that Burisch concluded was yes the cylinder seals were from Earth; however, the writing from the seals originated off world. Cassidy went as far suggesting the off world entities were the *Annunaki* for her obsession with the "reptilian threat;" however, he did not agree with her point of view and dismissed her idea. The cube or the newly added name "black box," was what he considered a variant of alien technology that changed with the presence of human emotion or feeling. If the human was unstable, the effects could be disastrous causing instability. If the human was not ready, one could imagine what the results could be.

This in turn, could be seen as potentially realistic since most human beings do not focus or care about long term decisions; we only tend to focus on the immediate situation. Burisch claimed that because of his "effort," abductions and Project Lotus experiments have been removed from the treaty due to the fact that he utilized the cube to see the potential effects of the future [48]. The question now is that he mentioned earlier that it was missing and was in the hands of "someone else" in an unknown location. How then did he get a hold of it? Was this transpiring before it disappeared, or during the time that the elite was using it as well? Why didn't they foresee the disastrous effects then? Why was he considered the only concerned individual? Lastly, he expressed his gratitude to the unknown "benefactor" for taking it away from human hands off world. This final comment indicated he knew who had possession of it. It is clear in order for one to show gratitude, one is aware of whom they are talking to.

The Future Timeline Predictions

Concerning the idea of time travel, Burisch decided to journey the human race back into timeline 1, which he saw as a positive notion. He gave his idea of a hopeful future stating that it was a "blank slate." As far as this theory went, all the previously knowledge introduced contradicted this belief system. We already know that hope is misleading and can create a false expectancy of a bright future for all humans especially when we do nothing to allow this to happen. We also need to remember that these groups are a result of catastrophic events that happen on a geophysical level, and cannot exist unless the events take place. He stated that these two groups were from timeline 2 earlier and as a result, split into two separate human survival groups that underwent physical and genetic changes due to environments they encountered (both underground and surface wise). If we were to venture into Burisch's timeline 1, we would not encounter ordeal with the upcoming predictions and beliefs of his ideas.

He still believed that we had challenges dealing with global warming, environmental issues, and other human activities; however, this didn't take away from all of the outlandish speculations he presented. These other concerns are realistic and are transpiring now as we continue down the path of over consumption and technology, while the rest of the Earth and its organisms take a backseat to human progress. He further clarified that he has been told "special" information by Chi'el'ah against the Majestic group's wishes, such as treaties that he had no knowledge about. He jumped to arguments that he had with the members of the group due to alien contact he supposedly experienced in May 2001 (when he claimed that the *Lotus* project was decommissioned). Changing the date from 2003 to 2001, Burisch strongly believed that the project was essential for the P45 Rogue group physical deficiencies. The P52 group could not be helped since they were too far ahead in time approximately seven thousand years. Never once before did he mention any problems genetically or physically concerning the P52 group which now raises a few questions.

Was not *Chi'el'ah* a P52 that he exclaimed had severe physical problems? How does he know that the P52 group is not able to use the project for their benefit? Does he have a "secret edge," which gives him the understanding of the intricacies of the anatomy of these future humanoid generations (over forty thousand years ahead of our time)? Why does he keep interchanging the terms human and alien as if they are nearly identical in nature? Why does Burisch also interchange the timelines and their numbers so frequently? Does he mean to confuse us, or is he clearly delusional? He assured that he was member MJ-9 of the twelve who replaced a former agent in that position (female), but refused to give a name. He claimed to be against the fact that every elite in the selected countries were given access to the cube, and used them for their own purposes. Did he not do the same in a way to stop them from using his secret "project?" This indicated that he used the cube for his own purposes whether they were for the "good" of humanity or not.

Environmental Impacts of the Present

He indicated that the cube itself was utilized since the 1950s to display the history of the human race. He also stated that "we all have the right to a future of our own will, and not by the will of the blue bloods." Did he not in fact defy his own belief by using the equipment to alter the future? Even wanting the people to have the upper hand, how can we take this man seriously? He mentioned the NSM 200 Report (National Security Study Memorandum Report) which in 1974, dealt with Henry Kissinger's plan to create food control genocide over the world population [49]. It has been mentioned and stated that Kissinger himself, was a participating member of the Majestic group [50]. This executive plan was set up during the Ford administration, and Burisch believed that they were implementing this plan now on the third world with the coined phrase: "food as a weapon." Burisch believed according to his supposed scientific knowledge, that if the world temperature raises two to three degrees Celsius, the northern hemisphere will have accelerated growth rates concerning food and crops [51].

If it supersedes beyond this number, it will decrease in the lower latitudes i.e., the southern hemisphere (mainly Latin America, Australia, and lower Africa) leading to starvation and crop loss. This may be an actuality due to the changes in the temperatures that are different from as far back as 1979 leading to the climate change argument [52]. On a side note, this could also explain all of the bizarre weather patterns that we have been experiencing over the last eight years according to figures by former NASA scientist *Dr. Roy Spencer* from UAH (University of Alabama in Huntsville) [53]. Could the two be related with employing the use of alien technology, causing these weather patterns to change temperature globally to destroy people without the use of nuclear weapons?

Are these powers that Burisch mentioned as future humans, engaging in the same practices as the movie *The Arrival* (1996)? We have heard of *Telsa* and his inventions including his weather control device that the Clinton Administration may have utilized to create floods in 1993 to take over farmlands and private lands (for the Federal wetlands project) [54]. He believed that the southern hemisphere would sustain heavy losses in human life according to his research; however, remained outside the realm of politics concerning the whole situation. Burisch also has the speculative belief that everyone on the planet is of equal worth. Through the natural process, only the best are selected genetically (as if selected by natural eugenics) if not created artificially.

The Origins of the Looking Glass

Bill Uhouse, who passed away in May of 2009, actually utilized the "Looking Glass" in the 1970s according to Burisch. He also worked in Area 51 and was responsible for the creation of AVR equipment and avionics [55]. The both interestingly enough, shared the same story concerning the interaction with alien life forms called "j-rods" and being scientists together in this underground facility. Jumping back to the subject of the cube, Burisch stated that it was discovered in the crash in Roswell, New Mexico in 1946. This initially contradicts his original statements a year earlier, stating that the crash took place in 1953. To make matters more confusing, the official reported that the crash happened in 1947 [56].

The cube was then given to Eisenhower by the P52 that Burisch believed the U.N. would receive it; however, the U.S. military kept it for themselves. The P52 group allowed this situation to transpire as he described as a "spirit of goodwill," but then regretted this due to the miss assessment of our emotional human state. According to him, they believed us to be more balanced; however this wasn't the case. This thought in any rational/logical view would be utterly ridiculous for two reasons: firstly, since the P52 group is the future version of the humans who undergo 2012, they would obviously have a chance to remember their past to not repeat the same event (this making his statement of "goodwill" inane). They would have a chance to view us through the "Looking Glass" technology, since it was their creation to begin with. This would allow them the opportunity to make the same mistake again, causing the death and misuse of power that humans are capable of.

A wiser more intelligent race would not make simple errors that they have originally done, lest they be naïve and inadequate. Since Burisch described the Orion as "brilliant, emotional, positive, less rudimentary, and more complex," they would not fit the description of the group who caused this. Secondly, he seemed to confuse the P52 and P45 agendas that he supposedly had a profound knowledge of. We remember that he previously stated that the P45 group was the initial enemy of the humans and wanted the event to transpire. Therefore it would make more sense for this group to give the cube knowingly to the humans expecting the future result that would allow them to essentially exist.

Burisch regretted the "Looking Glass" technology due to the claimed uses; however, praised the stargates due to the contact with the UFO groups. He then went into his intricate details of how he thought the stargate worked discussing ring position, barrel position, and the flow of energy [57]. Burisch described the machine as an onion and its layers; with every layer having bits of information (in this case, infinite layers). As the movement of energy transpired, one was essentially moving through the layers and could add or subtract by "tuning" the device up or down. This result would create two separate pictures at the same time (meaning outcomes or realities). He stressed the use of computers to help this process to transpire with success. With a "special program," one could determine the probability of events using a complicated and sophisticated scientific system. Once the system was conducted, every event probable or improbable was charted by the program to view every possible future in timeline 1 or 2. With this situation, Burisch put forth his philosophy of "just because we have the power to do so, should we" question.

There would be an answer for every move or situation created. Surprises, creative thinking, and imagination would no longer be fascinating or mysterious. Everything would be known at a certain length with many possible alternatives. This of course is no way to live life; without the element of surprise, humanity is deemed to live a drone existence of following orders mindlessly in fear that those in power know their every move beforehand. This comes close to Phillip K. Dick's vision of the Minority Report written in 1956, where crime is prevented before the actual person decides to execute it by three "mutants" (who could see into the future therefore creating alternate realities and paradoxes) [58].

Burisch believed that the stargates were used to pass inhabitants and information one way only, as humans were on the receiving end. Only two groups were allowed to transmit; the P52 and the P45 Rogues. The Republic Society no longer had a function in his story in any way concerning the events, humanity, or the fate of their own race. Was this possible due to their ability to operate on their own completely, eliminating themselves from any of their perspective P45 Rogue brothers and future P52 relatives? As far as venturing off world, Burisch claimed that humans were only allowed on the moon. He also stated that the P52 Orion knew that we were irresponsible (yet they gave us the cube anyway) and that our emotions affected our physical state, our orientation with available energies from the cosmos affect our DNA, and that our health state or rubric application was accessible to them onboard their craft (so we were essentially experiments to them as well). When Cassidy mentioned planet Serpo, Burisch ridiculed the assumption stating that the idea came from the movie *Stargate* (1994). He stated that written backwards "opres" was a K-4 code, and that the name is also a reptile park located in either Norway or Argentina [59].

Through research, the actual park is located in the Netherlands and was not a planet located in the Zeta System as Cassidy thought [60]. When describing his knowledge about the alien life forms, he altered the amount and type of alien groups to eliminate the Republic Society, and added what he called "interdimensional beings" (another flaw to his story). He also stated that a human using the stargate to travel to different locations was improbable because there would be complications and the equipment would collapse. The story is again altered to add that unless a "planetary uproar" occurred, the stargate could not be utilized to transport entities.

The Orion did not essentially trust humans and will not let us off this planet based on his belief system. The idea that aliens are running this planet and keeping us into submission (that Project Camelot promotes and interjects throughout the interview), was not in Burisch's belief. He strictly believed in the "good" and "bad" concepts of people fighting each other for geopolitical dominance. The Moon has an "ark" that was mentioned earlier containing several pieces that was transported from Earth and rebuilt on the lunar surface. It has in its contents genetic, tissue, and other products of biodiversity just in case a catastrophe could occur.

The only final advice that Burisch offered was to "pray," which was unfitting for this type of situation. If we are to take responsibility as Burisch also believed, praying would not release us from the result of our actions and in turn, contradict the initial goal. He believed that releasing this information may save humanity, which added more fuel to the fire of his insanity. It is clear that Burisch offered very few factual points in this story of his about fantastic adventures and sinister groups that rule the Earth with alien technology. The idea of time travel is not unrealistic; however, Burisch seems to distort and twist the concepts to fashion his world of high adventure. He ended with the final statement of humans "creating their own reality;" and if this was the case, he has done so on a massive scale. If we want to view his story as authentic, Burisch needs to recap from the beginning and work out every tiny detail in order for the entire event to flow. Only then, can we revisit his idea of time travel with open arms and interest. Even the little details are important, and if one wishes to fabricate the event a mastery of the art of lying is needed, and Burisch is still a novice.

John Titor Origins

Another great example of time-travel is the story of the man from the future called John Titor. Although many consider this man to be a complete fabrication about his life in the future returning to year 1975 under military orders to retrieve a special IBM computer, others think he is a genuine article traveling back in time to warn us of future events that will affect our species as a whole. By mid-2004, there were approximately fifty websites dedicated to the "John Titor" story [61]. The initial name however before January 2001, was "time traveler-0" (meaning that this could be in fact a different entity than a man). Only after January, many postings that appeared in Art Bell forums, did the name John Titor come into use. This was needed because a name was required for use on the forum to discuss and comment blogs.

Usually when choosing a screen name for any account, we have the tendency either to leave our own name with a number that follows, or a fantasy name usually depicting our favorite pop culture icon, mythical figure, or videogame character. During the blogs on the Art Bell forums, he was asked if the name was his real name (assuming it was a male to begin with), with the reply being: "John Titor is a real name." This response does not give any indication of a yes or no; it only further implicates that something is either amiss, or that whomever is behind this blog, does not want to be identified just yet. Do we quickly assume that this individual is human at all? Could it be an alien entity or even worse, an A.I computer system like Watson who was created by IBM ironically?

This robot was tested on the game show Jeopardy in 2011, and defeated the best human opponents that were past champions (who amassed a great deal of money) [62]. It has already been deemed by a few as a "horrible machine" simply because it acts, answers, and responds more than human. IBM believes that the technology that runs Watson's system could save future human lives. Is it possible that time travler-0 was merely a super computer made to run like a human being, and able to fool anyone not privy to this type of knowledge? The answer would most likely be yes, simply for the fact that this is the Digital Age. The more we immerse ourselves online, the less human contact we receive. Most automated machines are sounding more human, making it difficult to tell sometimes if we are being spoken to by a human or not. As we investigate further, we must discover just who or what John Titor is, and if he can help humans change our current predicament by sharing future events. This in turn would complete the goal for the betterment of humankind or as *Kevin Flynn* (the fictional character from TRON) states: "a digital frontier to reshape the human condition."

Titor's Mission Objectives

Titor was described as a soldier from the year 2036 living in the United States (specifically in the state of Florida), operating out of Tampa in Hillsborough County. He was sent by the military via a time machine back to the year 1975 to obtain an IBM 5100 computer. It was understood that this specific model and this model only was needed to "correct" software problems in his time. The 5100 had the ability to use the old IBM code to reconcile incompatible programming languages of the future. He further stated that his grandfather had something to do with the 5100's initial programming and assembly, making him the perfect candidate. One IBM engineer named Bob Dubke concurred with Titor's statement on the technicalities on emulating and debugging mainframes using the 5100 [63].

It is believed that a computer system is never perfect, and if we are dealing with artificial intelligence, then we have to worry as humans about a growing singularity (that could learn to view humans as inadequate). Many films (such as the Terminator franchise and Tron Legacy [2010]) dealt with different types of computer programs that strived for perfection and the "perfect system" for optimal performance. As a result, humans are not part of the equation thus must be eliminated to prevent corruption. As of 2008, there are approximately one billion computers in operation worldwide [64]. With the growing promise of change in the world due to technology, humans could potentially be subjects and slaves to a new system with the likelihood of the perfect model of thought. Most humans will accept this digital world due to the fact that their own reality may be seemingly dull and painful; however very few who desire growth, change, critical thinking, and emotional power will be torn between the promise of a digital utopia or a digital cell (void of any change except from the master control program).

Titor had mistakenly traveled back to the year 2000 instead of 1975 (probably due to miscalculations) thus violating his mission protocol. As he became popular in just a few months beginning in October, he discussed pressing issues that the world was dealing with at the time. He claimed that the United States would engulf in a second civil war by the year 2004, and would totally be eradicated by the year 2015 due to nuclear attack [65]. He stated that most major cities would be destroyed and the nation would split into five separate countries; each with its own president. He later stated that he meant to stop in the year 2000 to visit family members and collect old photographs in the civil war, and wanted to warn the people of the coming war(s) plus their current state of diet. These two subjects are hardly related to each other, which draw many questions. If he stated the war started in 2004, there would be no reason to stop four years before to collect these photographs, unless there was another personal mission.

With the diet recommendations, Titor claimed that many lives would be lost to CJD or *Creutzfeldt-Jacob Disease*. This disease is an incurable degenerative brain disorder which leads to the loss of brain function and death. This disease was due to the consumption of infectious particles of protein (or prions) comparable to BSE (*Bovine Spongiform Encephalopathy*) [66]. Another name for this condition would be Mad Cow Disease; which is a disease due to the ingestion of infected meat (which will be an epidemic in the future according to Titor). He never gave a specific date; however he knew extensively about a disease that recently caught wind in the world about the year 1999. This would be a detail that nobody would understand in such great detail since the disease was just introduced to the population that year.

It could then be postulated that indeed this individual could only come from the future if he had such an extensive knowledge about a disease that would not be considered lethal until 2003. A main problem was disobeying his original mission objective to take care of personal agendas, and tried to interject his ideals to warn the people of the past of the dangerous future. Another interesting fact was his interest in UFO phenomena. When questioned by online subscribers about them, he stated that they were mysteries but did not deny their existence. He even went as far to claim that they could be time travel visitors themselves. Adding to the UFO speculation, Titor stated that they had in their possession far superior time machine technology than those from the future government program of 2036.

Titor's Time Machine

The time machine that he utilized was discussed in great detail on his online blogs. He stated that the time machine was compromised of "two magnetic housing units for dual micro singularities [and] an electron injection manifold to alter mass and gravity." This process was distinct and unique or as in quantum physics was described as "a point in space time when matter is dense (infinitely)." Along with the first part, three computers were also added with a cooling and x-ray "venting system," gravity sensors, and a variable lock with four primary clocks containing caesium (which is described as a sliver/gold alkali metal used specifically for atomic clocks) [67]. The problem that Titor would have with this element, would be exposure (that causes hyperirritability and spasms) making it a mild toxic. According to modern science, these compounds are rarely encountered by people due to the similarity to potassium (at least not naturally). The registered lethal dose of caesium chloride would be 2.3g per kilogram tested in mice studies (similar to the effects of potassium or sodium chloride) [68]. If Titor were to be exposed to this element even in a controlled environment, he would be seriously affected by it.

All of this equipment was then mounted on the rear of a 1967 Chevy Corvette that had been described by Titor as a "pastiche of pop science technology [69]." The time machine was later moved to a 1987 truck that was not specified (having four wheel drive) for some unknown reason. There were photos of the time machine displayed on the blog, but most of them came out fuzzy, making the story less believable as the skeptics had a field day debunking this. Many parts were described to be purchased at a local military surplus store, and even the laser photo was considered fake due to the noticeable beam holding it in place (not coinciding with the pointer). There is however, a significant understanding of advanced quantum physics done by Titor. He knew plenty of information concerning black holes, vortex singularities, and zero point energy (which were the new "cutting edge" of research). More than half of the Manhattan Project scientists (creators of the first atomic bomb) believed that a nuclear chain reaction could not be stopped; however, instead it would set the atmosphere on fire and incinerate the Earth. After years of research, this theory was deemed inconclusive [70].

Since all new science was deemed by modern science as "nonsense" or "magic," many are shying away from the possibilities of these concepts being more than just theories or entertainment venues. Few scientists believe that time is like a river and sometimes forms whirlpools, vortexes, and ripples creating and providing "shortcuts" through both time and space. Titor through his detailed explanation of the time machine described what science called the *Casimir Effect* [71]. This belief demonstrates that when two electronically conducting metal plates brought together close in a vacuum, a sort of space is created that negates gravity. Since gravity and time seem to be interrelated, canceling one may cancel the other. UFO witnesses according to research done by *Jim Marrs*, often described the loss of time or the cessation of all electronic devices when they saw a UFO nearby [72]. Could these subjects all correlate with Titor and his ideas? How does he have such an understanding about a subject not yet fully accepted by the scientific community until many years later? This could point to a theory that Titor may not be so human after all.

Multiple Realities

Besides his nuclear prediction, and the contamination of meat products, he also acknowledged recent time travel theories by asserting "everything that can happen does happen in a multidimensional universe." Instead of the belief of one linear time-space universe, we have an infinite number of timelines like a "needle on an old phonograph record." Only while we perceive the groove in which the needle rests, we usually ignore that there are more grooves present. How would Titor have such an understanding about a concept just introduced to the world at that time? He would either need to be informed by working in the government, part of a scientific research team on a project involving this study, or being from a future timeline where due to this theory he traveled back in time. Titor also discussed something on his blog concerning the question of going back and "killing your grandfather theory" with his exact words being:

> *"Nothing would happen. The universe would not end and there are no paradox problems that threaten existence . . . temporal space-time is made up of every possible quantum state. The grandfather paradox is impossible. In fact all paradox is impossible. The Everett-Wheeler—Graham or multiple theory is correct. All possible quantum states, events, possibilities, and outcomes are real; eventual and occurring. The chances of everything happening*

someplace at some time in the **superverse** *is 100%."*
(John Titor 02/02/01, 10:09am)

This theory that Titor exclaimed, fit the *Everett-Wheeler Model* proving it to be correct in nature. The Princeton physicist named Hugh Everett along with his advisor John Archibald Wheeler researched the "many-worlds" theory due to the fact that all systems were defined by a wave function [73]. The result of this wave function gives itself through this model; with the probability of finding the system in one or an infinite number of 'quantum states' defined by its total energy, momentum, and spin [74]. In other words, with these three main calculations and the use of mathematics causes the wave function to collapse if not viewed at that precise moment; which in turn nulls the effect of the original belief that there was more than one system. This is due to the numbers become finite and infinity becomes one specific reality; while the others were only there for a brief instant collapsing onto themselves (according to the Copenhagen "interpretation" of quantum mechanics). In 1957, Everett proposed a new theory counteracting the original theory above to display that in fact the wave function never collapses; therefore creating an infinite bundle of alternate histories each time the quantum state of any particle in the universe changes with interaction [75].

Whatever decision one individual makes, the same individual in another reality, chooses the latter of the two creating a new interaction, a new timeline of events, and a completely new outcome. With this theory, the human being is just a passive agent following along the many possibilities of whatever event(s) transpire making the human dependent on the system rather than in control. Most humans would not accept this due to the inability of personal control. No one wants to have someone control their life consciously making the decisions for them.

The Copenhagen model stressed the opposite where the human became the observer and could make changes in consciousness, giving us only one possible state. The Schrödinger Cat Theory plays perfect in the way that it displays a human being deciding the outcome of the life of the cat in the box (which alters the cat's destiny to save it before the poison is released). The observer has a chance to stop the chain of events from occurring; in turn choosing the right to control the situation [76]. The human seems unable to understand such a system due to the pertinacity of relying on the emotional state, questioning the situation, and the brain's uniqueness to halt an acceptance of any system counteractive to one's own faith (being that this human observing the cat is different from the collective or hive mind mentality we now experience).

In turn, that human will try to halt the events in order to achieve the result in a way that copes with their beliefs, passions, faith, or feelings. The Movie *Source Code* (2011) dealt with this type of subject where a soldier supposedly serving in Afghanistan (Colter Stevens) awoke within someone else's existence in an unknown location. He had eight minutes within this human's experience or memory to prevent a disaster from killing millions of people in a populated metropolitan city involving a train with bombs. In effect, Stevens had to prevent a chain of horrific events from transpiring altering a timeline's future for the government.

It took a while for Stevens to accept that he was living in another's existence for only eight minutes due to the tragic event that caused this train to explode. On a positive note, he bonded with the other individuals that eventually he grew an affinity for. While he was doing this "mission," Stevens was curious on his location and why the agency involved would not give him the Intel on his situation. After discovering that he was dead, he existed as only a memory within another man's dead body (in which he had to prevent more chaos from transpiring). This deals with quantative states of alternate realities, specifically associated with sequential time. Since the event already happened, there was no stopping it as Stevens wanted to do; there was only a future timeline where he could prevent more deaths.

Being told that he would be released upon the completion of his mission, we find that in the end, he wasn't alive and that his brain (along with half his body missing) was hooked into a super computer system that looped only eight minutes of reality pertaining to the event. He did however stop the bomb from happening within the eight minutes saving those already deceased people from dying.

In turn, he created another timeline where no one died and the train continued to its destination. Sending a message within the other body, he told one government agent close to him that a bomb threat would be thwarted, the name of the bomber, and to tell his dead body that everything would be "ok" without worry. Within this new reality, stopping the events caused him not to take the mission and he continued past the eight minutes creating a new world within a different body (even though this was impossible). With this complicated explanation, could this theory be realistic? This paradox provided one question: since the body he inhabited was already deceased, did this only take place in his mind, or did he utilize relational quantum mechanics to change the outcome?

Failed Predictions?

Most of his predictions did not occur making either untrue, or he was essentially from a different timeline of events. He did not mention September 11th, 2001; however he did mention that huge arsenals of weapons were in Iraq prior to the 2003 invasion. Could it be that the death of three thousand people might not have been important to him (considering he was three years old)? His early assertions that the company CERN (*European Organization for Nuclear Research*) Fermilab, and Brookhaven would discover the basis for time travel sometime around 2001 with the creation of "miniature black holes" (about a half a year after his departure from our time) [77]. Burisch did mention the use of micro wormholes being used in the 1990s, so it could mean that Titor is essentially onto to something here.

The 2004 Civil War did not take place at all either during the presidential election of George Bush Jr. (with no further conflicts in 2008 as Titor predicted) [78]. He stated that a "Waco type event" would transpire every month with problems escalating "at everyone's doorstep" by 2008 which didn't happen either [79]. He also stated in 2011 as a thirteen year old, he fought with a group called the "Fighting Diamondbacks" (described as an infantry unit out of Florida) for the next four years. In other posts; however he described himself hiding during the war.vvCould it be that it is a computer error by a system made to react as human? His 2015 prediction of WWIII may have some truth as we now are experiencing tension between the countries mentioned:

> *"In 2015, Russia launches a nuclear strike against the major cities in the United States (which is the "other side" of the civil war from my perspective),*

> *China, and Europe. The United States counter attacks. The U.S cities are destroyed along with the AFE (American Federal Empire) . . . thus we (in the country) won. The European Union and China were destroyed." (John Titor 11/07/00 21:23pm)*

Remember that Green also believed that Russian submarines undetectable by radar were positioned on both coasts of the United States. Could Titor be discussing these events that would happen years from now in this timeline? He referred to the altercation as "N Day," where Washington D.C and Jacksonville Florida were destroyed due to nuclear attacks. After this war, Omaha Nebraska is considered the new capital of the nation. If the country splits into five separate nations, which one is he discussing? On 02/08/01 at 9:40 am, he talked vaguely about what exactly the reason was for the culmination of war that "dealt with border clashes and overpopulation." He did mention also, that the Arab/ Jew conflict would begin this war as well. As of late, Iran and Israel are displaying tensions and the possibility for attack on either side could happen anytime [80].

Titor mentioned strangely that after the 2004 events, no Olympic games would take place anymore even though the 2006, 2008, 2010, and the summer Olympics of 2012 happened [81]. His insignia also bore a strange display that are said to be of a military nature; with one version displaying the words "*Tempus Edax Rerum*" displayed below the insignia. The translation from Latin means "time devours all things." Is this an ironic musing used purposely to push the idea of time travel for reality? Will this be the new standard for future military agencies once time travel is no longer considered a hoax or theory?

Will time devour us all, or do we have a chance to change anything we see unfit? Burisch's cube already has the ability to see what a better future could be according to the individual user, so could Titor adapt to this theory as well? He seems to adhere to the same idea of a many-worlds theory giving both stories similarities. Titor essentially leaves us with a final quote before either traveling back to the year 2036, or going back to 1975 to finally complete his mission. This quote was in response to the criticism of his claims and the disbelief of his predictions:

> *"How can you possibly criticize me for any conflict that came to you, I watch every day what you are doing as a society. While you sit by and watch your constitution being torn away from you, you willfully eat poisoned food, buy manufactured products no one needs and turn an uncaring eye away from millions of people suffering and dying around you. Is this the 'Universal law' you subscribe to? Perhaps I shall let you in on a little secret . . .* ***no one likes you in the future, this time period is looked at as being full of lazy, self-centered civically ignorant sheep. Perhaps you should be less concerned about me and more concerned about that*** *. . ."*
> *(John Titor: A Time Traveler's tale, pg 21)*

Whether we want to believe his predictions or his story at all, these final words are a sad reality. It is a sad day in humanity when a future man describes to us what exactly we are made of, how we conduct ourselves, and what our foundation consists of in the current time period. Can we prove him wrong or is it too late to stop a bullet train heading down our current timeline? Can we as humans fulfill the role of "Stevens" and prevent the bomb that could possibly end our species?

As we close the argument of paradoxes and time travel, we must discover what we can learn from this experience. Most people are comfortable in their surroundings, which results in little interest to venture outside their safety zone to discover new things. This fact hinders humans from rising above to view reality in a way incomprehensible to the current human mind state. If we are ever to change our ways, we must seek out new paths, since the old current one damage us beyond repair. Whether Burisch is indeed mentally disturbed, through his insanity we can find out what we are missing from his our vague and obscure existence.

Titor can indeed show us even though considered untrue by most skeptics, a new way to sit back a view our current behaviors and how they destroy us. Most of us as humans believe we are fine and fail to see the need for a new road. If we are ever to accept the many-worlds theory, we must acknowledge the fact that we are not in control and not as important as we consider ourselves to be in the grand scheme of things. Let us look at the possibility that our concept of the "divine" is also based on our biases and prejudices altering its concept wherever we see fit. Can we alter our current timeline and fix our past mistakes? This would give us the opportunity to change and prevent certain events from taking place such as: losing a loved one, preventing a marriage/union, or preventing an event that forces us to pick an option we later regret. If we do not experience these trials and tribulations, we would never realize the need to be aware of the change, therefore making us stagnant without the concept of anything different about the present.

In the *Time Machine* movie (2002) based on the novel by H.G Welles, if Hartdegen never experienced the loss of his love Emma, he would have never had the need to build the machine to prevent the death in the first place. So he needed the loss of his love to undergo a metamorphosis into a more intelligent, critical, adventurous, and rational individual with a new learning experience. Is it true then that we need pain to grow into a better human? Sadly enough, if pain and suffering do not transpire on some level for humans, we will always be the same unaware, ignorant, innocent, and boring individuals. Concordantly, if we are not careful, the pain transforms us into empty somber shadows forever stuck in limbo with regret, and remorse. Some say "ignorance is bliss," however does the inquisitive mind also fit in this category? Only with our personal experiences we find that we are essentially alone in our travels; whether through time in this reality or in others.

End Notes

[1] "Project Camelot interviews Dan Burisch." *Projectcamelot.org*, Las Vegas Nevada (July 2006).

[2] Ibid 1.

[3] George Knapp. "Bob Lazar: The man behind Area 51." *8newsnow.com* (2000-2012).

[4] ufocasebook.com/danburisch.html.

[5] Sanford B. Steever. *The Dravidian Languages*. Routledge; Ns Ed edition (January 1998).

[6] "Dr. Dan Bursich-Area 51 scientist-A total fraud?" *rense.com* (December 2005).

[7] Ibid 6.

[8] Ibid 6.

[9] Ibid6.

[10] Eric Hoover. "Truth and Admissions: former MIT dean seeks to reclaim her name." *The Chronicle* (December 2009).

[11] Ibid 1.

[12] Ibid 1.

[13] Ibid 1.

[14] Ibid 1.

[15] Ibid 1.

[16] Ibid 1.

[17] Ibid 1.

[18] msscweb.org/Public/history.html

[19] projectcamleot.org/dan_bursich_summary.html.

[20] Lee Speigel. "Result UFO crash: there was 2 crashes, not 1 says Ex-Air Force official." *Huffington Post* (August 2012).

[21] Ibid 1.

[22] Ronan Hicky, Simon Berrow, and John Goold. "Towards a Bottlenose Dolphin whistle echogram from Shannon Estuary Island." *Biology and Environment: Proceedings of the Royal Irish Academy* 109B [2] (2009).

[23] Alejandro Acevedo-Gutiérrez, William F. Perrin, Bernd G. Wursig, and J.G.M. Thewissen. "Group Behavior" *Encyclopedia of Marine Mammals* (2nd Edition) Academia Press (2008).

[24] Ibid 1.

[25] Ibid 1.

[26] Ibid 1.

[27] Ibid 19.

[28] L. Spence. *An Encyclopedia of Occultism*. Carol Publishing (1993).

[30] Ibid 1.

[31] Ibid 1.

[32] Wendy Chapman "Who are the Indigo Children" *Ajna Spirituality* (August 2012).

[33] Bernard Foing. "Noah's ark on the Moon." *Moon Daily* (February 2006).

[34] B.J. Wolf, Albert Howell, and Dan B. Catselas Burisch. *Eagles Disobey: The Case for INCA City Mars.* Candlelight Publishing (August 1998).

[35] ufocasebook.com/2008c/meninblack.html.

[36] H.C. Van Ness. *Understanding Thermodynamics.* Dover Publications Inc. (1983).

[37] Ker Than "Bacteria may hold immortality." *Fvza.org* (September 2006).

[38] Ibid 1.

[39] Robert Brown. *Ganesh: Studies of an Asian God.* Albany: State University of New York (1991).

[40] Sailen Debnath. *The Meanings of Hindu Gods, Goddesses, and Myths.* Rup & Co. New Delhi (November 2009).

[41] J. Rostand. *Lazarro Spallenzani e le origen della biologia sperintale.* Torino Einaudi, (1997).

[42] Project Camelot. "Interview with Dan Burisch" *Projectcamelot.org,* Las Vegas Nevada (July 2007).

[43] Ibid 42.

[44] David Deutsch. "Quantum Mechanics near closed Timelike Lines." *Physical Review* D44 [10] (1991).

[45] Kip S. Thorne. *Black Holes and Time Warps.* W.W. Norton (1994).

[46] Nikodem J. Poplawski. "Radical motion into an Einstein-Rosen Bridge." *Physical Letters* B687 [2-3] (2010).

[47] David Kay. *Schaum's Outline of Theory and Problems of Tensor Calculus.* McGraw-Hill (1998).

[48] Ibid 42.

[49] Joseph Brewda. "Kissinger's 1974 plan for food control genocide." *The Schiller Institute* (December 1995).

[50] William Cooper, "Majestic 12 and the secret government." *Thelivingmoon.com* (2006).

[51] Ibid 42.

[52] epa.gov/climatechange/science/indicators/weather-climate/temperature.hmtl.

[53] Roy W. Spencer Ph.D. "Weak warming of the Oceans 1955-2010 implies low climate sensitivity." *Drroyspencer.com* (May 2011).

[54] C.B. Baker "Tesla weather control over America." *Rense.com.*

[55] Area51et.com/bill-uhouse.

[56] Ibid 20.

[57] Ibid 42.

[58] Philip K. Dick. *The Minority Report*. Gollancz: London (2002).

[59] Ibid 42.

[60] Serpo.nl/

[61] Jim Marrs. *Above Top Secret: Uncover the Mysteries of the Digital Age*. Disinformation Books (2008).

[62] Melissa Maerz. "IBM's Watson computer beats 'Jeopardy!' champions." *LA Times* (February 2011).

[63] "Time traveler most likely to be spotted in Rochester: IBM Engineer Bob Dubke on hidden features" *Rochester Magazine* (December 2005).

[64] Associated Press. "Worldwide PC use to reach 1 billion by 2008." *CBC News* (June 2007).

[65] John Titor 11/07/00 21:23.

[66] G. McDomel and P. Burke. "The Challenge of Prion Decontamination." Clinical Infectious Diseases: *An official publication of the Infectious Disease Society of America* 36[9] (May 2003).

[67] johntitor.strategicbrains.com/timemachine.cfm

[68] Law, J.C. Kasan, KM Fazil, L. Eberdy, A. Adomat and H. Gus ES. "Accessing the therapeutic and toxilogical effects of cesium chloride following administration to nude mice bearing PC-3 or LNCap prostate cancer." *Cancer Chemotherapy and Pharmacology* 60[6] (2007).

[69] Ibid 67.

[70] fas.org/syp/othergov/doe/lanl/docs1/00329010.pdf

[71] A. Lambrecht. "The Casimir Effect: A force from nothing." *Physics World* (September 2002).

[72] Ibid 61.

[73] Hugh Everrett. "Theory of Universal Wave Function." *Thesis; Princeton University* (1956, 1973).

[74] Ibid 73.

[75] Ibid 73.

[76] Carlo Rovelli. "Relational Quantum Mechanics." *International Journal of Theoretical Physics* 35 (1996).

[77] Robert Matthews. "A Black Hole ate my planet." *New Scientist* (August 1999).

[78] John Titor 02/27/01 17:25.

[79] John Titor 02/01/01 8:36.

[80] Ronen Bergman. "Will Israel attack Iran?" *New York Times* (January 2012).

[81] John Titor 01/29/01.

The heart is the chief feature of a

functioning mind.

-Frank Llyod Wright (1868-1959)

Be noble minded! Our own heart,

and not other men's opinion of us,

forms our true honor.

-Johann Von Schiller (1759-1805)

VII

Dr. Pete Peterson: The Problem Solver of "Spaceship Earth"

The UFO community is full of those who offer different points of view concerning the future and the 2012 endgame. An individual by the name of Pete Peterson speculates another view concerning human existence in a vast complicated universe. He introduces us to his past life with Robotics, UFO experiences, information on just how the heart is more than a muscle, the brain in conjunction with the heart, and the ways that we can prepare ourselves for what he called the "oncoming onslaught." The "end of days" belief, whether religiously interjected or not, has plagued humanity in fear for the last twenty-five hundred years. The Christians believed due to Harold Camping, that May 21st, 2011 was the day of the "rapture" where all devout Christians would ascend to heaven to leave all of the "non-believers" here to rot in the seven day war between Jesus and the Anti-Christ [1]. Camping, an American radio Christian broadcaster, owns *Family Radio* (based out of California) and is responsible for one hundred fifty markets all over the United States.

Due to considerable donations by his mindless followers, Camping was able to raise millions to get his "divine message" across to save the world. Camping did not have the ability (as he claimed) to predict the end of the world failing miserably. With his first two failed predictions of May 21st, 1988, and

September 7th, 1994, it was not surprise that he failed again in May 2011. He later changed his mind concerning the prediction and conveniently postponed the date to October 21st, 2011 where "god would destroy the universe." Moving ahead in 2012, he conveniently disappeared from the limelight leaving plenty of followers behind embarrassed and ashamed.

The religious dogmatic preacher pushed his asinine theory so intensely, that one teen in Russia actually committed suicide due to fear [2]. Many others ignorantly gave their possessions away, quit their jobs, and spent their money with one woman in Maryland spending her daughter's college funds on preparing for this religious event! She also sadly and ignorantly told her children that they were not going to "heaven" with her [3]. Our need to believe in these empty cults has prevented us from using our rational, emotional, and logical skills to prevent disaster in our lives. Even though most of these penniless, homeless, and jobless Christians suffered, they will most likely still believe in its nonsensical structure with zero positive results.

Peterson only discussed material science and a new frontier that may not help us prepare as a whole species, rather individually take into consideration that we cannot set a date on something too complicated by adding a "human touch." Maybe as individuals, we can look into our hearts and see that there is more to emotions than meet the eye; with the heart that throughout history has had different meanings both positive and negative [4]. We can find ourselves and form a new consciousness that may save our species from destroying each other. In a way, by discovering what the heart can help us do for each other and other organisms, we may find a sort of rapture where humans will be able to join a complex community of universal love. It seems we do not have enough sequential time to determine this; however maybe a few individuals will break the mold humans have shaped over our long morbid history.

Peterson's Spaceship Earth

Pete Peterson's story is an interesting one full of speculation. He stated that he has been involved with the U.S. government since he was thirteen years old. During his time there, he was considered a problem solver when faced will of the issues presented to him. He attributed this "ability" due to the fact that he claimed to have inventors on both sides of the family. Peterson claimed in his own mind, that most of his family took part in the changes in humanity on a technological level. His belief also extends to the country itself heading for a "meltdown," and school system deterioration with the motto "no child left with a mind."

Claiming that he served ten years in the Marine Corps (all ten years in combat zones), he felt he was equipped with the knowledge to make such statements [5]. The country according to his belief has completely turned away from its original purpose into a new socialist system where logic and reasoning were inadequate. His "inventions" have been helpful; however was suppressed by industry run government instead of the fabled "people" concept.

As all of the previous individuals we have gathered information from, Peterson was no different in the fact that he was interviewed by Project Camelot in June of 2009. He claimed that this was his only interview in depth to warn people of oncoming disasters. Peterson in the beginning of his interview, described himself as different from the rest of his family. He always had the belief that he was "dropped from the sky in a titanium egg" until the age of twenty-two [6]. His point of view was that people were stuck with him on this planet and that he was different from every other human being. Instead of a planet, Peterson considered this location "spaceship Earth" passing through the cosmos. Genetics according to his belief, was the main key in solving most questions on this planet. This point could be very accurate since modern science is now fortifying an already strong foundation, using genetics to cure human deficiencies [7]. His childhood as he vaguely described it, was mainly a home powered by solar energy with an atmospheric (temperature climate) pressure change environment. He called the structure a Mexican hacienda gallery, however covered. His father supposedly was also an inventor who constructed automobiles, the house itself, and was an engineer for the military.

At the age of ten, Peterson claimed to have built his first rocket and "naturally powered" fuel rocket (as he described an affinity for them and explosions). He attributed his unknown recognition to the fact that he never considered himself a businessman. Due to this naivety, certain people took his "inventions" away to capitalize on. Peterson also attributed his influences to *King Tut's tomb*, as it familiarized him with ancient cultures and technology. From this point on, he decided to become an anthropologist/archeologist. Later however, his fascination with ancient cultures ceased as one day he described a life changing event. Supposedly, at a family gathering he viewed a "flying saucer show" with many different shapes and sizes. They flew back and forth, dashed away at great speeds, and returned as if just for him to view [8].

Oddly enough, he decided to study science until he could build his own flying saucer. He claimed while mentioning this, he also built the Dr. Who "phone booth" or the TARDIS (*Time and Relative Dimension in Space*) before ever producing plans for a saucer. This in turn produced an interest for time travel, since the booth itself was used for this purpose making the user a Time Lord [9]. As we review the story of the Dr. Who universe, we remember that the Time Lords were an extraterrestrial civilization to which the Doctor belonged to [10]. Peterson is now hinting that he may have built the time machine before its inception from the BBC science fiction show. He also claimed to have worked for many government agencies, corporations, and now himself.

During the beginning, he stated that he was be sixty-nine years in 2009, and was trying to build his own laboratory to continue his research. He wouldn't state what the research was for, but stressed that it would be in a remote location without man made electromagnetic fields (that would allow his work to be done). If his age is to be considered correct, he would then be born in 1940 making him develop his rockets in 1950. He would also be within the U.S. government in 1953 (since he stated he was thirteen at the time). Could this be a story of "boy genius," or is he another disillusioned individual creating a fantastic adventure?

Technology, Religion, and UFOs

A number of governments according to Peterson have the technology of flying saucers by "peoples off planet" due to ancient knowledge. This could be an accurate statement since most ancient civilizations from the Egyptian, Incan, Aztec, Sumerian, and Rama (Northern Indian empire dated from about 10,000-15,000 BCE) all displayed flying devices or pictures within their texts, cuneiform, or hieroglyphics [11]. The three thousand year old structure named the New Kingdom

Temple located several hundred miles south of Cairo and the Giza plateau at Abydos, displayed ceiling beams that show glyphs of flying devices. Pakal the Aztec Astronaut is another example of technology found in ancient civilizations before our modern time.

Discovered in 1949 by Alberto Ruz in the Temple of Inscriptions Pyramid in Palenque Mexico, a strange sculpture found within the sarcophagus that archeologists only considered art, we find a description of an alien or god within a machine that resembles a spaceship or flying saucer [12]. The Rig Veda (an ancient Hindu bible) holds the truths concerning the Rama Empire, their technology, and could possibly be the oldest writings predating the Sumerian tablets [13]. Peterson himself stated that due to ancient knowledge, one Sumerian tablet displayed how to build a flying saucer and presented the speculation that modern physics did not apply. The legendary children of the *Uru* were said to have knowledge based on the Sumerian tablets in building flying machines [14] [15].

We have seen amazing wonders excavated from Iraq and Iran. Along with the U.S. reluctance to leave this area (by creating war and propaganda), these unknown reasons have caused the deaths of many innocents on both sides. The Baghdad Battery (one minute example of technology allowed to be displayed to the world) discovered in 1936, displayed the use of technology that supposedly wasn't "invented" until the 1800s by Alessandro Volta. Since Peterson claimed to have a PhD in natural philosophy (or physics), these ancient documents may prove that modern science is wrong and we as responsible humans must rewrite history. Regardless of having the degree or not, this statement is true even though history has already been rewritten by religious and secret society interests. They did not plan to share the knowledge of the past with everyone, in turn kept the secrets for themselves.

Even if we know the supposed truth, how are we to change anything without disastrous effects? What do we replace the last two thousand years of lies and deceit with the truth or another lie? History as we remember according to Green is just a story of the victor omitting the details (that would probably explain what we today consider mysteries). Like Maxwell, Peterson stated that the Vatican library contained documentation proving most things that we believe to be true were not so. Most of these documents were fashioned after surviving manuscripts from the fires of Alexandria (the rest were stolen by Arab/Jew interests and placed in archives at the Vatican and the National Library of Israel for their eyes only).

Peterson has even went as far to claim that somehow he obtained some of these documents, and involved himself with a machine to translate them [16]. He mentioned the *Annunaki* (which were giants according to his diagnosis) suffered from "genetic problems and errors" and how past skeletons did not have these anomalies. He was in fact hinting that the Titans of the past did not suffer from what current human giants suffer from: gigantism. This condition is due (according to medical science), to the pineal gland producing an excessive amount of growth hormone. Also known as Acromagaly, the skeletal and circulatory systems both suffer immensely due to this condition.

He also believed that DNA testing has been thwarted by religious schools and bodies who want to keep this information, in order to strengthen the lie. Against this belief system (and rightfully so), he was positive that radio carbon dating was one hundred percent accurate. According to modern science, cave men were considered the first people accepted by archeology and anthropology. However in the last eight years, science has discovered an ancient civilization three thousand years old with writing, language and technology that predates even cavemen (fully developed and seemed to "appear" out of nowhere) [17]. Although he doesn't attribute a name to this civilization, he could be hinting at the Rama empire or Sumer (that both existed more than six thousand years ago). If one studies the tablets or the Rig Veda, it displays the technology that would be considered to be from our current time or even more advanced.

Peterson's Diagnosis

Peterson switched the subject leaving his childhood behind to concentrate on some of the inventions he has claimed to create. The first machine he discussed was a device that measured the field around the human body, was able to locate all of the organs, view their health state, and developed a solution of up to fifty percent diagnosis for each. He stated that any diagnosis above fifty percent was impossible due to genetic errors within the human population. The only way to reach up to seventy percent was to use this procedure individually rather than in groups.

This makes sense as almost every human individual (although similar in certain ways), is unique in nature. Peterson concurs with modern science that only eighty-five percent of the human genome is charted and discovered. The other fifteen percent is unknown unlike anything else on Earth [18]. It can only be described as "alien-like," possibly due to solar radiation or ionized radiation (usually found in southern Utah, Nevada, New Mexico, and Arizona due to nuclear testing). He believed that the fifteen percent came from off planet with documents proving that "visitors" originated from extra solar planets, and galaxies. According to his knowledge, scientists have written documents (that he did not mention) about recorded events concerning this subject. He speculates that the alien DNA can be recognized due to the rejections of programs created by the U.S. government that allow for mind control (reprogramming people's minds), throwing them off balance and forcing people to believe events or things that would be ridiculous [19].

The mind control experiment according to him, works on eighty-five percent of the population making the other fifteen percent unharmed due to their alien DNA strain. The strain is not limited to one race or type of people; it is distributed throughout different cultures and races. If this speculation was true, that would make identifying the strain almost impossible due to the fact that research had to be done globally. The second device that he proclaimed was his invention, dealt with communication concerning what Peterson described as "lecture laundry;" which he supposedly designed to increase communication within "no noise" microphones.

As he described the contents of the device with two bands that recorded the information, the last band gave identification to the speaker. By installing a "knob" on the device, the interference that was once a problem, cleared producing a crisp sound that he described as "perfect." Peterson claimed that Christopher C. Kraft Jr., a retired NASA engineer and manager of Mission Control operation, specifically asked him to develop this "knob" to resolve the communication issue. Considered a problem solver in his own right, at no time does Kraft ever mention Peterson or this communication issue. Kraft was heavily involved in the space program during the 1957 Sputnik launch and was considered a mentor to the program [20]. Also during this time, Peterson claimed to have built a satellite tracking system that recorded the location of the first satellite (this would be Sputnik is his story was to hold water). He then supposedly contacted the U.S. government, which in turn gave him another contract to build robots for the Energy Commission dated from the years 1955-58. If Peterson was born in 1940, he would be too young to known Kraft or engage in the communication field, since his name was not listed on the thirty-five members of Project Mercury (the first of flight operators to put a man in space for the U.S.).

Preparations for the Future

He was secluded from the outside world surrounded by a three hundred sixty degree valley where supposedly no man made electromagnetic fields were present. He assured that this secret location was also deep within the mountains, highly defendable, and difficult to breach. Seemingly, Peterson was preparing for certain events to transpire as he was confident in the description of his location. What in the world could he be preparing for? His idea of the world "meltdown" was imminent due to the signs in movies, pop culture, and books. He claimed them to be cataclysmic events that would transpire between the years 2010-12 according to the Mayan calendar belief system. This disaster will initially take place on both political and geophysical levels [21].

Peterson briefly focused on the money issue and how the U.S. government was printing money without gold or silver to attain a value (he estimates in the trillions). He anticipated the fall of the dollar then very soon to his knowledge within the coming years. As far as the location went, his fortress of sorts had the four seasons, agriculture, meat products, and could easily be shut off from large amounts of people in a chaotic situation (looking for food, supplies etc . . .). It is apparent that whatever group he belonged to was preparing for these events preordained by ancient civilizations.

Peterson was confident in his location with plans already in effect; however, did he have a plan B? One can never fully prepare for anything with plans due to the order of the universe complying with another type of modus operandi. The term "never say never," is also undetermined concerning the human mind state, for we do not know how we will act until the situation arises. Unless a human being has experienced desperate, it is unknown how the mind will react in events such as these. Is he one hundred percent sure that the location will be totally safe from large masses of desperate humans, or was this pure speculation? Usually impossible places are eventually breached if the mob worked together for one common agenda: survival.

Survival is a human theme that can be achieved, since all organisms fight for their wellbeing in any circumstance. How does Peterson think he can defeat this natural process? Could it be through science or an illusion? It seems very unlikely that he is completely prepared for any situation, as plans always have flaws (because they are essentially human). He affirmed that he was preparing for future probable events (due to the school systems around the country not teaching the student body anything about real current events). The debt as he described, "will be finally paid in four generations of the American family." He also clung to the idea of a world problem due to economics failing worldwide with fiat money not having any value [22]. The idea of ethics and morality (if they are such things) in Peterson's eyes, were removed from the school systems twenty-five years ago for political reasons. He believed that they only teach anarchy and chaos. Some examples of this belief happen during riots that supersede beyond a safe point of restoring order. If this is the case, the National Guard is told to fire upon civilians if necessary. This has been done before during hurricane Katrina in New Orleans. With the support of the governor Kathleen Blanco, she was quoted with this warning to looters that they would be killed:

> *"These troops are battletested. They have M-16s locked and loaded. These troops know how to shoot and kill and I expect they will." (James Joyner, September 2, 2005; OTB)*

If this was the case, new young soldiers were taught to not have emotions while following orders. He also believed that senators and congressman such as Blanco were here to please what he called "splinter groups" (which are defined as either a religious faction or political faction separate from the "parent group") rather than the people. If the National Guard is told to fire on unarmed thieves looking for food and supplies, or armed civilians just the same, it is safe to assume that order is not meant to be established; rather elimination is the objective. Peterson supported the "one world currency" idea that we have entertained before. He stated factual evidence about the last four presidents belonging to the Council of Foreign Affairs, with NAFTA along with GAT agreements, would make Canada, Mexico and the United States "one government with three parts [23][24]."

The Amero (the currency that would be replacing the dollar) and the North American Union were certain to flourish soon according to many conspirators [25] [26]. Robert Pastor vice chairman of the Independent Task Force on North America (who advocated a greater economic and social integration between Canada, Mexico, and the United States as a region) even supported the belief and stated that "In the long term, the amero is in the best interests of all three countries [27]." Peterson's belief as of now was that the currency has been destroyed and was being replaced by another U.S. currency. Whether this is true or not, the idea still stands that international bankers would like to see the down fall of this economy to rule the entire globe under the dominion of their own monetary standard. The idea of "shipping people around" was another concept that he stated coinciding with Green's initial idea that concentration camps would be built.

The human population would be "chipped" as well for identification purposes. Peterson goes as far as to mention that a sort of hypodermic needle was now being used to "identify people;" which acted as a sort of Bluetooth technology for credit and financial type purposes. The first *RIFD* (radio frequency identification) that was "officially reported" happened in 1988 when English scientist Kevin Warwick used it to open doors, turn on/off light switches, and communicate verbally within a building structure (without the use of any other methods) [28]. It is now reported that this model is currently being displayed in the Science Museum in London. Verichip Corporation (or better known as the Positive ID Corporation) since 2002 has used this microchip technology successfully on human trials calling the product VeriMed in 2004. Approved by the FDA, the chip finally suffered a defeat due to the fact that the result led to cancer in all laboratory tests on animals [29].

Discontinued in May 2010, many other groups (most religious in nature) opposed this technology due to their belief of "satanic" implications ("mark of the beast" ideology) [30]. The more important reason for the ban of this technology by this corporation and government should not be based on religious ignorance, rather the idea of tracking, reporting and identifying all of an individual's history, location, and activities. Peterson added that the idea of "geo-location" and anti-theft purposes on people would be used as if we were products (concurring with Maxwell). Countries such as Mogadishu Somalia, Mexico, and the Mediterranean were using this chip in full effect according to his belief [31]. It seems we can expect in the future in terms of a new "shopping experience" or human "Onstar" program, just in case we lose or loved ones. The false ideas of freedom and justice would be eliminated for the sake of a new "national security" measure: the human being itself.

Proceeding with the subject of preparation, Peterson described his methods for surviving the 2012 disasters waiting to happen. He reiterated that currency issues (U.S. dollar fails, T-bills becoming null, and bonds being worthless) were the main factor. The European Union would fail due to bankruptcy especially the Icelandic financial crisis 2008-2012 and Greece saved from bankruptcy by European Central Bank [32]. He then mentioned a very bizarre description if his "expertise" in urban survival and has claimed to train others as well.

If he was in a secret fortified location, what would be the need for this type of training? Is he expecting a breach of his perfect defense? The true ideas that humans can take out of this "training," deal with the absence of community within the human habitat. Due to globalization, an expansion that superseded beyond small communities has been impacted. There are no more small towns where the people "know each other" as past history has shown. In times of chaos, the small town if well connected, would be able to work together to resolve their problems as best as possible. As we venture into huge areas where people barely know each other what guarantee does one individual have that his/her neighbor will not attempt to steal or even kill them to survive?

The highest probability would be the most realistic answer: a fact that everyone will be trying to survive and put themselves and their families first. If one is well financed with food and supplies, it's a good idea to assume that the less fortunate will not stop by and ask for products/supplies as they would eliminate you for them. The government according to Peterson expects this situation to transpire which is why they demonstrate the urgency to eliminate "unruly civilians" breaching national peace. We can safely assume that no human would like the fact of being placed in a concentration camp during these times, unless they have a submissive cultural upbringing. The whole process is very frightening; however one has to come in terms with realism and the logical outcome. This doesn't mean that fear should take over the senses ("I have to prepare for this everyday" theme), for it is not a way to live. The only preparation suggested would be awareness of one's surroundings, keeping supplies realistically within the parameters of one's own budget, not allowing the mind to enter desperation or fear, and not to trust anyone due to the fact their survival is beyond yours.

Sadly enough, the world is not as before where one could trust their neighbor, making the plight more than an individual's survival mission. Peterson exemplified the last five years of the hurricane Katrina incident and how unprepared the country was. Texas, New Orleans, Mississippi and Alabama have had occurrences where service stations have stopped, crowded highways emerged, no supplies available, and people were stuck [33]. This makes sense as during the chaotic dismay, all humans would try to escape the area and flood the roads blocking themselves and others. He stated also that the weather itself was changing becoming colder, with droughts.

Problems with water were also evident, meaning that it could become a commodity in short supply very soon. His suggestions of making copies of important documents, copies of pictures to ensure "continuity," and to come in terms with the idea that people will have to fend for themselves due to shortages of supplies was realistic at best. Communication is needed along with resources such as short wave radios to find out important information. He also recommended a "bug out bag" filled with medical supplies, food, gas, things to keep cool/warm, etc . . . for what he called a "small preparation [34]." He assumes that people are equipped to think, rationalize, and have the financial means for preparation.

Most live on a day-to-day basis, and are totally ignorant to any event around them relying on mass media outlets for information. Very few individual groups actually take the time to make any preparations based on research, religious dogmatic view of the end of times, or using critical thinking skills. If he was certain that supplies would be limited, this meant that not everyone would have the opportunity to survive. It seems that this plan for preparation was not well thought out. He did however; reiterate the point of relying only on oneself. Preparing mentally was also mentioned, assuming that most people have a controlled mental state to begin with. The only valid point that Peterson clarified was that when we rely on others the situation may or may not succeed; only with oneself can a probability for success be close to the hundred percentile range. Why is it that we cannot depend on each other? It is true that responsibility has been nonexistent for the last twenty years or so and religion along with government, has given the people false promises and claims instead of teaching them responsibility.

Peterson believes that the president has no idea or any control on what is to transpire soon and that Cassidy's idea of the illusionary "white hats" was inaccurate. He attributed this belief system due to the movies and entertainment industry that he believes are government funded to display what they want the population to know [35]. He also stated that the only real president of the United States was Washington (along with Jefferson being another valid candidate). The presidents after these two leaders were only puppets pleasing their masters to control the population [36]. Kennedy and Lincoln could be added to this list of real presidents, due to their reluctance to follow procedure of the "plan," which in turn cost them their lives. Peterson hinted at the possibility that Obama might disclose UFO truths in 2009; however this did not happen.

He mentioned also that many countries that have experienced UFO phenomena, ranged from contact to abductions. Brazil, Africa (didn't mention any specific countries), Russia, Germany, and the United States. He also claimed "massive sightings" were taking place and that Brazil had over three hundred. Recently, the Brazilian government has made plans to make all UFO sightings public for study purposes [37]. Peterson also stated that the 2001 fiasco was orchestrated by the government and that the building had nothing to do with the crash. The building was destroyed due to the fact that the basement had a large quantity of gold that disappeared [38]. He described that the wind pattern could not have affected this building, causing something elusive or planned for this building's demise. A few Arab freedom fighters were able to penetrate the defense so easily of one of the world's leading highly defendable countries, seemed impossible to say the least. Along with Jim Marrs' research and analysis on 9/11, there seems to be a diabolical scheme at play here [39].

Peterson's "Inventions"

Peterson strongly believed that he impacted the science community and the different agencies he "worked" for in his career. He described that he studied and worked with Russian scientists (formerly in the USSR) considered "top scientists," which were known by "invitation only" status. Peterson claimed that he was responsible for most of the technology that was moved out of the USSR into the United States, labeling them as "donations." The subject was labeled as material science that was used to generate alternate energy. He stated that the government was looking for new ways to operate motors and spacecraft, along with new ways to store electricity in capacitors (a lot of this was new technology or updated innovative designs). He mentioned that electric cars were part of this project and the process of energy was sent to the air as "heat," which then "broke" into different pieces and finally processed into a capacitor device. This in turn, recharged the battery to allow the electric car to move.

This technology didn't sound out of the ordinary as hybrid electric cars use this technology today in a similar way. Using an ICE (internal combustion engine) propulsion system along with an electric propulsion system, the car can operate fully without the use of fossil fuels (thus deeming it as a ("full Hybrid"). To believe that Peterson had anything to do with its initial creation could be questionable. He discussed his involvement with General Atomics and Pratt and Whitney Rocketdyne (PWR) concerning the Aurora Project stating that it was made in the USA [40]. General Atomics was a nuclear physics and defense contractor founded in 1955. They are located in San Diego California, where their main research involves fission and fusion. With expansion in other venues, they were involved in remote surveillance craft, nuclear fuel cycle, advanced electric, airborne sensors, electronics, and wireless and laser technologies. Although Peterson describes the Aurora Project dealt with spray gas emitting to the surface and "exploding it" in turn creating fuel, it is highly unlikely that this had to do with General Atomics as he claimed.

The *Aurora* (secret reconnaissance aircraft) was considered a black project and supposedly created by *Skunkworks* out of Lockheed. Although the government denies this project as purely "mythical," many sightings have been seen in England and the United States, stirring up some sort of controversy (this coincided with Dean and his discussion concerning the *B-2* craft developed by Ben Rich) [41]. Peterson could not be describing this craft, since he did not mention Rich or Lockheed (making it unlikely that he had anything to do with this project). Concerning General Atomics, the only leading projects on record that they were involved with were Project Orion, and the TRIGA (Training, Research, Isotopes, and General Atomics) nuclear reactor that Peterson didn't mention at all. The TRIGA nuclear reactor was their first project design led by Freeman Dyson in 1958 [42]. If Peterson had something to do with this, he would have been eighteen at the time, making him too young to have any sort of involvement.

Considered a "pool-type reactor," it was used as a research tool by scientific institutions in testing isotope production and was considered "nondestructive." The reactor is being made now for use in other countries and approximately over sixty *TRIGA* reactors have now been licensed by the U.S. Nuclear Regulatory Commission in 2008. Project Orion considered a nuclear propulsion project, was a study of spacecraft intended to work and propel itself on explosions of atomic bombs behind the craft (also called nuclear pulse propulsion). Although the initial proposals started in 1946 by the Polish scientist *Stanislaw Ulam*, the actual project started in 1958 by Ted Taylor at General Atomics; with Freeman Dyson again onboard due to his success of the TRIGA reactor [43]. With this technology, the performance of rockets could be of greater results than the original Saturn V rocket for the Apollo Moon missions.

The idea of low cost was also considered however by 1963, the Partial Test Ban Treaty (which prohibited the testing of nuclear devices in the atmosphere, outer space, or underwater) was said to have decommissioned the project. Peterson obviously mentioning very vaguely about the Orion Project, would again be too young to have taken a part in its conception, testing, or study, since he would not fit the time frame of his claimed age during these events. Rocketdyne, on the other hand, was a U.S. based company that designed and produced rocket engines that utilized liquid propellants. The company itself was formed in 1967 by the North American Aviation when it merged with Rockwell International, but was already a separate division beginning in 1955. Their major contributions were for the NASA space program and military weapon systems essentially creating engines, missiles, and rockets (that were utilized named Thor, Delta, and Atlas).

The F1 rocket engine used in the Saturn V rockets, were one of their famous engine designs. Since it was first developed during the years 1955-57 prospectively, it is highly unlikely even due to Peterson's claim of working at a young age for the government, partook in any of these projects. He diverted his attention back to the scientists, especially one he called I.M Frankovic which he described as a believer in quantum physics. This scientist never hired anyone who didn't believe in this theory [44]. Although no research or evidence could be found under this name, it could be possible that Peterson was fabricating this individual, being a pseudonym. He also stated that the only reason we as humans have went to space was due to UFO involvement and the fact that outer space technology we had at the time encountered man problems such as the amount of radiation, and the ionosphere during the "earlier period" (but did not mention when). He also believed that both sides partook in our daily lives within government agencies and events worldwide.

Peterson's Informational Field

For science in general, Peterson stated that many of the current technologies dealing with nano-electronics and microelectronics, were his area of "expertise." Most of our implants he stated, were not human based hinting at the possibility UFO technology. The implants are biochemical or organic (meaning "alive"), which he doesn't believe were created from an Earth-based origin. He mentioned James Clerk Maxwell and his theory of electromagnetism, pointing out that he was correct in his statements.

Maxwell was a Scottish physicist and mathematician. His most prominent achievement was stating that all electricity, magnetism, and even light itself are creations of the same phenomenon calling it the electromagnetic field [45]. He also demonstrated that electric and magnetic fields both traveled through space in the form of waves at the speed of light. Publishing his work in 1865 called *A Dynamic Theory of Electromagnetic Field,* ushered a new wave advancing the world of physics. Maxwell also contributed to the kinetic theory of gases; mainly the *Maxwell-Boltzmann distribution*:

which described the statistical meanings of particle speeds in gases who do not constantly interact with each other, but move freely within short collisions. With these two amazing discoveries, Maxwell led the way for modern physics; especially dealing with special relativity and quantum mechanics [46].

Peterson familiar with this scientist attributed all electric motors, receivers, TV, internet, and modern technology due to the theory of electromagnetism. He also believed that all of this information was passed down where "action was at a distance." This in turn meant that from point A to point B could have an unlimited distance between them. No energy would be required and information could be passed instantaneously at speeds faster that the speed of light. Peterson stated that without electromagnetic radiation, a new sort of technology would be needed due to a sort of "tuning" mechanism that had to be acquired. Information as he described, was unconscious energy in the known universe where each individual has a sort of "field" characteristic of the soul or spirit. Every field or individual is considered different and the definition is outside the understanding of organized religious thought. He believed that the spirit was not localized, was not a device, and not part of the neural (brain) reality; rather a separate entity all together [47].

Although it is centered on the individual, he firmly believed that it was not localized; hinting that it could only be considered as a sort of "aura field." This went against the former belief that the body is a housing tank for the soul making it fixed and identifiable. If this phenomenon wasn't localized, where would the source of energy come from since Peterson didn't consider it a device? If the brain had no connection, that meant that another unknown source would have to constitute a sort of point of origin where this energy began. The idea is very fascinating; however Peterson gave no explanation, or common ground for the scientific/nonscientific mind to work with. He described the DNA as merely a factory that generated the human body with possible regeneration (with the "proper technology"). The information gathered from the DNA was derived from the information field as "perfection." Is this the same field that he was describing in terms of where the soul emits from? If he stated that the source was not localized, that would mean the only other suggestion is that a huge field of energy is responsible for the creation of the DNA, (mainly our whole existence) and the essence of the soul. The source could also mean that it could be anywhere in the universe, or in fact be the universe.

Peterson also stressed the importance of brain tissue and the connection of how the heart carries similar information. He mentioned that after heart transplants, people who did not have a certain affinity for special tastes (i.e. chocolate, mustard, etc . . .) developed them based on the donor's preference. This could mean it could be possible that the heart sends messages to the brain and vice versa (if these allegations can be proven that a "feeling" for things, tastes and objects can be transferred). Interestingly enough, the brain neuron itself seems to match the creation of a cluster of galaxies or with what modern science calls the "creation of the universe" [48]. Peterson added that not everyone was the same, and could not communicate with this spiritual information field. He considered these humans "informationally wrong" or "troubled" noting that the cause would originate from their DNA. Could this hint at people who are considered "heartless" or void of emotion lack the connection between the brain and heart? Does the heart and brain connection allow communication with this field that Peterson believes in? It seems that according to Peterson, this field can be produced artificially within the realms of stem cell research, which heightens the field itself and can transform tumors or anomalies to benign or almost nonexistent. This also could mean that artificially induced fields only pertain to the body and not the spiritual aspect.

He mentioned a French scientist called *Jean Claude De Roche*, whom he called a "master of acupuncture," belonging to the French Institute of Science. The IFSA or French Institute of Administrative Sciences was created in 1947 by René Cassin (being the only existing organization in France). The science practiced here is moral and administrative science, not the type of science that Peterson was attributing to the organization. The name De Roche was also not recognized by the organization, hinting another pseudonym or invention. Nevertheless, Peterson stated that acupuncture and Chinese herbal medicine were very effective and worked well in curing aliments and physical problems. He stated that acupuncture meridians believed to be located within the veins, were in fact located elsewhere (and refused to state where). The body itself is biomechanical in nature, ionic in nature, and polarized (meaning the information pulsates and moves within the body). Acupuncture as a guide, sends these "messages of information" to distinct locations around the body relieving pain, causing pain, etc . . . Peterson claimed that with a smooth surface, one could essentially identify the problems above and below the joints in both hands and feet. By messaging the area, pain would be relieved and the trouble organs associated with pressure points, would also be relieved. By using metal, Peterson claimed this would be ineffective due to it discharging however, using *plastic* (which tends to charge), one could use this with what he called "electrets" (a magnet to an electric field; similar to capacitors) which could create permanent charge that would be "fixed" (for both hands and feet). This of course would put acupuncturists out of business if Peterson's claims were accurate. Peterson also recommended the extreme care of one's teeth as he believed that all points end where the tooth roots were located [49]. While one lost their teeth (due to negligence or improper care), he stated that the overall health would diminish and the use of man-made devices would be needed more to cure ailments and pain due to the absence of teeth.

Peterson's story filled with outlandish claims, unknown projects, advances in technology, and the future of our world, must be researched to connect the most advanced achievements given to humankind by entities unknown (and his belief of an intimate connection with them to humans). Firstly as we remember, Peterson claimed that he loved rockets, explosions and the latter. However by the age of seventeen, he supposedly created what he called a satellite tracking system even before satellites were in orbit! If he was born in 1940, this would make this alleged achievement created by 1957.

This "tracker" was supposedly built for the military the same year Sputnik went into space. He also claimed to have worked for the Atomic Energy Commission (which he referred to as a nuclear tests site) where he received contracts by the government to deal with robotics and the handling of nuclear problems in case of meltdown. For a seventeen year old, the speculation of responsibility in charge of the lives of all the plant personnel, including the civilians surrounding the city would be questionable. He then claimed that he worked in East Idaho between the years 1955-58. It doesn't seem possible that he could be in two different locations at the same time, unless he mastered time travel.

During the supposed stint in the AEC, he discussed how within the reactors, electromagnetic materials became insulators, how insulators became conductors, how stiff metals broke apart, and ashes became solid. During this "contract," he claimed to have built a device called a manipulator (which consisted of a pair of arms to move, grip, and no spill capabilities). Through research, *Arco* (Idaho) contained a device created earlier than his "contract" called the Experimental Breeder Reactor *1* (ERB-1) and earlier robotics were being developed in the year 1951. *Enrico Fermi*, happened to be the one responsible for the creation of the breeder reactor in the University of Chicago in 1941, when Peterson was supposedly one year old [50].

The robots were called "master slave" manipulators or MSM contrary to Peterson just calling them manipulators. The first company to make them was called Central Research Labs located in Red Wing MN, which constructed these since the 1940 [51]. At no time do they mention Peterson anywhere within the creators of this technology as he would be just an infant at the time. Peterson all added that his manipulator had wheels or tank treads that allowed for mobility. This robot supposedly worked at any distance between twenty and thirty feet, which also required wires (in his earlier "models"). He claimed to operate those using radio waves; however was unsuccessful in the nuclear facility due to interference.

The first MSM, called the Model 1, was publicly demonstrated by inventor Ray Goertz working at Argonne National Laboratory of the U.S. Atomic Energy Commission. Goertz also was a key scientist that developed *telepresence* (or *telerobotics* which meant remote controlled robots from a distance) just as Peterson claimed he created almost five years later [52]. With Argonne located in Illinois and not Idaho as Peterson claimed, there was an obvious mix up of location and dates. During the years 1975-6 Peterson invented a computer that was used in Tokyo as a flight simulator in different languages. He also stated that this was the first use of the microprocessor chip, which later he used for computer training devices for "tech" people on how to use the chip [53]. *Cyberdyne* (not to be confused with supercomputer defense system Skynet from the Terminator franchise) was another company he has claimed to work for as well. He stated without proof, that the movie was fashioned after his idea and that the movie was not far from reality.

Cyberdyne was a company founded in 2004 in Japan that dealt with robotics and technology. Also known as Cyberdyne Inc., it was responsible for releasing a new prototype robot in 2009 known as the HAL 5 hybrid-assisted exoskeleton. This robot was intended to assist the body by increasing strength up to ten times the normal strength of a human. With this cybernetic-type robot, the physical capacity for any human would be improved dramatically [54]. Their technology is strangely interesting due to the fact that the cyborg actually mimics the brain's operation in terms of nerve signals to allow the limbs to move.

With a sensor attached to the human skin, the cyborg "catches" these signals, and in turn sends the messages to the limbs, allowing them to operate as the human process does. This would be ideal for those with physical deficiencies; changing the world forever. It is safe to assume that Peterson did not have anything to do with the development of this technology due to the inconsistencies of his story. Peterson affirmed that the chips that he "developed," are still in use now making Intel chips unnecessary due to his chip acting more like a computer. He described the process as making the chip work required the right "language" and "computer design" (but gave no explanation or proof) [55].

He added that this process would allow for the creation of an A.I. chip called "fuzzy logic;" where the chip could decide what actions to take on its own without a human controller. Peterson claimed to have created these out of Idaho Engineering Labs (being the largest research facility in the U.S.) now called the Idaho National Laboratory (established in 1949). At this time he also stated that he partook in a mission that brought "super capacitors" out of Ukraine failing to mention dates or details. During the years of 1987-88, Peterson claimed that he tried to sell his manipulators and robots to the Japanese in secret because they were considered "Black projects."

He stated with a firm affirmation that the United States had the technology before the Japanese with the quote "we already had ours fifty years ago, (laughing) actually forty-three years ago." If this was the case, the year would be 1945-6, making him only five or six years old. If he didn't start working for the government until thirteen, and did not receive those contracts until 1955-58, why make such a ludicrous statement? This technology concerning robot standing upright or "segway," was invented by Dean Kamen [56]. Having the sensor with "FORTH" technology, was in fact not Peterson's creation at all. Chuck Moore from the National Radio Astronomy Observatory (*NARO*) was said to have developed this technology beforehand. In 1971, along with Elizabeth Rather, they co-founded Forth INC. FORTH is programming described as structured, imperative, reflective, extensible, "stack based" computer programming language and environment. Dealing in the realm of computer science, the program is ideal for execution of commands, and compiling sequences of commands for later execution [57].

Peterson seemed to be familiar with the subjects, but somehow forgot that actual research could be done to refute his claims. The explanation he gave for not expressing details or having dates was because of the alleged secrecy of these programs which he labeled "MK Ultra." Considering NASA all "idiots and clowns," claiming to be a member of the

Russian board of directors for the Astronomic Association for Mankind were also part of his delusions as well. It is true that NASA works for the government and has many faults and disinformation; however this does not constitute them for being considered idiots at all since bright minds are still employed. The fact that their job is to mislead people doesn't affect their intelligence at all, displaying that Peterson has lost all sense of decency. As far as the Russian association goes, no such organization exists anywhere. To make matters worse, Peterson suddenly became "pro" NASA and stated that most of the technology came from this agency and that it had materials twenty years ahead of its time.

Peterson left this timeline behind and traveled to another invention of his called a UFO detector. This supposed invention was done at the age of fourteen due to the government's request. He did not know if it was operational at all but stated that the model was not built on the Wilhelm Reich model (concerning Orgone energy) called a Cloudbuster. The Cloudbuster was meant to manipulate orgone (universal life force) energy in the atmosphere to produce rain [58]. This machine was also having said to attract or detect UFOs due to their attraction to orgone initially. Peterson stated that his detector was built on science, but of course didn't go into detail on his explanation. His device was so fantastic that according to his belief, could detect anything in the universe [59]!

His explanation for the government's disapproval was due to the detection of stealth or secret projects. Peterson mentioned that he hasn't seen any of it in operation, however would be able to know due to a certain signal it supposedly emitted. With the lack of explanation and details, how would he have known of its use if not by E-M (electromagnetic) radiation? What other sort of technology could substitute this? He did not give any clues on what had to be involved in this process. Peterson considered himself as an "instrument maker" that didn't replicate anything; however we are seeing the opposite where everything he stated to invent was created by others.

The Brain/Heart Connection

He also had the strange belief that he was protected on an "Earthly level," but was unsure of the other levels. Peterson claimed the government had experiments where they tested frequency and the use of electromagnetic waves. Eugene Oregon was one location that Peterson claimed these experiments were run. People had side effects to the testing including birth defects, headaches, and sunburn while sleeping due to strong psychoactive frequencies (which were meant to disrupt the appropriate thinking capabilities of the brain) [60]. Since electromagnetic waves decrease with distance, a "device" was made to prevent this disruption making the wearer unaffected. Peterson claimed that diplomats, military personnel, presidents, and high ranking officials carried that at all times (and of course, he included himself). Using an electromagnetic field, the mind could avoid a disruption by creating its own field to prevent this as well. In turn, mastering the frequencies of the brain would eliminate the need for Peterson's imaginary device.

This technique was Peterson's suggestion in case of not having the device handy, applying the technique to resonate the brain "in phase." With this new type of "neural-linguistic program," as he firmly called it, a different form of mind control was applied where the effects included reductions in IQ, short attention span, change of memory, the victim forgot the chain of events, and forced actions against the will of the victim [61].

Although the idea of mind control and UFO phenomena is not untrue with the fact that the U.S. government had been studying this under the name *Project Bluebook* since 1952, it is not unlikely these programs still continue under a different name (since the program was deemed decommissioned) [62].

The heart has an important connection to the brain as we have briefly mentioned earlier. They have a sort of passageway linking them together in ways we have never thought. Peterson discussed later towards the end of the interview on his belief system concerning the heart. He recommended the book *Magical Child* by Joseph Chilton Pearce for its importance concerning the brain, heart and child connection. In this book, Pearce suggested that a fatherless/motherless child could not become useful members of society outside the standard family structure. What does it mean to be a "useful member?" Does it mean to follow in the parent's footsteps going to college, or making a business/white collar move to become rich in the capitalist environment? As we have seen, most successful individuals such as Dave Thomas the founder of Wendy's franchise, was adopted and became a fast food mogul. So as far as the theory suggests, many anomalies can be found. Pearce also stated that inner city children didn't stand a chance due to the lack of the heart and brain connection [63].

What exactly does this mean in detail? Peterson stated some of his "ideas" that he believed were relevant to this conversation. After about sixteen days during the embryonic fluid break, the child is exposed to an electromagnetic field from the mother's heart. This "field" is modulated by the amount of brain cells in the heart and brain which amount to emotions. These are then transferred to the child (although he didn't state how; it could be through the umbilical cord). This method according to Peterson was a Russian study that stated the first sixteen to eighteen days were crucial [64]. If the mother raised the child in water at body temperature slowly to the mother's breast, the two hearts would be intact. If held at the breast for twelve to fourteen hours the child is said to develop speech by six months, and able to stand on their own.

Peterson claimed that Madonna used these techniques; however as we have seen she also adopted. His theory suggested that the adopted children did not receive this treatment, so they would not develop as fast as her biological children. Within the theory, the heart becomes an electromagnetic component as the body is bio-magnetic; making this relationship between these organs for more complex. Peterson also believed that both parents were necessary and if only one was present, it would not be enough as both components were necessary. Through research, there would be little evidence to support his theory. It would of course be an ideal world if all children had both parents who provided them with love, care, and feelings. However, one parent could essentially do both jobs providing love to help the child in developing emotional tides.

Unwanted children according to *Freakanomics* by Steven Levitt and Stephen Dubner, are more likely to become criminals and dangerous individuals. They also stated that legalized abortion has helped reduce the crime rates by not producing unwanted children that end up disowned or destroyed emotionally [65]. Their theory could be correct to the fact that if two individuals not interested in childbearing and only interested in sexual adventures, would not produce any connection through the brain and heart to the child because of the lack of desire/emotion. If the parents themselves are results of the same predicament, this would make the child essentially worse; since they do not have the capacity to offer any love, feelings, or emotions to the absence in their childhood. With results like these, a dangerous chain of events transpire everyday around the world when a child is born unwanted.

His reluctance to say where he lived only stating "somewhere in Nevada," displayed a sort of dishonesty and untrustworthiness in his character. The fact that Project Camelot was ridiculous in enhancing his image as a sort of genius, made the whole interview more choppy and illogical. Cassidy still wanted to believe in positive aliens, however Peterson was smart to reject this notion or have anything to say concern her wish for "saviors from above." The only thing Peterson did state that could be one of the few possible valid points in his entire fantastic adventure was that humans have done too much damage and that we are incapable of changing our behavior.

Closing this investigation of the "problem solver" he has failed miserably. Inside each of us, there burns a desire to be something out of the ordinary. While children call this imagination, some adults still keep this intact even dealing with society and its obstacles. The problem becomes severe when certain individuals concoct a fantasy based on imagination of others, or stories that are not original in nature. Peterson interjected himself into certain times and events that did not coincide with his birth year or existence. His vocabulary and expressions seemed to demonstrate a thinking process; however he still maintained a face of dishonesty and vagueness.

Having an imagination shouldn't be considered a negative attribute because it creates ideas, inventions, and new worlds for the human mind to explore. Many who have had dreams make them come true in our reality due to their imagination. Others steal these dreams in return for financial profit or recognition. How to determine the two is most difficult, since the heart and brain are not easily read by others without a sort of sixth sense. Hopefully, we as human beings are able to grow this ability if we earn it through experience, feelings, and emotional progress. It was obvious that Peterson tried to take credit for other people's work, but could not defend the fact that they stole the idea from him. He never stated this directly, however at the beginning of the interview he explained that most people considered him a fraud and a liar on the internet [66]. It seems that these convictions are correct based on the investigation to refute his claims.

It seems that whoever discarded Peterson from in space, probably lied to him about his whole life feeding him dreams and ideas from other beings; essentially making him an echo. Repetition was his main premise coining the new name "Repeat-erson" in order to identify his true nature. We on the other hand as conscious human beings, can learn from this by focusing on details. Details are forever important when telling any kind of event or story. They must coincide with one another even if the story is untrue to make it more believable. Most people today do not analyze, question, or investigate; which then paves the way for ridiculous stories and fabrications.

Humans will never rise to greatness without combining all of our different strengths under scrutiny, and extreme detailing of the spirit, mind, and body. It is apparent that Peterson believed in the words of Von Schiller where only in his world his opinions matter and not the rest of us analyzing him. Does he essentially have a true heart that isn't void of nobility, love, emotions, and feelings? In the entire interview, he displayed no emotions, or honesty. Many humans thrive on lying to themselves due to their boring existence and the need for a fantastic adventure. Are we not essentially all alone? Or can we connect with each other forming human communities of understanding to usher humans into a new age?

End Notes

[1] Dave Thier. "May 21 is judgment day? Harold Camping's latest prediction." *AOL News* (January 2011).

[2] Elena Garcia. "Fearful teen commits suicide due to Harold Camping's judgment day prediction" *Christian Post U.S.* (May 2011).

[3] Stephanie Samuel. "Rapture prediction to devastate Christian's faith?" *Christian Post U.S.* (May 2011).

[4] Galen. *On Usefulness of the Parts of the Body.* Cornell University Press (1988).

[5] "Project Camelot interviews Dr. Pete Peterson." *Projectcamelot.org* (June 2009).

[6] Ibid 5.

[7] Michael Boylan and Kevin Brown. *Genetic Engineering: Science and Ethics on the New Frontier.* Prentice Hall (August 2001).

[8] Ibid 5.

[9] John Nathan-Turner. *The TARDIS Inside Out.* Picadilly Press LTD. U.K. (1985).

[10] Mark Harris. *The Doctor WHO Technical Manual.* Random House U.K. (1985).

[11] Erich Von Daniken. *Chariots of the Gods: Unsolved Mysteries of the Past.* Berkley Books (Janurary 1999).

[12] Ibid 11.

[13] Ravi Shankar Mukkavilli. "Air Planes in Rig Veda." *Vedic Science* (November 2006).

[14] T.S. Garp. "Ancient Civilizations like Sumerians firmly believed in UFOS." *Helium.com* (August 2010).

[15] mysteriousaustralia.com/rexufo/uru-flying-machines.shtml.

[16] Ibid 5.

[17] "Advanced Ice Age Civilizations and Atlantis." *UFOTV* Special Edition (2006).

[18] John Stokes. "Scientists find Extraterrestrial Genes in Human DNA." *Rense.com* (January 2011).

[19] Nick Begich and Jeanne Manning. *Angles Don't Play This HAARP: Advances in Tesla Technology*. Earthpulse Pr. 1st Ed. (September 1995).

[20] "Science: Conductor in a Command Post." *Time Magazine* (August 1965).

[21] Ibid 5.

[22] The Mogambo Guru (Richard Daughty). "Losing Faith in Paper Money." *Daily Reckoning* (February 2011).

[23] Stephen Brown. "Paul believes in threat of North American Superhighway." *LA Times* (November 2007).

[24] "Canada, the United States and Mexico Diverted by Jelly Beans: No Sign of a North American Union." *The Economist* (August 2007).

[25] Drake Bennett. "The amero conspiracy." *New York Times* (November 2007).

[26] Herbert G. Grubel. "The Case for the Amero: The Economist and Politics of a North American Monetary Union." *The Frasier Institute* (1999).

[27] Robert Pastor. *Toward a North American Community: Lessons from the Old World for the New*. Peterson Institute: Washington D.C. (2001).

[28] Alex Pasternack. "Cyborg Professor looks to future of Bionic Technology." *CNN* (September 2010).

*[29]Todd Lewan. "Chip Implants Linked to Animal Tumors." *Washington Post* (September 2007).

[30] Alorie Gilbert. "Is RFID the mark of the beast?" *CNET News* (February 2005).

[31] Ibid 5.

[32] Reuters. "Euro Crisis 2012: Greece reportedly saved from bankruptcy by European Central Bank." *Huffington Post Business* (July 2012).

[33] "Hurricane Katrina devastates Gulf Coast." *The Telegraph U.K.* (July 2005).

[34] Ibid 5.

[35] Bruce Rix. *Hollywood vs. the Aliens: The Motion Picture Industry's Participation in UFO Disinformation.* Frog Books (January 1998).

[36] Ibid 5.

[37] Associated Press. "Brazil UFO Sightings to be Documented, Made Public." *Huffington Post* (August 2010).

[38] Audrey Gillan. "Gold, secret CIA arms and seized drugs in huge WTC basement." *The Guardian U.K.* (November 2001).

[39] Jim Marrs. *Above Top Secret: Uncover the Mysterious of the Digital Age.* Disinformation Books (October 2008).

[40] Curtis Peebles. *Dark Eagles: A History of Top Secret U.S. Aircraft Programs.* Novato CA: Presidio Press (1999).

[41] Ibid 40.

[42] Edward Teller. Memoirs: *A Twentieth-Century Journey in Science and Politics.* Perseus Publishing (2001).

[43] George Dyson. *Project Orion: The True Story of the Atomic Spaceship.* New York: Henry Holt and Co. (2002).

[44] Ibid 5.

[45] Peter Hartman. *The Natural Philosophy of James Clerk Maxwell.* Cambridge University Press (1998).

[46] Ibid 45.

[47] Ibid 5.

[48] David Constantine. "Science Illustrated: they look alike, but there's a little matter of size." *New York Times* (August 2006).

[49] Ibid 5.

[50] ne.anl.gov/about/modern-day-alchemy

[51] centres.com/company.htm

[52] "Table: Robot Milestones (extended)." *Bloomberg Business Week Magazine* (March 2001).

[53] Ibid 5.

[54] cyberdyne.jp/English/robotsuithal/index.html

[55] Ibid 5.

[56] Mary Bellis. "Segway human transporter." *About.com* (2012).

[57] Mahlon G. Kelly and Nicholas Spies. *FORTH: A Text and Reference*. Prentice Hall (1986).

[58] Myron Sharaf. *Fury on Earth: A Biography of Wilhelm Reich.* De Capo Press (1994).

[59] Ibid 5.

[60] Ibid 5.

[61] Ibid 5.

[62] Steven Ornes. "Whatever happened to . . . Project Blue Book?" *Discovery Magazine* (February 2007).

[63] Joseph Chilton Pearce. *Magical Child*. Plume (March 1992).

[64] Ibid 5.

[65] Steven D. Levitt and Stephen J. Dubner. *Freakanomics: A Rouge Economist explores the hidden side of everything.* William Morrow (April 2005).

[66] Ibid 5.

Afterword

The Final Word

Searching for answers concerning the topic of UFOs as we have seen is not an easy task. Dolan said it best as "responsible humans," investigation is needed and available if the individual looks hard enough. Some of the events could be fabricated; however there is evidence that is undeniable displaying that we are not alone in this vast universe. Although Project Camelot seems to interview these men in order to open the eyes of the people to tell the "truth," they lack consistency, intelligence, and frankness concerning the subjects at hand making disastrous claims and misleading ideas. Some of the men such as Dolan, Maxwell, and Green show a sort of sincerity in what they preach without taking the role of a savior or promising that "something will save us."

The main idea is present that we as humans, are not ready as a species to change our ways as we continue to destroy the planet in increasing numbers. There is even a report that labels humans a national security threat to the planet Earth. It seems that a new study concerning climate change is attributing man to the cause of ocean acidification and changes to the climate. Computer analysis display areas such as Japan, Australia, the U.S. and India show raises in temperature near oceans that are not a natural occurrence [1]. Fossil fuel consumption has been the culprit according to the studies over the last century.

On the other side of the spectrum, Burisch, Collier, and Peterson have speculated ideas about current events that people need to be altered to; however lack evidence, consistency and seem to invent a world where they expect people to believe them without proof. Burisch and Peterson fabricate their existence, the events, and include themselves in key historical accomplishments laid down by others and the alien agenda (helping humankind advance in technological ways). Dean and Greer fall under another light where they present great details about how the military and U.S. government are hiding valuable information on UFOs; however lean towards an unrealistic/idealistic future where all humans worth saving and the promise of hope in the future.

There is no doubt that alien and off world entities surround us every day in the real world. Sooner or later, the government will have to address these occurrences and anomalies truthfully with proper full disclosure. Retired U.S. Colonel John Alexander recently stated in his new book that UFO disclosure has happened already and that the government isn't hiding anything [2]. Although the ongoing war on UFO disclosure is stronger than ever, some have been infuriated by Alexander's testimony based on high security clearance documents and military practical knowledge [3]. He focused on the phenomena surrounding the mysterious nuclear missile launch failures that occurred such as the incident in California back in 2011, and the recent failure of North Korea's nuclear missile launch as possibility of contact. Alexander considered these "one-time events" that actually transpired and not to alarmed unless they happen frequently. He does admit that UFOs are real and are physical objects of unknown origin that transit our universe. With the current technological boom that human civilization has experienced over the last ten years, can we expect these alien interest groups to employ a type of laissez-faire attitude towards human progress? Will they help usher humans to the next level of progress for cleaner efficient energy without the constraints of pollution, human hierarchy, corporate policy, or monopolies?

We have to discover a new way of viewing things, discovering new passages, and open the mind for creative, logical and rational ideas. Life could be defined as bizarre and complicated requiring more than two simple realities that the human mind has been fashioned to believe based on our established institutions. Humans seem to utilize the R-complex brain (or triune) "fight or flight scenario" except for a few who surpass the basic functions and explore the mammalian brain (or paleo-mammalian) or the neo-cortex (neo-mammalian) [4]. Humans need to move beyond the simple function of the limbic system and expand on the ability to love universally, have compassion for all living things, and understand others despite their ignorance.

The ancients seemed to understand this concept, and the Native Americans utilized this practice. However over time globalization, cultural mixing and technological abuse have caused us to lose our way from where we ought to be in this universe/reality. Believing we are "special" doesn't constitute for greatness without the proper foundation. People need to feel special as we are left to fend for ourselves. We also lack the tolerance of one another, bent on judging each looking for our differences rather than our likes.

Is Project Camelot going to take the responsibility of replacing this system with a new one without causing more damage? The only beauty that the human has is the mind, heart and spirit; which we neglect or allow those in power to control. Why would a human being so complex and unique allow another human to designate their lives? We lack responsibility plain and simple; and we have accustomed ourselves to adapt to a smug reality. Life is seemingly not a simple and will forever remain in the way it is unless we finally take the actions necessary as individuals. We as men and women are defined by our actions, and to pass judgment on another human is not realistic and irresponsible. To describe what sort of life is beyond the physical realm is also based on speculation, individual interpretation, and an understanding of the fourth and fifth densities. We are involved with many different realities that humankind cannot fathom in its current state.

Religious and political hustlers utilized these ancient fairytales to explain the world around them. Because tribes were easily swayed by their explanations, they believed them. As we usher into the 21st century, people still cling to medieval superstitions when society has blossomed into a technological network of information. Many of these stories are not based on historical facts without proof; yet most people still want to believe. Although the very foundation of most human lives rest on their faith, this is the very obstacle hindering them from enlightenment. Once the facts emerged and proof destroys the fairytale belief, it will be time to grow and move on to discover what there really is. This is not to deny that the extraterrestrial presence wasn't rooted in the foundation of these ancient cultures; rather that these stories were altered over time by priesthoods removing the "alien concept" to replace it with an incompetent spooky father figure who watches us from the clouds. The less the people know about the actuality of events, the less trouble they will cause overall.

By imposing a belief (such as the "heavenly delusion") based on human error doesn't give us the right to impose this fantasy on the rest of the population. Everyone should discover this journey on their own, because we are alone in all we do no matter how much company we keep. We should learn from each other because this is the purpose of human pair bonding. We must grow, change, and work towards a more realistic outcome where on the individual can rise to prove their worthiness to venture in a new frontier that will hopefully help us discover our purpose.

Questioning, analyzing, and looking at the details are what can probably "save" us from complete failure and annihilation. This doesn't mean that we are to consume ourselves in details rather that we focus on what we can deal with as individuals. We are not all the same as we are led to believe, and human lives although tied by physiology and anatomy, having different worth depending on how far our mental and spiritual capacity grows. Our fear has engulfed us to do things by force distorting the conscious mind. Others that call it karma also believe this as well by doing what they call positive things. With this belief they are in turn helping the community and securing a position in the afterlife perceptively. Why do we as humans mix fear and responsibility whilst confusing them at the same time? Green stated the best possible scenario of reality by saying "help your own world, not the whole world." We cannot save everyone despite our best efforts and the enormous workload that potentially has to be completed on all levels of humanity.

Nature always has worked by proving the survival of the strong organisms and destroying the weak entities. Humans on the other hand, refuse to operate this way and tend to alter nature. These results are more disastrous effects that transpire as the meaning of life has changed into a morbid reality. Everything has to survive and life has to continue because we do not want to die. Our affinity for the physical body has misguided us away from the important part; the spirit which now humans seem to be void of. This is not a statement that the physical is to be neglected, rather take care of the one's own body we are given and focus on the internal as well creating a balance. This is a difficult task no doubt, but it can be done by playing society's game without losing oneself.

The mind, body, and spirit are all commodities in this human world where the controllers of society seem to want for their own desires. Our objective is to remain free of this bondage and attempt to communicate with our alien creators. This will hopefully reconnect us to them as we have conquered our humanity (and experience a metamorphosis beyond the understanding of the mind). They are out there, probably waiting for us to wake up in consciousness. If this is a mission called life, perhaps we must complete this in order to take our place among them by working towards changing our ways one human at a time.

With these results, we then can be saved by helping ourselves with no need for false hopes, external deities and dreams. We can do it, and we are capable of change. We must allow the reconnection of animal companionship, planetary union between humans and Mother Nature, and shatter this prison constructed by our own doing. Perhaps Titor is correct about our human behavior in the future tense, but are we the same in every reality or are there hopeful places one human can go to seek refuge? Would this be labeled as another means of escape or will it be another chance to start over? Time will tell, and as all of these men have put in one way or another: "time is running out . . ."

End Notes

[1] Susanne Posel. "U.S. Government Study: Humans are National Security Threat to Oceans and our Planet." *Blacklisted News* (June 2012).

[2] John B. Alexander Ph.D. *UFOs: Myths, Conspiracies, and Reality*. Thomas Dune Books (February 2011).

[3] Lee Spiegel. "Retired Col. says UFOs are real, but denies cover-up." *AOL News* (February 2011).

[4] P.D. Maclean. *The Triune Brain in Evolution: Role in Paleocerebral Functions*. Springer (January 1990).

Bibliography

Ackerman, Forrest J. *Science-Fiction Classics: The Stories That Morphed Into Movies*. TV Books (August 1999).

Alexander, John B. PhD. *UFOs: Myths, Conspiracies, and Reality*. Thomas Dune Books. (Feb 15th, 2011).

Allen, Gary. *The Rockefeller File*. Seal Beach, CA. Press (1976).

Allen, Gary and Larry Abraham. *None dare call it Conspiracy*. Rossmoor, CA: Concord Press (1972).

Ashe, Geoffrey. *Stonehenge: The Arthurian Encyclopedia*. Peter Bedrick Books: New York (1986).

Baigent, Michael, Leigh Richard, and Henry Lincoln. *Holy Blood, Holy Grail*. Dell (1983).

Ball, Desmond. *Pine Gap*. Allen and Uwin. Sydney (1988).

Barrett, Jeffery A. *The Quantum Mechanics of Minds and Worlds*. Oxford University Press (1999).

Begich, Nick and Jeanne Manning. *Angles Don't Play this HAARP: Advances in Tesla Technology*. Earthpulse Pr. (September 1995).

Bergrun, Norman R. *Ringmakers of Saturn*. Pentland Press: Edinburgh (1986).

Biancuzzi, Federico and Shane Warden. *Masterminds of Programming Conversations with the Creators of Major Programming Languages*. O'Reilly Press (2009).

Bramley, William. *Gods of Eden*. Avon. (March 1993).

Brown, David. *Prion Diseases and Metalloproteins: BSG, Scrapie and CJD Research (Harwood Infectious Diseases and Microbiology Series)*. Woodhead Publishing (October 2002).

Brown, Julian. *Minds, Mechanics and the Universe*. Simon and Schuster (2000).

Brown, Robert. *Ganesh: Studies of an Asian God*. Albany: State University of New York Press (1991).

Bussenbark, Ernest and Jordan Maxwell. *Symbols, Sex and the Stars*. The Book Tree (2010).

Collier, Alex. *Defending Sacred Ground: "Letters from Andromeda and Diversified Enterprises."* Val Verian Press (1998).

Clark, Jerome. *The UFO Encyclopedia Volume 3: High Strangeness, UFOs from 1960 through 1979*. Visible Ink Press (1996).

Collyns, Robin. *Did Spacemen Colonize the Earth?* Regnery: London (1974, 1976)

Coppens, Phlip. *The Ancient Alien Question: A New Inquiry into the Existence, Evidence, and Influence of Ancient Visitors.* New Page Books (November 2011).

Daniken Von, Erich. *Chariots of the Gods: Unsolved Mysteries of the Past.* Berkley Books (January 1999).

Daniken Von, Erich. *History is Wrong.* New Page Books (August 2009).

Daniken Von, Erich. *Twilight of the Gods: The Mayan Calendar and the Return of the Extraterrestrials.* New Page Books (July 2010).

Dawkins, Richard. *The God Delusion.* Black Swan New Ed. (2007).

Deardorff, James W. *Celestial Teachings: The Emergence of the True Testament of Jmmanuel (Jesus).* Wild Flower PR (May 1990).

Debnak, Sailen. *The Meanings of Hindu Gods, Goddesses, and Myths.* Rup & Co. New Delhi (November 2009).

De Kriuif, Paul. *Microbehunters.* Mariner Books (2002).

Dick, Philip K. *Minority Report.* Gollancz: London (2002).

Dolan, M Richard. *UFOs and the National Security State: Chronology of a Cover-up, 1941-1973.* Hampton Roads Publishing (June 2002)

Dolan, M Richard. *UFOs and the National Security State: The cover up exposed, 1973-1991*. Keyhole Publishing Company (2009).

Dolan Richard M. and Bryce Zabel. *A.D After Disclosure: When the Government Finally Reveals the Truth About Alien Contact*. New Page Books (May 2012).

Durazno, Manny. *Cosmic Multiverse: Zach Jonesmay Discovers the Parallel Universe Book I*. Createspace, (June 2010).

Dyson, George. *Project Orion: The true story of the Atomic Spaceship*. Henry Holt and Co.: New York NY (2002).

Essene, Virginia and Sheldon Nidle. *You Are Becoming a Galactic Human*. Spiritual Education Endeavors (April 1994).

Fondebrider, Jorge. *Versiones de Patagonia*. Buenos Aires Argentina: Emece Editores S.A. (2003).

Friedman, Stanton T. and Kathleen Marden. *Captured! The Betty and Barney Hill UFO Experience: The True Story of the World's First Documented Alien Abduction*. New Page Books (July 2007).

Friedman, Stanton T. and Dr. Edgar Mitchell. *Flying Saucers and Science: A Scientist Investigates the Mysteries of UFOs: Interstellar Travel, Crashes, and Government Cover-Ups*. New Page Books (June 2008).

Good, Timothy. *Above Top Secret: the worldwide UFO Cover-up*. Quill 1989

Good, Timothy. *Alien Contact, Top-Secret UFO Files Revealed.* Quill, 1994.

Glazebrook, R.T. *James Clerk Maxwell and Modern Physics.* MacMillan Press, (1896).

Graham M, Lloyd. *Deceptions and Myths of the Bible.* Citadel Press (June 2000).

Graves, Kersey. *The World's Sixteen Crucified Saviors or Christianity Before Christ.* Truth Seeker Co. Inc. 6th Ed. (June 1960).

Green, George and Benevolent Beings. *Handbook for the New Paradigm.* Bridger House Publishers Inc. Vol. 1 Ed. (May 1999).

Green, George and Benevolent Authors. *Embracing the Rainbow.* Gazelle Distribution Trade; Volume II edition. (June 1999).

Green, George and Benevolent Beings. *Becoming (Handbook for the New Paradigm, Vol.* 3). Bridger House Publishers Inc. (January 2000).

Greenbaum, Leonard. *A Special Interest: The Atomic Energy Commission, Argonne National Laboratory, and Midwestern Universities.* University of Michigan Press 1st Ed. (1971).

Greenwood, Norman and Alan Earnshaw. *Chemistry of the Elements (2nd Ed.)* Oxford: Butterworth-Heinemann. (1997).

Hall M. Jack, Richard E. Hewlett, and Ruth C. Hans. *Argonne National Laboratory*. University of Illinois Press (1997).

Hall, P. Manly. *The Secret Destiny of America*. Aziloth Books (April, 2011).

Hancock, Graham. *Fingerprints of the Gods*. Three Rivers Press. (April 1996).

Hancock, Graham. *The Message of the Sphinx: A quest for the hidden legacy of mankind*. Three Rivers Press. (May 1997).

Hancock, Graham and Robert Bauval. *The Message of the Sphinx: A Quest for the Hidden Legacy of Mankind*. Three Rivers Press 1st Ed. (May 1997).

Hancock, Graham and Robert Bauval. *The Mars Mystery: A secret connection between the Earth and the red planet*. Three Rivers Press (June 1999)

Harman, Peter. *The Natural Philosophy of James Clerk Maxwell*. Cambridge University Press (1998).

Hamilton, William. *Project Aquarius: The story of an Aquarian Scientist*. Authorhouse. (December 2005).

Harper, Charles L. *Environment and Society: Human Perspectives on Environmental Issues*. Prentice Hall 5th edition. (July 2011).

Harris, Mark. *The Doctor WHO Technical Manual*. Random House, UK (1985).

Henry, William. *Blue Apples*. Scala Dei (April 2000).

Hight, Craig and Jane Roscoe. *Faking It: Mocking Documentary and the Subversion of Factuality*. Manchester University Press (February 2002).

Icke, David. *Human Race get off your knees: the Lion sleeps no more*. David Icke. (May 2010).

Imbrogno, J. Philip, Dr. J. Allen Hynek, and Bob Pratt. *Night Siege: The Hudson Valley UFO Sightings*. Llewellyn Publications (May 1998).

Kean, Leslie. *UFOs: Generals, Pilots, and Government Officials Go on the Record*. Three Rivers Press (August 2011).

Kelly, Mahlon G. and Nicholas Spies. *FORTH: A Text and Reference*. Prentice Hall (1986).

Kent, Adrian. *One World versus Many: The inadequacy of Everettian accounts of Evolution Probability, and Scientific Confirmation*. "Many Worlds? Everett Quantum Theory and Reality." Oxford University Press (2010).

Klass, Philip J. *UFOs: The Public Deceived*. Prometheus Books (June 1986).

Klass, Philip J. *UFO Abductions: A Dangerous Game*. Prometheus Books (March 1989).

Koopman Jr., Phillip J. *Stack Computers: The New Wave*. Ellis Howard Limited (1989).

Kropotkin, Peter. *Mutual Aid: A Factor of Evolution*. London: Free Press (2009).

Levitt, Steven D. and Stephen J. Dubner. *Freakanomics: A Rouge Economist explores the hidden side of Everything*. William Morrow (April 2005).

Lide, David R. *CRC Handbook of Chemistry and Physics* (87th Ed.) CRC Press: Boca Raton FL (2006).

Lorgen, Eve. *The Love Bite: Alien Interference in Human Love Relationships*. ELogos & HHC Press (February 2000).

Mackenzie Donald A. *Triumph of the Sun God: Egyptian myth and legend*. Gresham Publishing Company (1907).

Maclean, P.D. *The Triune Brain in Evolution: Role in Paleocerebral Functions*. Springer (January 1990).

Marrs, Jim. *Above Top Secret: Uncover the Mysteries of the Digital Age*. The Disinformation Company, (2008).

Marx, Karl. *Critique of Hegel's Philosophy of Right*. Cambridge University Press (1970).

Maxwell, Jordan, Snow, Allen, and Paul Tice. *That Old Time Religion*. The Book Tree (2000).

Maxwell, Jordan. *Martix of Power: How the world has been controlled by powerful people without your knowledge*. The Book Tree (2003).

Maxwell, Jordan. *That Old-Time Religion: The Story of Religious Foundations.* The Book Tree (2003).

Miller Frederic P., Vandome Agnes F. and John McBrewster. *Caesium.* Alphascript Publishing, (November 2009).

Miller Frederic P., Vandome Agnes F. and John McBrewster. *Caesium 137.* VDM Publishing House LTD. (2010).

Moore, William and Charles Berlitz. *The Philadelphia Experiment: Project Invisibility.* Fawcett (March 1995).

Nathan-Turner, John. *The TARDIS Inside Out.* Piccadilly Press LTD., UK 1985.

Nichols B. Preston and Peter Moon. *The Montauk Project: Experiments in Time.* Sky Books: Westbury New York.

O'Brien, Christian. *The Genius of the Few: The Story of Those Who Founded the Garden of Eden.* Borgo Press, (1985).

Pastor, Robert. *Toward a North American Community: Lessons from the Old World for the New.* Peterson Institute: Washington D.C. (2001).

Pearce, Chilton Joseph. *Magical Child.* Plume (March 1992).

Perkins, John. *The Secret History of the American Empire: The Truth about Economic Hit Men, Jackals, and How to Change the World.* Plume (April 2008).

Peres, Asner. *Quantum Theory: Concepts and Methods.* Kluner Dordrecht (1993).

Plato and B. Jowett. *Plato's Republic.* New York: The Modern Library (1941).

Quigley, Carroll. *The Shadows of Power.* Appleton WI: Western Islands (1966).

Redfern, Nick. *The Real Men in Black: Evidence, Famous Cases, and True Stories of These Mysterious Men and their Connection to UFO Phenomena.* New Page Books (June 2011).

Rich, Ben and Lee Jones. *Skunkworks: A Personal Memoir of My Years at Lockheed.* Boston: Little Brown and Co. (1996).

Ridley Rosalind M. and Harry F. Baker. *Fatal Protein: The Story of BSE and other Prion Diseases.* Oxford University Press (1998).

Rix, Bruce. *Hollywood vs. The Aliens: The Motion Picture Industry's Participation in UFO Disinformation.* Frog Books (January 1998).

Rostand, J. *Lazarro Spallenzani e le origen della biologia sperintale.* Torino Einaudi (1997).

Rubenstein E. Richard. *When Jesus Became God: The Struggle to Define Christianity During the Last Days of Rome.* Mariner Books (July 2000).

S, Archaya. *The Christ Conspiracy: The Greatest Story Ever Sold.* Adventures Unlimited Press. (July 1999).

Sahagun, Louis. *Master of the Mysteries: The Life of Manly P. Hall*. Process (2008).

Schwaller de Lubicz. Sacred Science: The King of Pharaonic Theocracy. Inner Traditions (April 1982).

Sharaf, Myron. *Fury on Earth: A Biography of Wilhelm Reich*. Da Capo Press (1994).

Silberman, Neil A. and Israel Finkelstein. *The Bible Unearthed: Archaeology's New Vision of Ancient Israel and the Origin of Its Sacred Texts*. Touchstone (May 2002).

Sitchin, Zacharia. *The Last Book of Enki: Memoirs and Prophecies of an Extraterrestrial God*. Bear and Company (2004).

Sitchin, Zacharia. *The 12th Planet*. Harper Collins Publishers (2007).

Sitchin, Zacharia. *There were Giants upon Earth: Gods, Demigods, Human Ancestry: the Evidence of Alien DNA*. Bear and Company (2010).

Steiger, Brad and Sherry Hansen Steiger. *Real Aliens, Space Beings, and Creatures from Other Worlds*. Visible Ink Press (May 2011).

Teller, Edward. *Memoirs: A Twentieth Century Journey in Science and Politics*. Perseus Publishing (2001).

The John Titor Foundation INC. *John Titor, a Time Traveler's Tale*. InstantPublisher.com (December 2003).

Thau, William A. *Source Code*. iUniverse INC. (December 2006).

Thorne, Kip S. *Black Holes and Time Warps*. W.W. Norton (1994).

Van Ness, H.C. *Understanding Thermodynamics*. Dover Publications Inc. (1983).

Walton, Travis. *Fire in the Sky*. Marlowe and Company; 3rd Ed. (September 1997).

Wells, A.F. *Structural Inorganic Chemistry* (5th Ed.) Oxford Science Publications (1984).

Wolf, B.J., Howell Albert, and Dan B. Catselas Burisch. *Eagles Disobey: The case for INCA City Mars*. Candlelight Publishing. (August 1998).

Wood, Ryan. *Magic Eyes Only*. Wood Enterprises: Winfield KS. (November 2005).

Wood, S.G. *The American Revolution: A History*. Modern Library (2002).